REDEEMABLE

REDEEMABLE

A Memoir of Darkness and Hope

Erwin James

BLOOMSBURY CIRCUS

LONDON · OXFORD · NEW YORK · NEW DELHI · SYDNEY

Bloomsbury Circus
An imprint of Bloomsbury Publishing Plc

50 Bedford Square   1385 Broadway
London   New York
WC1B 3DP   NY 10018
UK   USA

www.bloomsbury.com

BLOOMSBURY and the Diana logo are trademarks of Bloomsbury Publishing Plc

First published in Great Britain 2016

British Library Cataloguing-in-Publication Data
A catalogue record for this book is available from the British Library.

ISBN: HB: 978-1-4088-1397-3
TPB: 978-1-4088-7295-6
ePub: 978-1-4088-4933-0

2 4 6 8 10 9 7 5 3 1

Typeset by Newgen Knowledge Works (P) Ltd., Chennai, India
Printed and bound in Great Britain by CPI Group (UK) Ltd, Croydon CR0 4YY

MIX
Paper from
responsible sources
FSC® C020471

To find out more about our authors and books visit www.bloomsbury.com.
Here you will find extracts, author interviews, details of forthcoming
events and the option to sign up for our newsletters.

Pay attention to your thoughts, because they become words,
Pay attention to your words, because they become actions,
Pay attention to your actions, because they become habits,
Pay attention to your habits, because they become your character,
Pay attention to your character, because it is your fate . . .

The Talmud

Sometimes you have to go back to know just where you have been . . .

Rise Against

I

All my life I had been a liar, a thief and a cheat. Now I had to face the rest of my life as a convicted murderer. Standing in the dock of court number one at the Old Bailey listening to Mr Justice Otton deliver his judgement was my darkest moment. I tried to keep my head up and hold the judge's gaze as he spoke, until he described me as 'brutal, vicious and callous'. Then I lowered my eyes. When he finished I took a deep breath and glanced around one last time at the courtroom full of strangers, all there because of me and my co-accused. Flanked and separated by prison guards he and I never once acknowledged each other in the dock. He blamed me for our crimes. I denied any involvement. We were both lying.

In the crowded court a small group of people sitting near the end of the lawyers' benches far to my right stood out. I'd noticed them coming and going on different days of the trial and it struck me that they did not appear to be part of the official proceedings. Neither were they press. Eventually it dawned on me that they were connected in some way to our victims – family or friends perhaps. I avoided looking in their direction. Their dignified conduct served only to intensify my shame.

Sitting directly in front of me and facing the judge, the prosecutor, a striking woman with dark eyes and an almost bleached white complexion, appeared quietly contented as she shared the occasional whispered comment with her assistants. She had been a formidable interrogator and I couldn't help but respect her for it. Back a row and to her left sat my QC, a man in late middle age whose thick grey eyebrows and corpulent face made him look much older than he probably was. He kept peering at the pile of papers in his lap. He had done his best, but he must have known there was little chance of success, not that he ever gave me any hint of what his true opinion was regarding my guilt or innocence.

To his right sat my co-accused's QC, a fierce, bulbous-eyed man with pale greasy skin whose barrister's wig appeared to be at least one size too small. His role had confused me at first; he was like another prosecutor. His cross-examination of me had been the most vicious, leading to an exchange between us during which I turned to the jury and said, 'Members of the jury, this man is being paid thousands of pounds to say these untrue things about me. I am innocent.' Turning to the judge I repeated the lie. 'Your Honour,' I said, 'I'm innocent.' The memory of my performance in the witness box shames me still. Later it would be recorded in my prison file that whilst giving my evidence I gave the appearance of being a character in an American soap opera, rather than a man on trial for murder.

To the right of the lawyers sat the detectives in charge of the case. They were clearly satisfied with the outcome. No doubt they would be out on the town that night celebrating their success, drinking with colleagues, backslapping and swapping anecdotes about their investigation. To them I was just another piece of society's rotten detritus.

The twelve members of the jury looked surprisingly subdued. They too had done their duty well. They had sat through eight days of evidence, listened to witnesses, asked a number of questions of the judge and watched me being cross-examined. The guilty verdict, delivered by their foreman, a thickset man wearing a crumpled suit and a severe haircut, had been unanimous. I was first to be sentenced and I knew the sentence that was coming was mandatory. I feared it as much as I had feared an acquittal. A 'not guilty' and freedom would have let me back out onto the streets to pick up the threads of my old life with all its chaos and dysfunction and would have been no freedom at all.

'Life imprisonment,' said the judge finally. He told me he was going to recommend to the Home Secretary that I serve a minimum of fourteen years. Then nodding to the prison officers on either side of me he said, 'Take him down.'

Before I moved I managed a quick look up to the public gallery where my father sat alone. He was fifty-one but at that moment he looked a whole lot older. The expression on his face reminded me of how he looked when he was drunk – his dark complexion becoming darker, his brown eyes squinting and blinking slowly as if he was peering into a secret place deep inside his head. He had a worn-out, haunted look about him. The trial began on my twenty-eighth birthday and he'd sent me a card wishing me luck: 'Don't worry, pal, we'll celebrate with a

Guinness when all this is over!' It was the only birthday card I could ever remember receiving from him.

The verdict must have wounded my father deeply. I wanted to smile to him, to let him know I would be OK. But all I could manage was a vague, meaningless grin. He looked down at me and then looked away. I had never seen my father cry before, but I was sure that I saw tears in his eyes. Were they for me, I wondered, or for him? I guessed they were probably for us both.

Marshalled by the prison officers I stepped through the door leading to the steep wooden stairs connecting the dock to the holding cells below. It was too late for apologies. I'd had my chance. Yet as I ducked beneath the doorway I had a sudden urge to turn back and tell everyone I was sorry. But would anybody listen? Would anybody care? I doubted it – and anyway the truth was I could not wait to get out of that courtroom, out of the public glare and away from my accusers. As usual whenever there were hard choices to be made, I just wanted to turn my back and run.

What I hadn't anticipated as I walked down those steps to begin my life sentence was the sense of relief that washed over me. By the time I reached the bottom of the stairs the realisation hit me that my life outside was finally at an end. It had been a painful life – but worse, other people's lives had been painful because of me. People were grieving because of me. I daren't even think about that. I was just so glad my life was over. One of the prison officers stepped in front of me to pull open the gate into the barred holding enclosure (known as the cage) especially reserved for high-risk prisoners. I was a Category A prisoner, or 'Cat A', the highest security category in the system, and the officer seemed a little anxious about how I might react to the sentence. He needn't have worried. I was too dazed to be anything other than totally compliant.

'You all right?' he asked before ushering me inside.

'I'm fine,' I said.

The officer then pushed the big gate closed behind me and turned the key.

Sitting on the long wooden bench that ran along the back of the cage, I stared at the cigarette butts on the floor and the graffiti on the bench and the walls. In one way I felt I had been released, freed from a life I wished I'd never had. But then I thought about my father, imagining him making his way out of the courthouse, head down, shoulders heavy. It would have been a strained and lonely journey back to his one-roomed apartment in Surrey. I had loved him all my life, but hated him too for a good part of it. That was something that I never really understood – how you could love and hate someone at the same time.

2

Later that afternoon I was taken back to Brixton Prison where I had been held on remand since my extradition from France five months earlier in November 1984. As the prisoner transport wagon sped through the busy London traffic I looked out of the tiny shaded cubicle window and had the sensation of having passed over into another dimension. I could see and hear life all around me but I knew I was no longer a part of the real world. I was still numb from the sentencing but my thoughts continued to dwell on my father. As a son I had never amounted to much but had always been desperate to achieve something in which he could feel some pride.

After committing my crimes I fled the country and joined the French Foreign Legion where I hid for almost two years. I sent him photographs of me in my Legion uniform taken during basic training in the South of France, and others taken when I was on manoeuvres in Corsica or on operations in Africa with my regiment, the 2nd Foreign Parachute Regiment – the *2ème REP*. He used to show off the pictures to his drinking cronies. It pleased me that he thought I had done something that he could be proud of at last. But I was never under any illusion that my Legion persona was anything more than a charade on my part – and now he knew it too.

In Brixton Prison before and during my trial I had been held in A SEG, a small special secure unit within the main prison that housed around a dozen or so Category A prisoners at any one time. When I was taken back to the prison after my trial I was assigned to D SEG, also a secure unit for Cat As, but much smaller than A SEG. As a remand prisoner I had been allowed to wear my own clothes, usually trainers, shorts and T-shirts. Now I was a convict things were very different. At the prison reception desk after handing over the grey suit my father had provided for me for my trial, I was kitted out with prison clothing – cheap, well-worn denims, a blue-and-white-striped shirt, scuffed, ill-fitting shoes and tiny nylon socks. Most humiliating of all was the underwear, big baggy under-pants that hung to my knees. The tiny semblance of normality that it had been possible to maintain as an unconvicted prisoner was gone.

I was given a meal of cold chips, pie and peas and then locked alone in a glass-walled waiting room. I'd barely finished the meal when a bald man in a suit and carrying a briefcase arrived outside accompanied by two prison officers. I thought he was a governor. An officer opened the door and let the man in. I made to stand up but he waved his hand. 'Please don't get up,' he said. His eyes darted around the room and he started slightly when the door was closed behind him. He seemed nervous. 'Er, just a quick word,' he said. 'I'm a doctor, a psychiatrist. I just need to assess you to see how you are coping with your sentence.'

I sighed deeply. 'Sure,' I said.

He sat down on the adjacent bench and pulled some papers out of his briefcase. His hand was shaking. I was trying to think of something to say to make him feel at ease, when he dropped the papers and then quickly bent down to retrieve them. 'Sorry,' he said. Now I was getting irritated and I sighed again. Finally he rested the papers on his lap and took out a pen. 'I just need to know . . .' he said. 'Are you having any thoughts of wanting to take your own life?'

I closed my eyes. I was tempted to say that I hadn't until he walked in, but managed to keep my cool. 'No,' I said. I wasn't going to tell him that I'd had those thoughts in the past, many times, but never had whatever it takes to actually do it, though his question did make me think of it as an option for the future.

Mentally at that moment I was still in no-man's-land. I hadn't had time to consider my situation in any depth. My brain felt like it was frozen. I didn't want conversation or questions. He asked me how I felt.

'Fine,' I said. 'I'm fine. I just want to get out of here and back to a cell.'

He wrote something down, ticked some boxes on a second sheet of paper and then signed a third sheet before passing it over to me. 'Could you sign this too, please,' he said. When I asked him what it was he said, 'It's just to say that you have been seen by a doctor. I've declared that you are fit to serve your sentence.' I took the paper and as soon as I had signed it he turned to the two officers outside and called, 'Yes, please,' and then he was gone.

I was still wondering what the chat with the psychiatrist was all about when four prison officers turned up and entered the room.

'Pick up your gear,' said the biggest of the group. I gathered up my bedroll and the large plastic mug containing my plastic knife, fork and spoon before they escorted me through the prison to D SEG.

My new cell had two doors: a conventional outer one and a heavy inner steel gate. Both were banged shut as soon as I stepped inside. Bolted to the floor was a standard single metal cot-bed with a wafer-thin mattress. The table and chair were made of pressed cardboard. On the floor by the far wall a stinking plastic toilet pot that was missing a lid revealed a puddle of the previous occupant's piss. It was a grim beginning and made me focus my thoughts more forcefully on what might lie ahead. I still carried a heady sense of relief that I did not have to go back out into the world again. But there was no getting away from the fact that spending years and years in this stark environment was going to take some getting used to. I made the bed and long before lights out crawled beneath the one coarse blanket that made up my bedroll. I was exhausted and despite the leanness of the mattress soon after I closed my eyes I was sleeping like a dead man.

When I woke up the next morning my brain seemed to be thawing out and my head was filled with all that had happened over the past few months. There was so much to think about, almost too much. After 'slop-out' (the ritual of emptying the toilet pot in a communal sluice) and breakfast of toast, a small pat of margarine and a hard-boiled egg, I was allowed out onto an exercise yard enclosed with wire mesh. It was a sharp sunny morning and I paced slowly back and forth while four prison officers stood watching me from strategic points on the other side of the wire.

Eventually I sat down in a corner from which I could see across to the caged yard of A SEG where the unconvicted men I'd been held with were being let out for exercise. In their colourful T-shirts and jeans and shorts they still looked like real people. Someone saw me and waved. The outcome of my case had been on the radio news. Somebody else shouted, 'Stay strong.' I raised a hand, but it felt like there was a chasm between us as wide as an ocean.

I'd been back in my cell for just a few minutes when a man identifying himself as the Deputy Governor appeared in the doorway. The main door was fastened wide open and he spoke to me through the bars of the secondary gate. 'How are you?' he said. He was small and pointy-faced with neatly combed oily hair that glistened under the fluorescent lights. His glasses looked as if they were meant for someone with a bigger head. He wore a brown jacket with a large check pattern and as he spoke to me he held his hands behind his back.

I nodded. 'All right, I suppose,' I said. I wasn't sure what to say.

'Do you need to see the doctor?'

I wondered if this was a test. I told him I'd already seen one. 'And he said I was fine.' What I wanted to know was how long I was going to be held in Brixton, in this grimy cell with its lingering stench of human waste. Brixton was a remand prison for unconvicted prisoners. As a convicted prisoner I was sure I should have been taken somewhere else from the Old Bailey.

Before I could ask him he began to explain. 'We've been told to keep you and your co-accused apart,' he said. 'He's gone to the Scrubs. We're just waiting for the Home Office to say where you are going. Shouldn't take more than a week or two. We'll let you know as soon as we hear. In the meantime just let one of my officers know if you have any problems.'

Any problems? Was it possible to have any more? I had no space in my head to think about my co-accused. He and I had never been friends. We were just two failed human beings whose paths had crossed with devastating consequences. He had been the first to be arrested when property stolen from the home of one of our victims was found at his mother's house.

Questioned by detectives he admitted being involved in our crimes but said he had acted under duress from me, and then bizarrely told them he had joined the Foreign Legion with me. His defence at our trial was that he was terrified of me, that I had dominated him and pressured him. Although I was voluntarily extradited from France, when I read the version of events he had given the police in the case depositions and was told by my solicitor that the prosecution case against me was going to be based on his testimony I felt like I was backed into a corner. That was the main reason I pleaded not guilty. There was no evidence to back up his story, not enough to convince the jury, who found him guilty of one count of murder and one of manslaughter. As we stood in the dock together however, his short, slight stature contrasted sharply with my tall, heavy build – and in the eyes of the judge at least, our physical differences lent some plausibility to his claims. But I was no better than him. His lies had simply made it easier for me to tell my lies. Now all I wanted to do was lie down on the bed and sleep.

I didn't want to talk or to think. I turned away from the Deputy Governor and began straightening out the bed cover. He continued scrutinising me through the bars of the gate for some moments and then turned on his heels and walked away. Over the next few days I tried hard to blank out the reality of my situation. It was impossible. I spent long hours lying on my bed drifting back over the months since August when I was first taken into custody.

It was my father who had first alerted me that I was a wanted man. He had just spent several days in Calvi in Corsica, the home of my regiment's base, Camp Raffalli, after arriving without warning to pay me a surprise visit. The day after he landed I was in the gun room cleaning weapons when a stocky Spanish sergeant called Sanchez came to see me. He told me my father was in town, creating '*un bordel*' (Legion slang for a bout of violent troublemaking, almost always involving alcohol). At first I didn't believe him. 'Oh it is your father,' he said. 'A mad Scottish man.' That was enough to convince me.

He told me that my father had been drinking in different bars around the town and was telling anyone who would listen to him, 'I've come for my boy.' He'd got drunker and drunker and then passed out down by the harbour. Two associates of mine on Legion military police patrol had kept an eye on him throughout the night as they did their rounds. Sanchez said he had told the duty adjutant that I had a family problem and should be granted a special twenty-four-hour pass to go and see my father.

I changed from my combat denims into my dress uniform and took a taxi into town.

As I scoured the backstreet bars and cafés I picked up little stories about my father's behaviour the day before. In one bar he'd fallen into the company of a group of Legionnaires and then taken a white kepi from the hat stand and walked out of the bar with it on his head. The men he had been drinking with took it in good humour and followed him into another bar where a band had been playing. Whilst the band members were having a drink, my father had climbed onto the small stage, picked up a guitar and started singing songs by his hero, Hank Williams. At another bar, still with the kepi on his head, he had mounted a bicycle left by the entrance and tried to ride it away, only to tumble and crash just a few yards down the cobbled street. The angry owner had to be held back from giving my father a beating. These antics were so typical of him when he was 'on a bender'. Sober, he was the most charming and likeable of people. But drink changed his whole personality. The only good thing was that, now he had lost his health and aged prematurely, he was no longer violent when drunk.

Eventually a bar owner called Lydia told me he had been in her establishment that morning and seeing the state he was in she had insisted on booking him into a boarding house round the corner. She gave me the address and off I went to find him. I had been anxious when I first realised that he was in Calvi, even more so when I heard what he had been up to. But as I climbed the stairs up to his room the same old feelings of excited anticipation began rumbling in my belly.

I knocked on his door and heard him shout. When I went in he was lying on the top of his bed wearing only his blue jeans. His glasses were perched on his nose and he was reading a paperback Western.

'Hello, son,' he said, stretching out a hand.

'Hi, Dad,' I said as I shook it firmly. It was good to see him, even like this. 'For fuck's sake,' I said. 'What have you been doing?'

He just smiled innocently and protested, 'What?'

'You know what,' I said. 'You're lucky you didn't get shot.'

He jumped up from the bed laughing and I waited for him to get dressed. He was ready for a drink, he said, and so was I. It was the only way we could communicate. We spent the day drinking in bars around the town and talking nonsense. When I left him to go back to camp he was smashed but in the company of two Corsican women who, though unable to speak English, appeared to be enjoying his bantering. I was just tired from having to act with him like I had had to in the years before I fled.

I saw my father a couple of times over the next few days. Each time we sat and drank for a few hours before I had to rush back to camp. He palled up with a number of English-speaking Legionnaires who liked his playful manner. He was 'a good laugh', they said.

'It must be great having a father like him,' one man said to me.

'Yes,' I said, 'we're like mates.' What a lie that was.

The day before he was due to return to the UK, I persuaded the duty adjutant to give me a pass to go looking for him so I could say my goodbyes. I searched all the usual places, but in vain.

Nobody had seen him. I checked his boarding house. No luck there either. Finally I gave up and caught the slow open-topped train that ran across the brow of the beach from Calvi right along the coast and passed within a few hundred yards of Camp Raffalli. The scorching sun sparkled off the sea and the golden sands were heaving with tourists – families, couples, friends – all shapes, sizes and colours, all living lives they understood and appeared to be enjoying. I envied them so much.

I was jolted out of my reverie by the sight of a figure I recognised instantly. My father was curled up in a ball on the sand, bare from the waist up, his eyes closed. Around him lay empty bottles. As the train trundled past I thought how pathetic he looked, pathetic and vulnerable. It was hard to believe that this weak, shrivelled man had inflicted so much hurt on so many people over his lifetime. Seeing him unconscious on the beach that day was the first time I had felt pity for him.

Two days later I called him from one of the camp telephone kiosks. I needed to know that he had arrived home safely. His telephone was a coin-operated public box that was attached to the wall in the communal area outside the door to his tiny apartment. He always took a while to answer. When he did my bogus existence was brought to an end. 'Son,' he said. 'You're wanted for murder.'

3

My father told me that on his return to the UK he had been stopped by detectives when he got off the plane at Gatwick Airport. Information from my co-accused had led them to him. Since we had exactly the same names the police thought the passenger they were waiting for might even have been me. They took him into custody and questioned him for some hours. 'They fucking stripped me,' he said. When he arrived home he found that his apartment had been ransacked in their search for clues to my whereabouts. They had taken letters and photographs I had sent him from various places I had been with the Legion. They now knew exactly where I was.

'You weren't involved, were you, son?'

My head spun in panic. It was the moment I had been dreading since I left England. I felt so much for my father, but in that instant I just could not bring myself to tell him the truth.

'No,' I said. 'No, of course not, Dad.'

After replacing the handset I thought about going to my captain and explaining the situation. I'd heard about another Legionnaire who was wanted for murder in his own country and came close to being apprehended by French police after he was recognised by a countryman whilst on leave in Paris. When he was questioned the wanted man ran, pursued through the city by the police right up to the doors of Fort de Nogent, the Legion recruitment depot in Vincennes. He was moments from being arrested when the door opened and he disappeared inside. Despite protestations from the police the Legion guards refused to hand him over. Instead the big door was shut tight and he was spirited away, never to be heard of again. But my conscience had driven me half mad already and now that I knew that the British police were on to me I didn't think I would be mentally strong enough to stay on the run for much longer.

That night I walked out of Camp Raffalli on the pretext of going into town for a drink. I would not be returning. A few weeks earlier, after our regiment got back from a four-month tour of duty in Chad, central Africa, I had been in front of our company captain who had asked me where I wanted to go next. The Legion had a construction regiment in Tahiti with a guard complement protecting the French nuclear-testing site at Mururoa Atoll and that was where I asked to be sent. He said he was going to recommend that I undertake a full corporal's course beforehand and that he would be expecting me to make sergeant before the end of my five-year contract.

I'd had a number of big *bordels* during my time with the *REP.* Once, after a drunken fight with a regular French Army sergeant in the Chadian capital N'Djamena which left the bar we were in totally wrecked, the same captain had asked me, 'How would you like to be a civilian?' But he stood by me when I said I would make twice the effort to maintain good conduct worthy of a Legionnaire. He would be disappointed when he learned of my departure, but when he found out why maybe he would understand my extreme ups and downs.

I knew that on the other side of the island there was a regular ferry from Ajaccio to mainland France. Uplifted by the idea that my days as a fugitive were coming to an end, I planned to disembark at Nice and hand myself in to the British authorities at the nearest embassy. I was never the perfect soldier, but the values the Legion had taught me had given me a flavour of the importance of moral responsibility. The knowledge that I was now a wanted man was the only trigger I needed to give myself up. Whatever was waiting for me in England, I knew that going back was the right thing to do. That night I slept in a derelict shop on the outskirts of Calvi, covered by an old tarpaulin. As I lay in the pitch-dark I felt something heavy crawl over my chest. I thought it was a rat, a big rat. I didn't flinch.

Early the next day I made my way carefully back into town looking for somewhere to buy clothes. They had to be cheap as we were a week from payday and I had little cash left. I found a tiny, run-down-looking shop run by an elderly Corsican woman where I bought some jeans, a couple of T-shirts, some shorts, some sandals and a floppy hat to cover my '*boule zéro*' haircut – the instant giveaway of a Legionnaire in Corsica, however he is dressed.

The woman looked at me knowingly. She clearly took me for a deserter. '*Légion, pas bonne?*' she asked.

There was still great resentment of France among the significant numbers of Corsicans who wanted independence. But generally the Legion was tolerated, though there was little fraternisation between Legionnaires and locals.

'*Au contraire*,' I said. '*La Légion est très, très bonne.*'

She turned up her mouth and lifted her eyebrows before handing over my change. I joined the Legion for ignominious reasons but I loved the life it gave me. Stashing my uniform and treasured white kepi behind a wall felt like an act of sacrilege.

Wearing civilian clothes made travelling in daylight a little less nerve-racking. Legion military police patrols were always on the lookout for deserters and I was desperate not to be apprehended on the island. That would have been disastrous. There was no way of knowing how the Legion would react to a request from the British police to hand me over. The last thing I wanted was to be ghosted overseas to a regiment in Africa or South America and lose control of the situation. Whatever fate was waiting for me I was determined to go back and face it.

I took a train all the way from Calvi to Ajaccio and then bought a ticket for the next available ferry to Nice. When it was time to board I mingled with the tourists and nonchalantly strolled up the gangplank. Half an hour later the big engines reverberated throughout the ship. As it pulled away from the harbour I was filled with trepidation.

The ferry took just under four hours to reach the mainland. I spent all of that time out on the decks, staring across the water, looking at seabirds and watching as the coast grew closer and closer, wondering what was going to happen to me. I knew I was going to be locked up, but my fears were not just about prison.

More daunting was the idea of facing up to the truth. By the time we reached the shore my anxiety was unbearable. I stepped off the gangway and instead of seeking out the appropriate authorities I headed for the nearest convenience store. I bought bread and cheese and a couple of litres of cheap wine and then went in search of a quiet spot on the beach where I could sit and try and slow down my thinking.

For the next three nights I stayed on the beach trying to figure out what to do, hanging out with a motley group of itinerants I stumbled across who had put together a makeshift camp. All day long I drank wine and dozed in the sun or swam myself clean in the warm sea. At night somebody played a guitar and others joined in the singing around a driftwood fire. A couple of times they tried to get me to join in, but I declined. I had no desire to sing and I knew that all I was doing by staying among them was putting off the inevitable. At noon on the fourth day I made my decision.

I walked along the Promenade des Anglais looking for a policeman and spotted a white-gloved traffic patrolman standing next to his parked motorcycle. When I asked him where I could find the British Embassy, he shook his head. '*N'est pas ici,*' he said. He explained that there was no embassy in Nice, only an honorary consul, and then kindly radioed his station to obtain the address for me. He wrote it down and I thanked him. I expected at least an office. Instead I discovered that the Consul, a pink-faced, silver-haired gentleman, operated from his own private apartment in an exclusive part of town.

'Yes?' he said, upon opening the heavily ornate door.

It was an awkward moment. 'Er, I was in the Foreign Legion,' I said. 'I'm involved in a story of murder in England and I'm wanted by the British police.'

The old man's eyes widened. He asked me what I thought he could do about it. I said I didn't know. He said if I was telling the truth I should go to the *Consulat Général* in Marseille and talk to someone there, or hand myself over to the French police, something I hadn't considered until then. The only problem was I had spent the few francs I had with me when I left the camp and had nothing to pay for fares to anywhere. Marseille was maybe a hundred miles away. I turned round to think for a moment and heard the door close behind me, bringing an end to my consular assistance.

It was going to be a long walk along the Riviera, I decided. I only had the clothes I had bought from the old Corsican woman. On manoeuvres with the Legion we marched sometimes for forty or fifty kilometres a day in full combat gear carrying heavy sacks on our backs, weapons and ammunition. The sandals I had on were meant for nothing more testing than a stroll along the sea-front. With no money and no alternative plans I set off for the main coastal highway. Head down, I walked on for mile after mile, counting down the kilometres marked on every road sign I passed. I tried my hand at hitchhiking but not a single vehicle showed even a hint of stopping for me. After nearly three hours I passed Antibes, a distance of around ten miles. I paused only once for water at a public drinking fountain. Ignoring the hunger pangs I set off again and an hour and a half later reached the outskirts of Cannes. Across the luscious hills overlooking the sea were some of the most beautiful houses I had ever seen, all bathed in brilliant sunshine. Everywhere I looked it seemed people were living wonderful lives. I searched for picnic areas close to the beach and rummaged in the bins for food. There was a surprising amount left to eat. Tied in little refuse bags I found cheese and bread, half-full jars of olives and other delicacies – I even found wine dregs and napkins.

After eating and drinking my fill I moved on. Marseille was still more than eighty miles away. I had covered about fifteen miles so far and decided to walk until I was exhausted and then find somewhere to get my head down for the night. I saw the signs for Saint-Raphaël indicating a distance of twenty miles or so. That was going to be my target for the day. Ten miles later I gave in when the sandals finally fell apart and I was down to walking on my bare feet. A barn close to the road offered shelter for the night. I snuggled up between bales of straw and covered myself with a heavy weatherproof overcoat I found hanging. Soon after closing my eyes I settled on a change of plan. Darkness fell and sleep came quickly.

The traffic was busy the following morning when I went back to the highway. But instead of walking I stood and faced the passing cars. I waited for almost an hour until I saw a jeep approaching with the livery of the gendarmes. I raised and crossed my hands and minutes later I was sitting in the back seat on my way to the gendarmerie at Sainte-Maxime, a pretty seaside town a short drive from Saint-Tropez.

Apart from the desk sergeant the small gendarmerie was empty. The two gendarmes who took me in were friendly and charming at first, but were unconvinced by my urgent pleading to be handed over to the British authorities. They asked their colleague to make me coffee and allowed me to sit in the glass-fronted reception area with no restriction of my movements. Certain I was a Legion deserter, they chuckled and told me they had already contacted Legion headquarters in Aubagne and that a patrol had been dispatched to collect me. Aubagne was only an hour's drive away. I knew I had to tell them more. '*Mais, Je suis recherché en Angleterre – pour meurtre,*' I said. 'I'm wanted in England for murder.' They laughed again. I urged them to contact Interpol – I was sure there would be an international arrest warrant out for me. I raised my voice. '*Téléphonez!*'

The older of the two stopped smiling and stared at me for a couple of seconds, a serious look on his face for the first time. He picked up the phone on the counter and tapped on the number pad. Somebody answered and he asked to be put through to central office. Someone there gave him a number and he hung up and tapped the pad again. We waited in silence. I could hear the faint hum of the ringing tone from the handset. It rang and rang but still no answer. Eventually he gave up. '*Putain!*' he exclaimed. 'Do they not work on Sundays?'

I had lost track of the days and hadn't even realised it was the weekend. The fact it was Sunday explained the slow pace of life outside the big windows. But the idea of Interpol being closed for the day was ridiculous. I began to feel panic rising. Unless the Legion had been contacted by the British police, they too would assume I had merely deserted. I could see a whole range of complications developing. '*Monsieur*,' I said solemnly. In my best pronunciation of his language I implored him to telephone Scotland Yard in London. All three officers looked at me at once and began nodding at each other. '*Ah, oui, oui*,' they said almost in unison. Good, I thought – they had heard of Scotland Yard.

The older officer again went through his procedure with his control centre and soon a telephone was ringing in an office somewhere in police headquarters in London. A female voice answered. The gendarme began to explain, apologising for his limited English. He spelled out my name a couple of times, but didn't know the English for 'murder'. He had to ask me. He repeated what I had said to the person on the other end of the phone and then there was silence. The woman spoke again and must have asked him to confirm some details. '*Oui*,' he said. 'Er yes, *mais deux?*' He squinted hard at the phone. I hadn't told him there were two murders being investigated. We waited and then a male voice came on the line. The voice sounded animated. Without taking the handset from his ear the gendarme turned to his colleague and glanced at his sidearm. I had no intention of moving a muscle. The younger man was standing about ten feet away from me. He unclipped his gun holster and drew his weapon carefully before pointing it directly at the centre of my chest.

'*Restez là, Monsieur,*' he said calmly.

'*Pas de problème,*' I said, keeping perfectly still. At least now they believed me.

While the younger man kept me in his gunsights the older man replaced the telephone handset, drew out his handcuffs and shackled my wrists to the back of the chair. The younger man replaced his weapon, took two more sets of handcuffs from the desk sergeant and shackled both my ankles to the chair legs. Once I was secured the three men relaxed. Out of my earshot the gendarmes had a quick discussion with lowered voices and a fourth colleague was summoned from a back room. Together the four men then lifted me in the chair and carried me through a swing door and into a corridor.

There were four cells in the corridor all of which had their doors wide open. Grunting and cursing, they manoeuvred me through the doorway of the nearest cell and laid me down on my side on a wooden bench that served as the bed. Exertions over, they exited the cell, slammed the door closed and slid over a bolt before leaving me in silence – still chained to the chair. Within moments of being left alone I had a powerful sense of being at peace and an urge to go to sleep, but real sleep would have been impossible. The pain from the handcuffs was increasing, especially from those that held my wrists. Though I knew it would be pointless, I wanted to shout out. Instead I tried to mentally block the pain – I doubted they would be returning in a hurry. But just a few minutes later I heard footsteps and voices and then a key turning in the cell door. They were back.

Whatever they were planning, there was very little I could do to stop them. The older gendarme was the first in. I braced myself for some more manhandling, but to my surprise apologies were offered for my discomfort. They could take no chances of losing me, the senior gendarme explained. It would have been too embarrassing, he said, if I'd made a dash for it and escaped. Between the four of them they unfastened the handcuffs and lifted the chair from me, allowing me to flop down on the bed. Later they brought me a couple of blankets and food and coffee and spoke to me politely before leaving me alone once more. As soon as I'd finished eating I stretched out on the bed and pulled the covers up over my head and tried to sleep. I heard the door open some hours later and a pile of magazines was dropped onto the cell floor. All I wanted to do was sleep and kept my head well under the covers. Apart from the spyhole in the cell door sliding open intermittently throughout the night there were no more disturbances.

In the morning a gendarme I hadn't seen before brought fresh coffee and a *pain au chocolat* and informed me that I should get myself ready to go as I was being transferred to a prison. He handed me a worn pair of tennis shoes. '*Où ça?*' I said. He couldn't tell me where, he said. I'd find out once I was there. I tried on the shoes. They were a size too big but I tied the laces tight and they were fine. With something on my feet again I felt a little less vulnerable. '*Bonne chance,*' said the gendarme as he closed the cell door. Half an hour later I was back in the reception area.

It was a boisterous departure. News of my capture had been relayed to other gendarmes and as well as the two who had brought me in and four members of the new shift, there were another half-dozen who'd turned up to have a look at me. The reception area was so crowded that the main doors had to be kept open to accommodate the overspill. I stood handcuffed squeezed up against the reception desk whilst relevant documentation was signed and witnessed.

The two who had brought me in were congratulated many times by their colleagues for their '*bon travail*'. The mood amongst all the officers present was buoyant. Everybody was happy it seemed with their big catch. Another pair of handcuffs was produced and I was double-cuffed to a young gendarme from the new shift before being taken outside and guided into the back seat of an unmarked car. Two others climbed in the front and soon we were speeding towards Draguignan, a journey of around ten miles during which nobody spoke. There was no hint of any personal animosity towards me and there was no reason for me to be especially defensive. The process for my return to the UK was now in motion. All I had to do was wait.

Draguignan Prison was ancient but relatively comfortable. I was taken to the lower ground floor where there were just three cells under a big alcove and all were empty. The cells had no doors, only gates with rusting bars. The glass on the window of the cell I was allocated had been painted over a dark green and the window bars were rusty. The walls were damp, but there was a quaintness about the place. The old table and chair were made of solid oak, as was the bed frame, and under the window there was a large enamel washbasin on an oak stand. The fabric of that part of the prison was poor – but the attitude of the guards was laid-back. They brought me fresh salad and fruit and as much coffee as I wanted. I was kept there for two days and on the third day three plain-clothes detectives from the *Police Municipale* arrived to take me to court for the extradition hearing. Again my wrists were handcuffed together. I was double-cuffed to one of the detectives and placed in the rear seat of their car. The courthouse was only a mile or so away and we were there within minutes.

It was a brief hearing, all conducted in French, naturally. The court resembled any magistrates' court in Britain. The *juge d'instruction*, a grey-haired man with gold-rimmed spectacles, presided alongside a middle-aged blonde woman, who appeared to be advising him. First he asked me if I was fluent in French. '*Oui, Monsieur*,' I said. Legion French is famously littered with *argot*, slang, and words adopted from other languages. My conversational French for polite company still needed some work, but I could understand most of what was being said. The judge asked me if I needed an interpreter. '*Non, Monsieur*,' I said. There were one or two legal terms which went over my head but I got the gist of the proceedings. I was asked if I intended to oppose my extradition. '*Non, Monsieur*,' I said again. I explained that I hoped that the process could be carried out as speedily as possible. He seemed a little surprised by my cooperation, but continued reading out various parts of the documents he had in front of him. He read out the charges I would be facing and then asked me if I understood everything he had said. '*Oui, Monsieur*,' I said.

Less than two hours later I was back in the rear seat of the police car, handcuffed to the same detective as before. This time I was driven to a police station in Marseille. I was held there for just the one night, but late in the evening the lead detective of the three came to my cell alone, unlocked the door and invited me to join him in his office. I thought I was going to be questioned and saw no reason to refuse. I followed him out of the cell area and into his office where I sat down facing him across his desk.

'*Voulez-vous boire quelque chose?*' he asked. I nodded. He then took a bottle of pastis and two glasses from a drawer in his desk. He poured us both two fingers of the aniseed-flavoured liquor and then added water from a dispenser on the wall behind him.

'*Merci,*' I said when he passed me the drink.

'So,' said the detective in English, 'you like France?'

I told him in French that I liked France very much.

'And the Legion?'

I said I liked the Legion very much too. '*C'est ma famille,*' I said.

'*Mais pas encore,*' he said, reverting to French and smiling.

We chatted for a while about nothing in particular. He complimented me on my skill with his language and expressed some sympathy for my 'predicament'. I told him I had brought it on myself and then he wrapped up our little chat before taking me back to my cell. The next day the same three detectives took me to Baumettes Prison in Marseille, the *Centre pénitentiaire*, at the time the biggest prison in Europe.

4

Baumettes was a concrete and steel fortress. It held around fifteen hundred prisoners, mostly three or four to a cell. It was a filthy place. All I knew about it beforehand was that it was the site of the last execution in France. It was hard to believe that the state killing had taken place only seven years earlier in July 1977 and the condemned man had been put to death by guillotine. This was my first taste of serious prison. Security was tight but the guards appeared reasonable enough. I was locked in a cell with two other men who were being held on remand. I was given no basic necessities such as toiletries or underwear. Such requisites had to be purchased, I was told. Since I had no money this could have proved awkward as prisoners even had to provide their own toilet paper. Luckily my two cellmates were kind enough to let me share some of their provisions.

Exercise in Baumettes was taken in rows of square cages that held ten men at a time. It entailed pacing up and down the ten-metre length of the cage for an hour in the morning and an hour in the afternoon. Conversations were conducted by one of us walking forwards and the other walking backwards – and then vice versa for the return. The pace could get hectic and there were plenty of arguments about space and elbows. I discovered that my arrest and the terms of the warrant on which I was being held had been reported in all the local papers. Once word was out in the cages that I was '*le Légionnaire*', I attracted some attention. People wanted to know more about my story. But I was uncomfortable with those around me knowing why I was among them. From the moment my father had told me that I was wanted, all pretence that I was a bona fide soldier evaporated. I had been found out. Almost immediately my sense of self reverted to what it had been when I had been loose on the streets in the UK. Insecure, detached and cowardly – I was again a base criminal failure.

I spent the next few weeks keeping myself to myself, fending off unwanted conversations with grunts and sullen looks. In the cell I read and listened to a radio belonging to one of my cellmates. I had no idea how long the extradition procedure was going to take. Then without warning one day the cell door opened and I was told to pack my kit.

Since I now wore mostly prison clothes and had nothing but a toothbrush, soap and towel, it was not long before I was in the reception area and, along with several dozen other men, being processed for the next part of the journey. We were handcuffed together in twos and taken in a convoy of coaches to the main Marseille railway station. Police armed with 9mm MAT machine guns manned the gauntlet as we were led from the coaches along the platforms in full view of the other passengers and on to two especially reserved carriages. An armed policeman sat at either end of each carriage and that was how we stayed for the next few hours until we reached the Gare de Lyon in Paris where the same security measures were taken to get us off the trains and on to waiting coaches.

Fresnes Prison was only slightly smaller than Baumettes. This time we were four to a cell and there were a lot fewer exercise periods. When I first entered my cell the conversation between me and the other three was interesting and animated even. One man who had been a professional tennis coach and robbed banks in his spare time was a real joker. His name was Pierre and he and I became quite friendly. He'd been in that cell for almost three years awaiting trial. Long remand periods were the norm it seemed in the French system. The other two had been waiting almost as long. After a while the conversation trickled away to just occasional chats between Pierre and me. I read a lot of books that were brought around on a trolley by a trusted prisoner. Most of the time the others spent sleeping – and eventually so did I.

It was three months almost to the day since I left Camp Raffalli when the time for my formal extradition finally arrived. French detectives took me from the prison to Orly Airport where I was handed over to three detectives from the UK. During my spell in the French prison system I had relaxed slightly. The attitude of the French authorities towards me had been neutral. On the plane I was seated at the back, handcuffed to one of the British detectives, and I felt threatened by the phoney friendly chit-chat. They had brought British newspapers to show me the reports of my capture. Not surprisingly they appeared upbeat. 'You made the headlines this time,' said the man in charge.

The lead detective tried to engage me in conversation a number of times during the short flight to Heathrow. I was polite, but nothing he said gave me any confidence that I'd be safe talking openly to him. Whenever he brought up the subject of my crimes I clammed up. When the plane started to descend his manner changed. 'Shit or bust then, is it?' I said nothing. 'Well it's life you're looking at now, Erwin,' he said.

Once we'd landed at Heathrow and the rest of the passengers had vacated the plane the detectives produced a blanket from a small holdall. 'For the press.' I was walked awkwardly along the aisle of the plane and then just before we exited the blanket was draped over my head. With a detective in front of me holding on to my handcuffs and the man in charge behind me I trod cautiously down the steep aircraft steps. I found out later that this was the image that was broadcast on at least one national television news programme. They kept me under the blanket as I was ushered into a waiting unmarked car and driven to an anonymous part of the terminal.

There the blanket was removed as I stepped out of the car and was made to stand in front of a group of customs officers and plain-clothes police. One man stood out – a detective constable who was over seven feet tall. He had been summoned especially to be my personal guard and looked nervous and embarrassed as one of his colleagues handcuffed our wrists together. They were not taking any chances. On paper I was clearly a very dangerous individual. The police had in their possession photographs I had sent my father in which I appeared with formidable-looking comrades in a variety of colourful locations, and loaded with heavy-duty weapons. Yet in truth I could not have been a more compliant prisoner.

Papers were checked and signed before I was guided back into the car with my giant escort in tow and driven away through a series of lanes that eventually led to a checkpoint. The barrier was raised and soon we were gunning along the motorway heading in to London. The journey to the north London police station where the detectives were based took just over an hour. There I was charged with the two counts of murder and robbery and put in a cell overnight. The next morning I made an appearance at Bow Street Magistrates' Court where I was remanded in custody to await trial. Soon I was back in the unmarked car and once more speeding through the busy city traffic, this time towards Brixton Prison where I was to be located on A SEG.

My experience of the criminal justice system before these events had consisted mainly of drunken overnight stays in police cells and appearances in front of magistrates' courts usually resulting in fines and probation or 'community service'. I'd had a couple of stints of custody as a teenager – six months in a detention centre for car theft and burglary when I was seventeen and the following year thirteen months of 'Borstal training' for similar offences. The only adult-prison time I'd served was six weeks among the winos and vagrants in Pentonville Prison for non-compliance of a community service order. I had never been through a trial and had never known people who made a living from professional crime.

Many prisoners in A SEG were surprisingly open about their criminal activity, lots of nods, winks and hints. In criminal parlance they were 'heavy' characters in the main, men who attacked security cash vans, robbed banks, or killed for money.

If they had known me in my previous existence I doubt that any of them would have considered me a worthy associate. But being charged with two murders and spending time in the French Foreign Legion apparently afforded me a measure of criminal credibility. One man in the unit even had a copy of photojournalist John Robert Young's recently published book about the Legion on the back of which was a photograph of a platoon of Legionnaires marching in dress uniform. When I walked on to the unit he said, 'Oi, there's a picture of you on the back of my book!' Sure enough, in the top right-hand corner of the back cover there I was, white kepi on my head, bright red-and-green epaulettes flashing on my shoulders and a bayonet-fixed rifle across my chest – marching alongside men I knew well and who had become like brothers to me. It gave me instant, but uncomfortable, acceptance in the group.

I was unaware before I joined them of how high-profile the crimes were with which many of the men I was with in A SEG had been charged. Along with two associates being held at another prison, there were two Israelis reportedly connected to Mossad, the Israeli secret service agency. They were accused of kidnapping the former Nigerian Transport Minister Umaru Dikko in London. One of the kidnap gang, an anaesthetist, was said to have rendered the man unconscious with drugs before he was bundled into a large wooden packing case which was then loaded on to a jet at Stansted Airport. Dikko had been rescued moments before the jet was due to take off.

Two others, Kenneth Noye and Brian Reader, were accused of murdering the policeman John Fordham in the grounds of Noye's home as Fordham was investigating the £26m Brink's-MAT gold bullion robbery at Heathrow Airport. Another was said to have supplied the weapons used in the same robbery. Two more, one of whom was the Great Train Robber Charlie Wilson, were awaiting trial for their suspected involvement in large-scale organised crime; and three others were members of the gang alleged to have carried out what was then Britain's biggest ever cash robbery, the £6m raid on the Security Express depot in Curtain Road, East London. Noye, Reader and Wilson were eventually acquitted, while the men accused of the Security Express robbery were found guilty and sentenced to long terms.

One of the biggest personalities in the unit was a man accused of killing two people in a restaurant after closing time. The prosecution said that he had used a sword to decapitate one of the victims. 'St Valentine's Day Massacre!' screamed one tabloid headline. Each evening as his trial progressed he would return to the unit and regale us with accounts of his fiery exchanges with the prosecutor. 'It's been cut and thrust all day,' he joked. Two weeks after he was acquitted he sent us all a postcard from Spain.

Despite the seriousness of the crimes with which we had all been charged, life in A SEG was not altogether disagreeable. The men held there had a greater level of maturity, either in age or attitude, than the average prisoner I had come across on French prison landings. Some of them had businesses outside. One owned a taxi firm. Another ran a chain of small supermarkets. Those who could afford it paid for lavish cooked meals to be delivered to the unit and shared the food among us. Few of us were forced to eat prison food. As well as being allowed to have food delivered we were allowed to have alcohol brought in: a daily allowance of two pints of beer or a pint of wine. On top of the legitimate quota, vodka or gin was injected into oranges and grapefruit and delivered by visitors – and cans of soft drinks were pierced and emptied and then filled with spirits by syringe. The tiny hole in the can was plugged with putty and covered over with a price tag. There was so much booze on the unit that every few evenings before bang-up there was a 'party' in at least one cell, when tongues became loose and even role-playing to practice for the high-pressure cross-examination we would all be facing in court was acted out, sometimes with darkly humorous results.

Said a 'prosecutor' to a 'defendant', 'Can you please explain to the jury what those guns were doing under your mother's bed?'

'Yeah. She shoots grouse.'

'With three Uzis and a Kalashnikov?'

'There's some fucking big grouse on Romney Marsh . . .'

A man of Middle-Eastern origin was being held on charges of manufacturing electronic bomb-timers for export to Libya. He presented as a gangly, guileless soul who appeared massively out of his depth. Quickly nicknamed Radar Ronnie, he was taken into the fold and given as much space as he needed to share his apparently heartfelt and genuine protestations of innocence. His arrest and confinement in A SEG was generally perceived to be a 'bleedin' liberty' and further evidence if any was needed of the unjustly heavy hand of the state. At his trial his jury were unconvinced. After their guilty verdict his judge awarded him fourteen years.

Then two men arrived on the SEG who had been striking miners. I hadn't realised that the miners' strike had been such a huge issue for the country while I had been away. The two were charged with the murder of a taxi driver who had been killed when a lump of concrete was thrown from an overhead bridge. The taxi driver had been taking a strike-breaking miner to work. The men on the SEG were on the side of the miners.

Some of the men in A SEG really were innocent. Three young RAF aircraftmen who had been arrested in Cyprus and accused of being part of the 'Cyprus Spy Ring' were obvious cases. All three were looking at thirty years apiece if convicted. Fortunately for them, the jury saw through the dodgy prosecution case. The system worked as it should and they were all acquitted.

Facing up to the horror of my crimes was always going to be hard. By the time I was extradited and remanded to Brixton I was seriously having second thoughts about handing myself in. Then I received my copies of the case depositions and witness statements and read the lies of my co-accused. When the first solicitor who came to see me in Brixton told me that 'nobody ever pleads guilty to murder' it was like the choice was already made for me. I was finished either way. With nothing to lose I decided on shit or bust. I had handed myself in to the French authorities with what I thought were good intentions. But in the end it was all about self-preservation.

As for my shameful performance in front of the judge and the jury, I'd been able to stand up to cross-examination during my trial thanks to one of the men in A SEG who slipped me a couple of tranquillisers before I left the jail on the morning I was due to go in the witness box. I swallowed them without water and by the time I got into court the sedative effect had calmed my anxieties and suppressed my inhibitions. Use of the tablets was widespread on the unit. The man who gave them to me had been on trial some years earlier for murder. On that occasion he'd been found not guilty. 'Take the bastards on,' he advised me. 'You're innocent, remember. How would an innocent man act?'

I only wished I knew.

5

My movement order came through exactly two weeks after I was sentenced. The same governor who'd welcomed me to Brixton gave me the news. I asked him where I was going. 'I'm afraid we can't tell you that,' he said, 'but it's not far.' In reception they had me strip-searched and fitted for transfer by a doctor in under half an hour. On board the transport wagon and locked in a cubicle again I was glad to be leaving Brixton behind at last regardless of where they were taking me. I wasn't on the move for long. We had hardly got through half-a-dozen traffic jams before I spotted a sign that signalled my destination. Soon the wagon was trundling through the massive gateway into the dark heart of Her Majesty's Prison Wandsworth.

The reception process in Wandsworth was more demeaning than in Brixton, but only because of the aggressive manner of the prison officers. I walked into the brightly lit reception area and the first thing I noticed was the row of toilet-sized cubicles, some with doors open and some with doors closed. Almost immediately an officer with the peak of his cap 'slashed' so it sat low over his forehead almost covering his eyes steered me into one of the tiny enclosures. He banged the three-quarter door shut behind me and slid over a bolt. I could sense other bodies behind the closed doors on either side of me but there was no interaction between any of us.

I sat on the narrow bench seat fixed to the back wall and listened to the chatter of the prison officers. Other officers arrived and joined in. There was laughter and talk about a particular 'con' that they didn't like. He'd been their tea boy. Behind his back they called him the 'Twat'. They needed another 'Twat', said one with a cackle. Their conversation became more animated. 'Fucking Cat As,' said another. 'They think they own these fucking places.' I knew that only one Cat A prisoner at a time was ever allowed in a prison reception area and today it was me. I was already subdued. The impact of the trial had numbed my senses and two weeks in Brixton hadn't done much to thaw me out. The relief I felt after my sentencing had long since ebbed away. But I'd never felt intimidated in prison until my introduction to Wandsworth.

My Legion persona had served me well in the French prisons. It served me even better in Brixton's A SEG. Fellow prisoners called me 'the Legionnaire'. It gave me a feeling of protection – and an odd sort of reassurance that I was more than what I was. Now in the reception cubicle in Wandsworth Prison I was aware that I had no status or protection at all. To the prison officers I was just another 'fucking Cat A', just another 'Twat'.

I'd been in the box for over an hour and my backside was stiff when I heard the bolt slide back.

'Sorry to keep you waiting,' said the man who opened the door.

He pointed to a spot in front of the reception counter and told me to stand over it. Including him there were five officers present – he and two others hovered around behind me while I stood facing the two standing on the other side of the counter.

One of them winked at me and nodded. He was chewing gum, a little nervously, I thought. 'All right?' he asked.

'Yes, I'm fine,' I said.

Their benign behaviour was in stark contrast to their spiteful banter while I was in the cubicle.

'How long you doin'?' the chewing officer asked while the others stood in silence.

I knew that there was no way in the world that they would not already know the answer. 'Life,' I said.

The officer sucked in his breath and said, 'The big one, eh?' He told me I was going to be in Wandsworth for a while. 'So long as you don't give us any shit you'll be all right here,' he said.

My 'prop box' with the lid open was on the counter alongside a standard property-logging sheet over which the nodding officer was poised ready to record all my worldly belongings. In the box were the suit, shirt, tie, shoes and socks I had worn at my trial. There were some letters sent to me from some of my former comrades in the Legion, some letters from my father, some photographs and several T-shirts and pairs of shorts and sports socks that I had mostly worn in Brixton's A SEG. It took the officer just a few minutes to record the items on his sheet. There was also a small transistor radio that my father had brought in to me on a visit at Brixton and my watch, another gift from my father which had been taken from me when I left Brixton. These were the only two things in the box that held any value for me.

'OK, strip,' said a voice from behind.

I turned slightly and saw that the person speaking was the officer who had let me out of the cubicle. I had come straight from a prison where I had been strip-searched before leaving and I was wearing prison clothes.

'I had a strip at Brixton,' I said.

'You're not in Brixton now,' said the officer. 'You're in Wanno.'

I sighed and began to undress in silence. I placed the shabby prison clothes item by item on the counter in front of me until I was standing completely naked.

'Now squat,' said the same officer.

As I bent my knees and slowly lowered my buttocks to the floor instead of feeling humiliated I felt angry at this crew of bullies – angry and helpless, but at least the anger helped to offset my surging anxiety.

Once dressed I picked up the bedroll that had appeared on the reception counter and the rest of the bits and pieces I was allowed to keep 'in possession' and set off for the wing in single file between two of the prison officers. We walked in silence broken only by the rattle of their keys and the clanging and banging of steel as we passed through half-a-dozen barred gates along the stark corridors on our way to the cavernous central chamber of the prison known as the 'Centre'. The prison had a typical Victorian panopticon layout with five main wings four landings high, holding up to two hundred and fifty men or more each. The Centre floor was a shiny steel hexagon and the point in the prison where all the wings merged.

We were greeted on the Centre by a tall, well-built prison officer sporting a large handlebar moustache. He was older than those I had encountered so far and unlike his bullying counterparts had a reassuring calmness about him.

'One on, Mr Barker sir,' said my lead escort as he opened the final gate. 'He's for D2.' D2 was the landing reserved for Category A prisoners.

'Thank you, sir,' said Mr Barker, then turned to me and said, 'Follow me, lad.'

I followed the big officer along the narrow gantry, glancing at the information cards on each cell door we passed. This was 'big bird' territory and no mistake. The atmosphere felt heavier with each cell card I read. Eighteen years, fifteen years, twenty-two years, eighteen years . . . one card with twelve years on it stood out as a relative short-termer. When we reached the cell that was going to be mine I glanced at my immediate neighbour's information card. His sentence was twenty-four years. Mr Barker took my card and inserted it into the small metal frame on the wall at the side of the cell door. One word which looked like it had been written in haste with a ballpoint pen announced my sentence: 'LIFE'. Mr Barker stepped back.

'It could be worse, lad. Twenty years ago you'd be going on E Wing.'

I stepped into the cell and Mr Barker banged the door shut. I knew the prison still had a working gallows, but I didn't know that the old death cell was on E Wing.

My cell contained just a chair, a small wooden table and a bed with a thin foam mattress wrapped in a heavily stained, cream-coloured cover that was ripped in several places. At the head of the bed was a raggedy lump of black sponge that I guessed must have once been a standard-issue pillow. The cell walls were coated with light-green emulsion paint which flaked everywhere. High up on the back wall natural light fought to make an impact on the gloom through three grids of iron bars. I noticed the faint whiff of urine and bent down, spotting the source under the bed – a brown lidless plastic bucket, the 'slop bucket', that would serve as my toilet. I pulled it out and was instantly hit by an eye-watering waft. When I opened my eyes again I saw that the bottom and sides of the bucket were heavily encrusted with dried urinary deposits. Whoever had used it last had sprinkled in some kind of cleaning powder which made the smell of ammonia even more potent.

I sat down on the bed and stared at the bare wall in front of me. Time came to a standstill. An almost physical weight pressed down on my shoulders. I wish I could say that I wanted to get down on my knees and beg for forgiveness, for mercy even – but all I could do was think about how I was going to manage to live like this, in this dead time zone, with a head full of shame and misery, for years and years on end. If the death penalty had still been on the statute books I surely would have been sitting in the death cell on E Wing – and the truth is I wouldn't have minded.

6

I unrolled my bed pack and made up the bed. I didn't want to think about anything and just lay on the top cover with my eyes closed. I hadn't been lying there for long when I heard what sounded like the rumbling of distant thunder – the cell doors were being unlocked for the evening meal. I was already on my feet when my door was opened. I stood in the doorway and watched as dozens of men dressed just like me in striped shirts and old denims streamed along the gantry. Some were chatting, some were shouting across the wire to associates. I stepped out and followed. A metal staircase at the end of the landing led down to the ground floor to the servery. A number of prisoners dressed in grubby 'whites' stood behind trays of food wielding ladles and scoops. I picked up a steel tray from the pile on the end table and joined the queue. On offer was a helping of mashed potato full of black lumps that hadn't been removed during peeling and a dry crusty pie, along with a clot of almost fluorescent peas and a gob of dark, glutinous gravy. I had no appetite for it but I was determined to eat just to hang on to my health and strength.

Making my way back to my cell was nerve-racking. Communication between prisoners was loud and aggressive; body language appeared threatening and even when anyone laughed to me it sounded intimidating. With my tray loaded I was eager to get back behind my door. But just as I was about to climb the staircase at the other end of the landing I heard the call of a familiar voice. When I turned round I saw it was Alex, one of the Israelis who I knew from the radio news had been convicted of kidnapping Umaru Dikko. He'd been sentenced to fourteen years. He hurried to catch up with me.

'Hey, Legionnaire!' he said in his familiar pronounced accent. 'You got life!' I shot him a wry smile.

'I know,' I said.

'How is it feeling?'

'It's feeling great,' I said. 'How are you doing?'

'Here it is fucking easy,' he said. 'We sleep all day and sleep all night. Fucking piece of piss!'

He told me his co-accused, Felix, who got twelve years, was also on our landing. 'So is Bobby D, Coxie and Terry P.' In the press Bobby D had been labelled the 'inter-city bank robber', after his MO of travelling to and from his targets by train. He was wounded in the shoulder during a shoot-out with the police before he was captured. His arm was still in a sling when he went on trial but he got no sympathy from the judge when he was found guilty. His eighteen-year sentence was pretty much the average for persistent armed robbers. Coxie had hidden some of the guns used in the Brink's-MAT gold bullion robbery and got a relatively lenient eight years. The guns had been found under his mother's bed. Terry P was one of the gang who had robbed £6m in cash from the Security Express Depot. He got twenty-two years. Since the day of my conviction I had spent all of my time in my head, thinking and trying not to think. News bulletins and newspaper headlines aside there had been no reason for me to spend much time thinking about any of these men. We had nothing in common but our Category A security status and long sentences.

None of us who had become acquainted in A SEG were close friends, but I hadn't realised until I heard Alex's voice how much I had appreciated their company. Knowing that some of them were here in Wandsworth gave me some comfort.

Alex had more years on his sentence than Felix because of his behaviour during their trial – that was the general opinion on the landings. He was the mouthy one, the braggart. He'd made himself out to be the leader of the kidnap gang. Their attempted kidnapping of Umaru Dikko had made national and international headlines and in jail he seemed to enjoy the notoriety his case brought him. The only thing that gave me any real credibility was the fact that I had spent some time in the French Foreign Legion and had a measure of physical presence. In A SEG Alex and I regularly conversed in French and often discussed weaponry used by different armies around the world – it was all a load of bull – but he was knowledgeable about various conflicts across the globe and when he told me he had operated as a mercenary he sounded plausible enough. During his trial he and the others had denied being Mossad agents and claimed to be mercenaries working for Nigerian businessmen. Whatever the case, he was no trouble to me. So long as I didn't involve myself in any of his business and he didn't involve himself in mine, there was no reason we shouldn't be able to get along just fine.

I had no strategy for how I was going to adapt to life inside. The routine in Wandsworth was mind-numbingly repetitive. The cell doors were opened for just a few minutes at a time each day: to empty the toilet bucket in a communal sluice and to collect washing water and breakfast; for exercise (Cat As exercised separately from mainstream prisoners – we had half an hour walking in a circle in the yard so long as the weather was not 'inclement', a word I had never heard before I went to prison); to collect lunch; to collect the evening meal at around 4.30 – and then briefly later in the evening when tea, nicknamed 'diesel' because of its foul consistency, was brought to the cell doors by an orderly and poured from a bucket into our plastic pint mugs.

Alex told me that I should ask for a change-of-religion form at the wing office and register myself as a Mormon. 'Mormons get fucking cocoa at night-time instead of that fucking diesel shit,' he said. He also said I should become a vegan, another word I had never heard of. 'You want to see something green on your plate that is eatable?' he said. 'You join the fucking Vegan Society for 25p and give your member's card to the kitchen. Then you get lettuce.' These were schoolboy dodges, but in all my life cocoa and lettuce had never seemed so appealing. A couple of weeks after that conversation I was officially a vegan and a Mormon.

It was a lonely existence but I was glad of the solitude of my cell. The days revolved around the door-opening times which though brief were long enough for incidents of violence to take place. A 'nonce' (sex offender) or a 'grass' (informer) being ambushed in the toilet recess area was a regular occurrence. Prison officers always took their time to respond and rarely before serious damage had been inflicted on the victim. You never knew when a confrontation might happen. I always felt a surge of apprehension whenever keys jangled outside the door, pre-empting unlock. My survival plan was to keep fit and strong by performing push-ups and sit-ups. I lifted my bed up on its end and tied it to the bars of the window with a pillowcase creating an exercise apparatus on which I could perform pull-ups and dips. Every day I would run on the spot for up to an hour – and then use the bowl of cold water collected in the morning for my strip wash. Whenever the door was opened I strolled out, body pumped by exertion, appearing confident and bold. It was the only way I could camouflage my fear and anxiety.

We were allowed one shower a week and one change of socks, underwear and shirt. Every Saturday morning we were taken six at a time to the prison library where we could choose six books. I spent the time in my cell reading, thinking, listening to current affairs or drama on my little transistor radio – and exercising. When we got our half-hour out in the yard I walked with the other Cat As I had known in A SEG, joining in the gossip, the prison politics, the finger pointing – totally lacking the confidence to offer counter-opinions during hypocritical conversations about who among us was a 'wrong 'un' and who was 'staunch'. Prison had its own language and it felt dangerous not to go along with it and adopt the mannerisms and demeanour of a 'con'. Prison officers were 'screws', to be addressed as 'guv', or 'boss', and any familiarity noticed between a prisoner and member of staff would be condemned immediately and the culprit shunned or worse. My cell was my only refuge.

My first visit from my father in Wandsworth was tense. Cat As were not allowed to have visits alongside regular prisoners in the main visits hall. Instead our visits took place in an empty cell on D2 landing. I was escorted there by two prison officers. When I entered my father was sitting at a small table in the middle of the cell. He stood up when he saw me and I walked straight over to him and hugged him. I didn't want him or the officers to see that my eyes were watery. I held him tight and wished I didn't have to let him go.

'OK,' said one of the officers, 'sit down, please.'

My father and I sat down on opposite sides of the table while an officer sat close behind each of us. He broke the silence. 'How's it going?'

I widened my eyes. 'It's all right, Dad, how are you doing?' I said. 'I'm so sorry for causing you all this stress.'

He screwed up his eyes and shook his head. 'Shhhht,' he said. 'It's you I'm worried about.'

I still hadn't talked to my father about my part in the crimes. I knew he wanted to believe I was innocent and it was easier for me to let him think that. One of the prosecution witnesses had been the French policeman with whom I had shared the glass of pastis in his office the night before he and his colleagues took me to Baumettes Prison in Marseille. In his evidence the officer told the court that during the encounter when just he and I were present I had confessed my guilt to him. I remembered telling him I was responsible for my situation but I had no recollection of the detailed confession he described and I denied it. After an hour of deliberation the jury returned to ask the judge if the policeman had made any notes of my confession and if so, could they see them. 'The officer made no notes at the time, members of the jury,' said the judge, 'but he has twenty-eight years' service in the French police force. I think we can take his word for it.' The idea that any police officer would not have thought to take notes of a 'confession' to double murder was enough for my father to give me the benefit of the doubt.

Most of our conversation during that first visit played out in short sentences and forced smiles. Finally I told him I had applied to a judge for permission to appeal on the grounds that the French policeman's evidence should have been inadmissible, seeing how he hadn't written anything down at the time and neither had he cautioned me. 'Fucken' right,' said my father. I didn't have the heart to tell him that I had not a hope in hell of getting to the appeal court.

Before we knew it our half-hour was over and we both stood up when prompted by the prison officer.

'Thanks for coming, Dad,' I said.

'Just you take care in here,' he said, 'and don't forget, when the going gets tough the tough get going.'

I smiled. It was typical of his fatherly advice. He passed on his first bits of wisdom to me when I was barely seventeen. 'The first thing to do when you arrive in a new town is to find a skipper,' he said – meaning a safe and secluded hiding place to get your head down for the night when you have to sleep rough. 'And always remember the golden rule – you can eat the drinking money but never drink the eating money.' This was his most sensible rule but I was never sensible enough to pay it any heed.

As he made to leave the visit cell I grasped his hand. 'I'll do my best, Dad,' I said. I had no idea what I was going to do my best at. I just said it hoping to reassure him that I would manage. Minutes later I was locked up alone again in my cell trying not to think about the visit. When the judge I had written to rejected my application to appeal I was finally resigned to my fate. I never told my father.

The days were long in that cell and the nights were longer. Sleep came slowly as I tried to figure out how I had become what I had become. I was sure that I hadn't been born bad – but I was woefully ignorant of my early family history. My family were all originally from Scotland. I knew that. My mother and father were from relatively large, quite poor families. I wasn't sure about the details of their backgrounds, other than what I had picked up over the years from various relatives. My mother was from Paisley, near Glasgow, and my father was from Stevenston on the west coast of Scotland.

All I knew about my own beginnings was what my father had told me many times but only when he was drunk. He and my mother met when they were teenagers. They were together for a while and then my father joined the Army and was sent overseas to Korea and Malaysia. While he was away my mother married a man called Sandman. Upon my father's return he was discharged from the Army and went looking for my mother. When he found her she left her husband immediately and hitchhiked alongside my father to England where they planned to begin a new life.

Previously my father's sister, my aunt Rena, met and married Nelson, a Traveller, who built them a log-cabin house on a small piece of land he'd bought in Yatton in Somerset where they finally settled down. In 1957 my father and mother moved in with them to stay until they found their own place. I learned from my birth certificate that my father worked as a driver and labourer with the local electricity board and my mother worked as a cleaner in a village pub. When my mother went into labour with me on the 18th of April that year my father borrowed Nelson's old Studebaker and drove her the five or six miles to Clevedon where he checked her into a private maternity clinic.

My father told me that in the dead of night two days after I was born he returned to the clinic in the Studebaker to collect my mother and me. He threw stones at her window, he said. When she came downstairs all the doors were locked and so she had to pass me out through a ground-floor window before climbing out herself. He said he raced away from the clinic and into the night with tyres screeching and my mother hanging on to me for dear life. 'Ah've still no paid that fucken' bill,' he'd say laughing.

My past was a vague, miserable place that I'd always tried to blank out. My prison dreams brought it all back.

7

I'm eight years old standing on the pavement staring at a derelict house. It's raining. I know the house well. I used to live here, with my mother, my father and my baby sister Alison – number 84 Thompson Street, Shipley, West Yorkshire. The cobbled street is one of several smoke-blackened hilly terraces on the south side of the Aire Valley overlooking the mills and livestock warehouses nestled alongside the Leeds and Liverpool Canal. The canal flows parallel to the river. Number 84 is near the top of the street and from our front gate you can see right across the valley. When we lived here I sometimes stood outside the gate with Rowdy, my dog, a bouncy black mongrel, and gazed out to the horizon.

Now the dark damp sky casts murky shadows over the home I loved. Water from the broken guttering cascades down the front wall over the entrance doorway. The gate has gone and the front door hangs open. The windows, upstairs and downstairs, are broken. The outside toilet in the front yard has long since dried up, the pot smashed to pieces. The coal bunker by the side of the steps leading into the house is crammed with rotting garbage. Dodging the waterfall I duck inside. On the floor of what had been our living room jagged slivers of glass crunch under my feet against the tattered linoleum. I'm looking for traces of us. I was happy here. Now the furniture, the chairs, the deep wrinkled sofa, the little glass cabinet full of ornaments that my mother was forever getting out and polishing have all gone. The grate in the fireplace where roaring fires used to crackle is missing. Some of the tiles covering the hearth and the mantelpiece are missing too; most of the rest are cracked and chipped. The nail from which the mirror used to hang above the fireplace is still there, but now it's bent and rusted and pokes out of the middle of a brown stain. Some top edges of our faded blue wallpaper that have become unstuck curl away from the ceiling. In other places long curved strips have been torn away leaving dirty white scars that reach almost to the skirting board.

It was here I sat in my father's lap in my cowboy suit watching Westerns on our tiny black-and-white television or listening to him telling me stories about 'Angus the Scottish cowboy' whose golden gun he said fired silver bullets. It was on this floor that my father tickled me until I was ecstatically exhausted while Rowdy, named after a character in our favourite Western series *Rawhide*, barked excitedly. When Rowdy was run over by a car and killed it was in this room that my parents spent hours comforting me.

It was here my mother never tired of fussing around us, feeding us, keeping us clean and loving us. It was in the small scullery at the back of the living room that one morning my sister signalled her arrival. My grandmother, 'Maw', was staying with us. My father was at work. My mother was hanging up washing on a line above the big white sink when she bent over and screamed. Maw looked after me while my mother rushed out alone to the nursing home on Kirkgate, just around the corner from the top of our street. We watched her from the front window as she scurried over the cobbles in her slippers, shoulders hunched, hair unbrushed, dressed only in her long blue dressing gown that had no buttons. With one hand she clutched it together tightly in front of her swollen belly – in the other she carried a small bag. The pained look on her face increased my pangs of anxiety. 'Don't worry, son,' said Maw, holding me tight. 'She'll be hame soon enough.'

When my sister Alison was just six months old it was here she had her first Christmas and her big present, an inflatable Bambi, fell into the fire. I can still see Bambi's face melting in the flames and my mother and father frenziedly shifting the rest of the presents away from the hearth. That was to be our last Christmas at Thompson Street, our last Christmas together as a family and the only one I can remember. A sudden draught lifts wisps of gritty dust from the floor and blows against the door of the closet in the far corner of the room making it creak until it's almost closed. I'm looking for ghosts.

I walk over to the closet slowly, hopefully. Pulling the door open I see it's empty, except for a little pile of shit near the back wall – human shit. Flies hover on and around it. I kick away the crumpled bits of smeared newspaper that have been used as toilet paper. There is no smell. Dark and crusty, the shit looks as if it's a few days old. I stare at it for a good couple of minutes trying to figure out who would do such a thing in our closet. A noise in the room above – my old bedroom – catches my attention. I turn and run to the doorway at the bottom of the stairs then stop and listen. One step at a time I climb the dark narrow staircase, straining to keep my hard breathing quiet. Halfway up I begin to sprint. In a moment I'm at the open door, shouting, 'Yah!'

But the room is empty. No bed, no cupboard, no coats that had kept me warm on cold nights – just more broken glass and stones and other debris that must have been thrown through the shattered panes. A piece of shredded curtain hangs from one side of the window that looks out onto the street above the front door. It flaps making a sound like a big bird's wing every time there is a fresh gust of rainy breeze. The other curtain lies in a soggy heap against the wall underneath. I remembered the curtains – and the window where I had stood one night less than a year before and listened as a policeman below told my grandmother that her daughter, my mother, was dead.

My special friend at Thompson Street was a mixed-race boy called Micky. He was the same age as me. He was brown, my father explained, 'Because he was left in the oven too long after he was born.' I wasn't sure why, but he thought it was great fun to prompt me to recount this to other grown-ups who also thought it was funny. Micky lived in the street next to ours, Wycliffe Avenue, in the house nearest to the connecting passage. His older brothers and sisters, all of whom were white, were wild and boisterous. His mother, Madge, always looked tired, but welcomed me warmly with bread and jam or biscuits whenever I called for Micky. I never saw his father. Micky said he didn't have one.

He and I spent all our free time on the undulating waste scrub-land at the side of his street known locally as the 'Delf' building dens or hunting rats. Sometimes we roamed further afield looking for new adventures. One day we made it to the sheep pens by the canal. We climbed over the metal barriers and began jumping on the backs of the panicked animals, screeching with excitement, seeing who could stay on the longest. Then the police arrived, two plain-clothes officers who put us in the back of their car and took us home. I was dropped off first. A mild chastisement was all my mother gave me – and then hugs and kisses. There were always plenty of those. I took Micky to the top of our street one day and pointed to the distant skyline where I could just make out the silhouette of a high gabled house with tall chimneys at the tip of either apex. 'That's where I used to live,' I said. 'That's Scotland.'

I believed that the house on the horizon was the old farmhouse in a rural enclave in Scotland where my parents and I had once lived. After their first attempt at a new life in Somerset failed they returned to Scotland and ended up at a place called Riverbank in Blairgowrie, Perthshire. I was happy at Riverbank. As well as the old farmhouse there were outbuildings where mill-workers, berry-pickers and other casual farm labourers stayed. We shared the big house with seven other families, some of whom were our relatives who worked in the mills, and Maw presided over all of us. I was three or four years old and being the only tot in the bedraggled community ensured I received huge amounts of loving attention. There was long grass and sunshine, rabbits and butterflies. There were campfires on long summer nights and singing and dancing. My father played the guitar and wore a cowboy hat. I loved having the same name as him. He was 'Big Erwin', and I was 'Wee Erwin'.

I never noticed the dire poverty in which we all lived. I thought everybody was as happy as I was.

Shipley was our second chance. As she had done in Somerset my mother worked again as a cleaner and later as an operator in the cotton mills in Saltaire and Bradford. My father laboured on building sites and then had a job driving a van delivering paint. They saved their money and put it into 84 Thompson Street. That was where I thought I would always live. My father used to bring his van home and sometimes took us out in it for picnics. One weekend he took me and my mother out for a drive over the moors around Shipley. It was a windy day and my mother, heavily pregnant, needed the toilet. 'Go on, Jeanie,' said my father, imploring my mother to go behind a rock. The moor was deserted but my mother was adamant that she was not going to pee outside. My sister must have been pressing hard on her bladder because suddenly she leapt up and raced over to the rock, crouching behind it quickly so that we could only see her head.

'Stop looking, you two,' she shouted to my father and me as we chuckled mischievously.

My sister was beautiful, with rosy cheeks and a mass of curly hair, and I loved her as soon as I saw her. We were often photographed together, both of us inveterate smilers. After she was born there seemed to be more uncles and aunts staying with us intermittently, newly arrived from Scotland. Maw stayed a lot – so did Uncle Jim, my mother's youngest brother who was only sixteen or seventeen. He arrived in his Army uniform wearing a kilt, a sporran and a jaunty Highland cap that had a ribbon dangling from the back. My aunt Janet stayed a while, so did my aunt Sheila, another of my mother's sisters, who got a job in Norman's, a popular working-men's café in the town. Micky and I often trekked down there. When Aunt Sheila saw us she sneaked us a chocolate bar each from behind the counter, telling me, 'Don't tell your mother.'

Uncle Archie, my mother's oldest brother, stayed too, so did my uncle Frank, my mother's middle brother. He met an Englishwoman and went to live in Bradford. He and my father were close. My father called him 'Ged'. He called my father 'Big Ged'. They laboured on building sites together. My father and Uncle Frank laid a concrete floor in the basement of 84 Thompson Street and turned it into a kitchen. I helped, shovelling concrete with my plastic spade, filling my little bucket and handing it to my father who patted me on the head and ruffled my hair. 'Good boy,' he said. 'Aye, he's a good wee boy,' my uncle Frank agreed.

My parents both spoke with strong Scottish accents and until I started going to school so did I. For a while I went to an infants' school, Albert Road, in Saltaire, but not long enough to have a single memory of what I did there. I must have started to try and change my accent in order to fit in with the other kids because one day as I played in our small front yard with Micky my father appeared from behind and shouted, 'Jeannie, look! Oor Erwin's talking English!' I blushed, but I didn't mind.

He was a great father. He made me a go-cart out of bits of wood and old pram wheels and in the attic built me a train set, which we both had great fun playing with. Sometimes he'd pick me up and let me sit on his shoulders as he danced whilst my mother sang her favourite song, 'The Tennessee Waltz': "'I was dancing with my darling to the Tennessee Waltz, the beautiful Tennessee Waltz . . .'"

It's the night of the crash. My mother and father are out for the evening. Maw is looking after me and Alison who is days from her first birthday. I turned seven just six weeks earlier. Once Alison is tucked up and asleep Maw tells me stories about Scotland. 'It's a braw place, son,' she says. 'Never forget that's your real hame. You're Scottish just like me and all your family. You mustn't ever forget that.' It's spring but the nights are still cold and to keep me warm the usual pile of coats has been laid over my blankets. As my mother has taught me, just like every other night before getting under the covers, I crouch on my knees at the side of my bed and say prayers for all the people I love. It's a long list. 'Thank you, God, for looking after us,' I say as Maw tucks me in and kisses me before I crawl under the blankets, safe and secure under their comforting weight.

A knock on the front door jolts me awake. I push my head out from underneath the covers into the pitch-dark and listen. Whoever it is knocks again – this time louder. I hear footsteps downstairs so I jump out of bed and run to the window. Pulling the curtains to one side I see a black police car parked outside our front gate. It's facing up the hill and its blue light is flashing.

The front door opens and I hear a man's voice. 'Mrs Williamson?' After a pause the man speaks again. 'I'm afraid there has been a road accident.'

Then I hear Maw: 'What? Who?'

There's another pause and the man speaks again. 'It's your daughter, Jeanie. I'm sorry to tell you she was killed tonight, along with the driver of the van in which she was a passenger.' The man continues, 'Jeanie's husband was also in the van. He's in hospital. He's . . .' but before he can finish Maw screams.

She begins howling like a wounded animal, shattering the hush of the street. On and on she wails, crying out my mother's name. 'Oh no, no, no, no . . .'

I stand in the dark listening to Maw's cries and I know that I am never going to see my mother again. Finally I hear the door close and then watch the two policemen who brought our bad news walk down the path, close the gate and climb into their car. The blue light is switched off and the car pulls away from the kerb. I hear it turn at the top of the street and accelerate away. I listen until its engine fades to nothing. All I can hear now are Maw's heavy sobs from the living room below me. I stumble to my bed and crawl back under the heavy covers, curling into a tight ball and holding my knees and my chin tight to my chest. There I lie weeping quietly until I fall asleep.

Nobody told me my mother was dead. No one talked to me about the crash. But in the days afterwards I listened in carefully on adult conversations until I knew for sure. It happened on the 29th of May. Near the end of their night out my mother and father argued. My mother left my father and went with my uncle Frank to the fish and chip shop at the top of Leeds Road. When my father got home worse for drink and found no sign of my mother he was annoyed and decided to go and fetch her. My uncle Jim was staying with us. He looked up to my father almost to the point of hero-worship. Jim followed my father as he set off walking down the hill to the house where his friend Charlie Rogers lived, near the bottom of Thompson Street on the same side as us. I knew him as Uncle Charlie. He drove a grey Bedford van with sliding doors and had a big collection of toy cars in a suitcase which me and his two nephews used to play with. Charlie was a kind man.

Charlie was in bed asleep after his own evening of heavy drinking when my father started banging on his door. He hammered and shouted until Charlie dragged himself out of bed. Ignoring Charlie's drunken state my father persuaded him to take him and my uncle Jim to the chip shop in his van. When they arrived my father went into the shop while Charlie kept the engine running. My father found my mother with my uncle Frank and ordered her out and into the van. Charlie's driving to the chip shop was so erratic that my uncle Jim refused to get back in for the return journey.

My father climbed in after my mother and Charlie set off for home. About a mile and a half from our house, still on Leeds Road on the long straight slope leading into the town, the van slewed across to the other side of the road and smashed head on into a steel telegraph pole. Charlie was killed instantly. My mother was thrown out through the windscreen and died when her head hit the pavement. My father was trapped inside and eventually had to be cut from the wreckage by the fire brigade.

My mother was buried five days later on a sunny June day. My father was still in hospital. It was the day before my sister's first birthday. Nab Wood Cemetery was a blaze of colourful blossom and the air was filled with the scent from the flowers. Birds cheeped and warbled. I hung on tight to my uncle Frank's hand. There was quite a crowd around my mother's grave. Maw cried the loudest. My aunts cried too and so did I – but I cried quietly so nobody could tell.

8

While my father was in hospital Maw and my aunts looked after my sister and me. I ran wild with my pal Micky. There was no school and no regularity to my life. One day I went with Micky to the crash site. It was opposite a pub called the Traveller's Rest. The tyre marks where the van had skidded were still on the road. They led to a dented and scratched green-painted telegraph pole. Tiny particles of glass littered the gutter at the edge of the pavement near the point of impact. Nearby on a light-coloured pavestone was a large stain that I knew was blood. I tried to take in the whole scene, imagining what had happened and trying to work out where my mother had landed. I decided the bloodstain marked the spot where her head had hit. I could see her lying there, her shattered body and lovely face still and lifeless.

When they learned my father was coming out of hospital my aunts and Maw became agitated. Before he arrived home I heard them talking about him, blaming him for the crash and my mother's death. They said it was my father being angry with my mother that must have distracted Charlie, but I had never seen my father angry with my mother before. Charlie's dogs lived in the back of his van and they said my father's shouting at my mother might have upset the dogs and Charlie had lost control as he tried to calm them. I hated the thought of my father shouting at my mother for any reason and couldn't believe that was true.

Almost as soon as he arrived home my father started getting drunk. My Maw and aunts got really annoyed with him. I overheard my aunt Sheila say she was going to don a white sheet and pretend to be my mother's ghost emerging from St Paul's Churchyard on Kirkgate to frighten him when he was making his way home from a drinking session. My father came and went on his crutches, sometimes not returning for days at a time. When he was home he drank more and punched holes in the doors, shouting, 'Jeannie! Jeannie!' Once he punched the wall so hard he broke his hand and had to go back to hospital. He was drunk more often than he was sober.

One night, about a week after he got out of hospital the second time, he pulled me out of bed and took me outside on to the street, leaving his crutches and dragging his plastered leg. He was swaying and slurring his words. 'Look, son,' he said, pointing up to the clear dark sky with his bandaged hand. 'Look at that star. That's your mammy.' It was the brightest star in the sky. Through teary eyes I stared at it with agonised longing.

A few days later I went with my father and Uncle Frank to collect my mother's shoes. They had been gathered up and left in the crashed van. The van had been recovered to the yard of a garage that was just a ten-minute walk from our house. When I saw the van I felt sick and started to sob. 'Erwin son, it's OK,' said my father. 'Don't greet. We just need to get your mammy's shoes. We'll no be here long.'

The front of the van had a deep V-shaped indent where it had impacted on the lamp-post. Both sliding doors were jammed open. I looked at the gaping hole where the windscreen had been and imagined my mother flying out of it. I saw her head hitting the pavement. I could see her face bruised and bleeding. I started to cry out loud. Uncle Frank picked me up and hugged me to him. 'Here, Ged,' he said, passing me to my father, who leant his crutches against the side of the van and grasped me tightly, pressing his lips hard against the side of my head. Uncle Frank retrieved the dark-blue open-toed sling-back shoes, and we left. Later I visited the van alone several times before it disappeared. I used to stand and look at it, angry at what it had done to us.

All the people who had been staying at our house began to leave. Maw was the last to go, leaving my sister and me in the care of my father. I cried when Maw left. My sister cried a lot too, but she was too young to know what was happening to us. The biggest surprise was when I returned from playing out on the Delf one day with Micky and found my father in the company of a woman I had never seen before. She had my sister on her knee.

'Erwin son, come here and meet your new mammy,' he said.

She had blonde hair piled high on her head and huge round eyes that smiled from her welcoming pink face. 'Hello,' she said. 'I'm your aunt Stella.'

She beckoned me over to her, throwing her free arm around me and hugging me close to her and my sister. She was fleshier than my mother and smelled strongly of sweet perfume. 'How would you like to come and live with me?' she said.

The idea horrified me. The last thing I wanted to do was leave our house, the street, the Delf, Micky. I stepped back from her, pulling myself out of her hug. 'No thank you,' I said.

'Erwin,' my father growled. 'This is your new mammy and we're all going to live with her. She's even got a new brother for you.'

I didn't want a new brother. I had my own sister. I started to cry.

'Erwin!' my father shouted at me and I cried louder.

The woman grabbed hold of me again and held me close to her. 'Shhh,' she said gently, reassuringly – except I didn't want to be reassured. I wanted to stay at 84 Thompson Street.

The next day Aunt Stella arrived to take me and my sister to her terraced house, which was off Coach Road at the bottom of the valley on the other side of the river. My father had got us both ready, filling a couple of plastic carrier bags with our things. He said he would see us later. 'Don't worry, son, we'll all be back together again soon.'

The walk to Stella's house didn't take long. Stella pushed my sister in her pram while I walked along beside her in a sulk. The house, on Grimdale Avenue in the shadow of the gasworks, was smaller than 84 Thompson Street. Its front door opened from the living room directly out on to the street like ours, but it also had a back door that opened from the kitchen out into a small yard and on to another street. I had to share a bedroom and a bed with my 'new brother', Danny, who was a year older than me.

'Hi,' he said when he saw me.

'Hi,' I replied with some reluctance. He too had a baby sibling, Darren, who was younger than my sister and spent most of his time in a pram with huge wheels. And he had a dog, a fluffy brown-and-black sheepdog cross called Gyp.

'Go on, you two,' said Stella. 'Go and play.'

Aunt Stella was not my aunt and she would never be my mother. Danny was not my brother and never would be. But he and I got on well enough, though he was the dominant one in our relationship. Not just because he was older than me, but because he was more confident and worldly. He belonged. It was his home. It was his mother in charge of us. He knew about films like *Mighty Joe Young* and *King Kong* and recounted them to me in great detail. And his dog was alive. I was in thrall to him. When we played it was with his toys. If we played a game, he decided which one. Whenever Stella called us it was always 'You two' this, or 'You two' that. I had become part of a pair, but I was never an equal part.

More than a week passed before I saw my father again. When he came in there was no great reunion between us. He seemed to hardly notice me or my sister. He and Stella went out drinking and left me and Danny to babysit the two youngest. Being left on our own with our young siblings became a regular way of life for us. When the adults were out we stayed up late and often fell asleep in front of the television. When they came in the smell of alcohol and tobacco flooded the house. Sometimes they brought friends back with them and drank more bottles of beer while my father played his guitar. Stella's laugh when she had been drinking was loud and rude. Danny and I hid and watched and listened.

I was enrolled at Coach Road Primary School in the year below Danny. The school gate on Coach Road was only a hundred yards or so from our front door. Danny had been there a while and introduced me to some of his friends as 'our Erwin'. I became self-conscious at school and almost stopped talking unless I was spoken to. I didn't want to be with any of these children. They all had their own families and seemed to know where they belonged. I wanted to be back at my home, playing in the street and on the Delf with my real friend Micky.

Six weeks after I joined the school during a Monday morning assembly, we were singing the hymn 'All Things Bright and Beautiful', while a large, red-haired lady accompanied us on the piano. Each time she hit a chord I felt a stab of pain in my head. I began to feel dizzy. I wanted to lie down. The singing sounded like it was getting louder and louder. I could feel my stomach bubbling. I thought I was going to break wind and let out a giant fart. Instead my bowels erupted making it impossible for me to stop what felt like a geyser of hot wet shit spurting out of me and forming a lake in the seat of my best short trousers.

I started to run, barging through the rows in front of me towards the cloakroom and the toilets at the front of the hall. I could feel the shit, first just a dribble, squeezing out from beneath the legs of my underpants. I ran faster and within a second the shit was cascading down the back of my legs like molten lava leaving a trail behind me on the shiny parquet floor while the whole school sang on. Their voices rang in my ears like a chorus of chastisement. By the time I made it into a lavatory cubicle the piano playing had stopped. The singing petered out and I heard footsteps rushing into the toilet and a woman's voice shouting, 'Erwin! Don't be worried. Don't be frightened.' I wasn't worried or frightened, just mortally embarrassed.

There were no locks on the cubicles so I had to lean against the door with my shoulder to stop anyone getting in. Soon the floor of the cubicle was a thick grid of shit smears. It covered my shoes and socks and absolutely stank. I didn't think I would be able to face anyone at the school ever again. I was in the cubicle for about an hour before I agreed to come out. While one of the women teachers washed me down with a flannel in a washbasin others came and went, scrutinising me and making various soothing comments. I felt numb and just stared at the floor. Eventually I was presentable enough for the teacher to walk me home.

When Stella answered the door the teacher explained what had happened by saying I had had 'an accident'. The stench that hung around me soon made it clear to Stella what sort of accident it had been. After the teacher left Stella made me strip naked in the kitchen. She boiled some water in a pan and told me to wash all my shitty clothes in the kitchen sink. I had to stand on an upside-down milk crate to reach.

'I'm sorry, Aunt Stella,' I said.

She said it didn't matter. 'Just don't go doing it here.'

I dreaded going back to school the following day but when I did nobody mentioned what had happened. The teachers were kind to me, but I felt odd. I felt different to the others. At playtime I kept my own company. While groups of kids mingled and played and others skipped or hopped, I mooched about the playground, head down, hands in pockets, kicking stones or standing on ants.

My father got a job as a lorry driver which meant he was away from home for days at a time. When he came back at weekends he and Stella went out drinking. It wasn't long before he was punching doors and walls again. Danny and I lay in bed listening. Not scared exactly, just puzzled. In the morning there were cracks in the door panels and knuckle indents in the plaster on the walls. Then he started hitting Stella. Then we got scared. He punched her and kicked her. We heard him roaring at her, comparing her unfavourably to my mother. He shouted my mother's name. Stella screamed, in pain, in fear. One night the fighting sounded like it was coming up the stairs. Bodies were hitting against the walls.

Stella shrieked, 'You can't take them!'

The noise, the scuffling and shouting, became louder.

'Get fucking off me!' my father yelled.

The sound of a thump followed. Stella screamed again. The bedroom door crashed open. 'Erwin son, come on,' said my father. He was drunk, staggering and breathing heavily. His normally neatly combed hair was hanging down from each side of his head and all the buttons had been ripped off his shirt. 'Erwin!' he commanded. I jumped out of bed and pulled on my school clothes. By now my sister was awake and crying loudly.

'Don't!' said Stella.

Ignoring her, he pulled my sister out of her cot and wrapped her clumsily in one of her blankets. 'Come on, son,' he said to me.

Hooking my sister under his right arm he tumbled down the stairs, leaning his other shoulder against the wall to stop himself from falling forwards. I followed as closely as I could. Stella shouted from behind us, 'Well fucking go then, but if anything happens to those kids it will be your fault.'

Soon we were in the dark outside and walking fast into the deserted night. I held on tight to my father's hand. I had no idea where we were going. We headed over the bridge and towards the town. I knew the area as it wasn't far from Thompson Street. I got excited momentarily when I thought maybe we were going home. But instead of turning right at the Leeds Road junction he walked straight on and up the slope towards the town centre. My father was swaying and tripped a couple of times, muttering swear words and grunting. The town centre was deserted. We passed the shops and the row of bus shelters, crossed over the car park that became a marketplace on Fridays and Saturdays and finally, cold and tired, we turned up at the glass entrance doors of Shipley Police Station.

My father told the desk sergeant that he had nowhere to go. 'We've been thrown out,' he said. 'We need a bed.'

The sergeant looked down at me and smiled. He went away and returned some minutes later with a colleague. 'We can let you stay for just one night,' he said to my father. 'But you'll have to sort this out tomorrow.'

The sergeant left his desk and appeared at another door which led down two flights of concrete steps. Still with my sister under his arm and me in tow my father followed. At the bottom of the steps we turned and walked along a narrow corridor with doors either side. As we passed one door I heard someone behind it cry out, scaring the hell out of me. The sergeant arrived at a door that was wide open and stood to one side as we all entered.

'I'll get you some blankets,' he said to my father.

Inside the room the walls were covered entirely with white brick tiles. The bed looked like a long wooden box and was about three feet high with a thin mattress on the top of it. Jutting out of the back wall was a toilet pan with no lid and no seat. The sergeant reappeared and passed my father some thick, rough blankets.

'Thanks,' my father said.

The policeman left the door slightly ajar and my father lay down on the bed, cuddling my sister close to him as he faced the wall. I huddled up behind him and pulled some of the blankets over me. I was so tired I quickly fell asleep. The next day with my father sober and washed from the water in the toilet pan we left the police station and headed back to Stella's. Soon we were back in the same routine. I went to school and in the evenings played outside with Danny. Sometimes we played out by the gasworks, or wandered up to the woods behind the terraced streets. At weekends my father and Stella went out boozing as usual – and as usual they argued and fought when they got home.

One night they arrived back by taxi and all seemed good. Danny and I went to bed and listened as they laughed and joked with each other downstairs. It was a relief not to have to listen to all the shouting and bawling for a change and we fell asleep quickly. It didn't last. Loud thuds and the sound of breaking glass and furniture woke us up. We both sneaked downstairs to have a look. Peeking through the gap in the slightly open door at the bottom of the stairs we could see that my father had hold of Stella by the throat. She was struggling to free herself and trying to scream but couldn't because she was choking. She had one hand on one of his arms and she was reaching out desperately with the other. Her hand fell on a plastic pig-shaped bottle of baby talcum powder on the sideboard where she often changed nappies. She grasped the pig tightly and then began fiercely beating my father across the head and face with it until the bottle burst like a bomb and a cloud of talcum powder engulfed them both. My father began spluttering for breath and let Stella go. Blinded and breath-less he started roaring. Me and Danny raced back up the stairs and hid under the bedclothes.

In the morning nothing was said about what had happened the night before. It was always the same whenever there was violence or an argument; afterwards they carried on as if nothing had happened. But Stella's behaviour towards me began to change. She overheard me telling Danny one day that I wished I still lived at 'aity-foor Thompson Street'. She'd been sweeping the kitchen floor and still had the broom in her hands when she appeared in the doorway. She looked at Danny and told him to go outside. Danny protested. 'Out!' she called. Reluctantly he obeyed.

'Right,' she said to me. 'What did you just say?'

I could feel the fear building in my chest. She had told me plenty of times before that I had to stop speaking 'fucking Scottish'.

Danny called his mother 'Mam', and I had been thinking about calling her that too to see if it would make her like me more. I wondered if I should try it now but then thought better of it.

Instead I looked up at her and said, 'Nothing, Aunt Stella.' My nose began to run and I sniffed loudly; 'snooked' was her term for it.

She shouted at me, 'And what have I told you about *snooking*?'

I was too terrified to answer.

'Eighty-four . . . say it,' she said. I trembled. She yelled. 'Say it!'

I took a sobbing breath and tried to do as she commanded. 'Er, ai . . . ai . . . ai . . . aity-four.'

She lifted the broom and screamed, 'EIGHTY-FOUR!' before swinging the handle and crashing it against the side of my head. In the instant I crumpled to the floor I saw flashes of tiny sparks behind my tightly shut eyes. As I lay cowering in a heap she swung the broom handle again, hitting me across the shoulders. 'Eighty-four!' she shouted, before returning to the kitchen and finishing her sweeping. It was the first time anyone had ever hit me.

9

On my first Christmas Eve at Stella's house Danny and I were left to babysit Alison and Darren while Stella and my father went out drinking. Stella had put them to bed before she left. We stayed up late and eventually fell asleep in front of the television. I woke up first. The television was making a loud hissing noise and the screen was black and mottled with silver dots. I turned it off and then shook Danny awake.

'They haven't come home,' I said. The house was in silence.

'Let's look for our presents,' he said.

For the next hour we searched like two little burglars, rummaging in drawers and cupboards until we found what we were looking for at the back of the top shelf of the wardrobe in Stella and my father's bedroom: a space pistol each that lit up red, green and orange and screeched when you pulled the trigger. Soon we were chasing around the house, hiding behind the sofa, barging up the stairs, bouncing on the beds. The racket we were making woke up the toddlers who both began to scream. Still we played on.

A loud rapping on the door brought a stop to our play. We listened, whispered. By now the toddlers were howling. There was another rapping, louder this time, followed by a voice, 'Hello? Can you open the door, please?' We whispered again, frightened;

we waited. 'Hello?' said the voice. 'It's the police. Can you please open the door?'

I looked out of the window while Danny lifted the snib on the door and pulled down the handle. Outside there were three black police cars like the one I had seen outside Thompson Street the night my mother was killed. I began panting and then panicking I ran for the door, forcing out a scream. The door opened and I barged into the policeman who was trying to get in. Behind him were two more policemen and two policewomen. The first policeman picked me up and I struggled and kicked in his arms.

'Whoa,' he said. 'Stay calm, stay calm, everything's OK.' He held down my arms and I stopped kicking.

I wanted to ask him where my father was but I couldn't speak for sobbing. The two women pushed past and made their way upstairs to where Alison and Darren were crying while the policeman who was holding me placed me gently back on the floor.

'There's nothing to worry about,' he said. 'Your mum and dad are a bit busy and they've asked us to come and get you and take you somewhere safe.'

They took Danny and me to Stella's mother's house where we stayed for the next few days. We didn't see the toddlers until Stella and my father turned up with them in a taxi and took us all home with no explanation as to what they had been doing or where they had been.

Their drinking continued but their arguing seemed to slow down. Danny and I were back at school. I hated the school. I hated being so alone. Then Stella said we were moving. 'The council is going to demolish this house and give us a new one,' she said. The idea of moving away terrified me. I could see Thompson Street in the distance on the other side of the valley from outside this house. Looking at it gave me comfort. I daydreamed about my old life with my real family and Micky. I said nothing, but the next day instead of going to school I sneaked off in the rain to visit my old house.

I'm upset at the shit in our downstairs closet and decide to go upstairs and investigate the noise I thought I heard in my old bedroom. Standing by the window I look out on the rain-lashed cobbles, remembering the policemen who brought the news about my mother. I hear somebody laugh. I look up the street and see two boys vying to shove each other off the pavement. I step back a little behind the flapping, raggedy curtain and watch until they stop outside our house.

'Fuck off, Podge,' says the smaller of the two. His hair is bright ginger.

'Go on, you scared bastard,' says Podge.

They're both older than me, maybe by two or three years. The taller boy, Podge, bends down and picks up a piece of brick. 'Watch this,' he says, before pulling back his arm full stretch and hurling the missile at my bedroom window. I jump back quickly as it explodes against some shards of glass still left in the window frame, shooting them around the room like bullets. Terrified I press myself against the wall. I can hear the boys giggling and swearing at each other as they chuck more missiles at different windows. When they stop I hope they have moved on. I sneak a peek from behind the curtain and see instead that they are heading down our short path towards the front door. My heart begins to thump.

I hear the crunching of feet stepping on the broken glass covering the floor in the room below me. They laugh again and again. Then it goes quiet. I wait. I hear more crunching footsteps. Then silence. I listen intently but all I can hear is the sound of my breathing. It seems so loud. Without moving from the wall I stretch my neck to have another look out of the window and see the smaller boy leaving. He goes out of the gate and turns to walk up the hill. I wait again and when I'm sure I can hear nothing I tiptoe to the top of the stairs and listen again. Step by gentle step I make my way down. At the bottom I push my head cautiously round the door frame until with half an eye I can see into the living room. It's empty. I start walking towards the front door when a voice calls out from the basement below me.

'Ginna!' I stop dead. It's the taller boy, Podge. He shouts again. He must think I'm his friend Ginna returned. 'Ginna, you fucker, get down here.'

I hurry across the room and seconds later I'm out of the front door, through the gate and walking fast down the hill.

A shout behind me makes me jump. 'Oi!' When I turn round I see Podge standing by our gate. He's shaking his fist and pointing at me. I dash off down the hill. The main road at the bottom of Thompson Street is always busy and I know I'm not going to be able to stop or he'll get me. When I reach the edge of the road I pause and chance a quick look behind me. Podge is bearing down fast. I run into the road causing cars to swerve and screech. Dodging and weaving between them I only just make it to the other side.

I remember the tunnel behind the Falcon pub that leads underneath the railway line. Micky and I had used it to get to the sheep pens. I rush into the tunnel and race towards the light at the end. Bursting out I turn a sharp right, running alongside the railway track, and then hop over the low wall at the top of the bank on to Baildon Road. As I land on the pavement I manage another glance behind me. Still Podge is chasing. He swears and calls me a 'little cunt'.

Further down Baildon Road I know a short cut to Coach Road across the adjacent cricket pitch. I scramble over the wall and skid down the bank on to the pitch. I'm on the home stretch and only a few minutes from the school gates. Halfway across the open space I start to flag and have another quick look behind me to see where Podge is. He's standing still on the other side of the wall watching me. I slow down and then stop and bend double trying to get my breath back. My lungs are on fire. Podge turns and heads back the way we came.

Mightily relieved and feeling safe I set off, walking steadily towards the big wall at the side of Coach Road behind which a double-decker bus has pulled up where I'm going to climb over. People on the top deck are looking at me – they must have seen me being chased. I scale the wall and hang down the other side before letting go and landing in front of the queue of people boarding the bus. My school is right across the road.

I bounce up and step out in front of the bus while trying to think of an excuse for my absence – and then suddenly I'm floating, tumbling through space, weightless and free. I look down and see the school below me. It feels like I'm dreaming. I look up at the clouds and there I see my mother with Rowdy, my dog. My mother is smiling and waving. I want to wave back but I can't move my arms. I want to shout to her but no words will come out of my mouth.

I hear a bang and open my eyes. I'm lying sprawled out on the road by the side of the bus peering up at a crowd of strangers standing over me. A woman lifts my head and places something soft underneath it. The people are jumbled, pushing against each other, all wanting to get a better look at me. I stare back at them and feel so special. I'd forgotten how good it was to be the centre of attention.

The crowd parts and a large man appears. He's bald and wears glasses and his black shirt has a round white collar. He kneels down beside me and strokes my head. His hand is shaking.

'I'm sorry,' he says. 'I'm so sorry.' He starts to cry and says over and over, 'I'm sorry. I'm sorry.' I don't understand why a vicar should be crying and telling me he is sorry.

An ambulance takes me to the small cottage hospital on Saltaire Road, about two miles from where the vicar's car hit me when he overtook the stationary bus. I never felt a thing. My father turns up at the hospital shortly after me. The nurses make a fuss of me which is nice and tuck me into the softest bed I have ever lain on. Everything is so clean and bright.

'Erwin son, are you OK?' asks my father.

I nod that I am. It's wonderful to have his complete attention and be so cared about again. I'm not in any pain. I just feel light-headed and special. An ambulance takes us home a couple of hours later and I'm put straight to bed. Even Stella seems worried about me.

In bed Danny tells me that the car that hit me was a dark-green Ford Zephyr. He knows about cars. 'You went twenty feet into the air,' he says. I remember seeing the car parked on the opposite side of the road near the front of the bus as the ambulance men picked me up. 'You should have seen your dad jump when the police came and told him what happened,' he says. 'He jumped over the sofa and sprinted out of the door.' I liked hearing that.

A couple of days later Danny comes home from school and brings me a pile of papers. Each of the children in my class has written me a get-well letter. I sit up and read every one.

Then Stella makes an announcement. 'We're going to live in a maisonette,' she says.

I don't know what a maisonette is, but whatever it is I don't want to go there. I'm still worrying about the maisonette when my father shouts for me to come in the house.

'Sit doon, son,' he says. He tells me that soon he's going away for a while but that I have no need to worry. He'll be back before too long 'and we'll all be together again'.

I start to cry. I don't want him to go away. I don't want him to leave us.

I O

The next time I see my father he is in prison. Nobody told me he was in prison. Aunt Stella said he was working away 'in a castle'. But I've already picked up plenty of information from listening to her conversations with grown-ups about why my father is no longer around. On the Christmas Eve they never came home there had been a fight in a pub called the Royal Oak. A man called Larry was hit in the face with a beer glass. My father was arrested and charged and when he went to court he was found guilty of wounding this man, although I heard some people saying afterwards that he had taken the blame for someone else.

Stella takes me and Danny on a train to see my father, leaving the two little ones with one of her friends. We get off the train at Lancaster and then walk the rest of the way. When we get there it looks exactly like a castle with a huge arched entrance and great big turreted towers on either side. Men in black uniforms wearing peaked caps, who look to me like guards, ask Aunt Stella questions and then usher us through a narrow gateway and into a corridor.

Inside we sit at a table in a room that looks like a school dining hall. At one end some of the uniformed men are sitting behind a raised desk. Danny and I chase each other around the table while Stella stares at a door at the side of the raised desk. The door opens and a stream of men dressed in blue denims and identical blue-and-white-striped shirts emerge. I see my father and run up to him. 'Dad!' He ruffles my hair and then picks me up, carrying me to the table where Stella is waiting. He puts me down and then ruffles Danny's hair, before reaching over and kissing Stella. It's the first time I've ever seen him kiss her. As I watch I feel my stomach tense, almost to the point of cramp. I try to remember him kissing my mother but can't.

A long hour and a half follows. On the way back to Shipley, back to number 8 Moody Lane into which we moved while my father was in jail, I hardly speak. I can't get the image of him kissing Stella out of my head.

Moody Lane was where I became a thief. I'd been a liar for a while already. After Stella hit me with the broom handle at the house on Grimdale Avenue I made sure I always answered, 'No, Aunt Stella,' whenever she asked me if I'd been speaking Scottish. The truth was I didn't know if I had or not. I just spoke. I'd practised saying 'eighty-four' the way she told me to, but I never tried to say it in her presence in case I got it wrong. She also asked me sometimes if I'd been snooking. 'No, Aunt Stella,' I told her. I never snooked in the house or anywhere near where she might hear me, but as soon as I was safely on my own I snooked away to my heart's content.

Stella often left me and Danny on our own at night with Darren and Alison. When we were bored with the television we went out into the dark and stole bicycles. We had a simple method – creeping and sneaking into gardens and outhouses – that's where most people kept their bikes. Some nights we travelled for what seemed like miles on the nicked bikes, whizzing along footpaths and down deserted streets, taking care not to stray on to any main roads. Stealing the bikes was exciting. Stella had no money to buy us a bike.

There was so little money around while my father was in prison that to decorate the maisonette she suggested we drew pictures on the walls with crayons. We drew a great big moonscape complete with craters and mountains across the whole of the back wall of the living room and then carried the picture on with other planets and spaceships all the way along the hall to the front door. There was rarely much food in the house. Once Stella had fed the little ones, the best she could manage for us was chips with everything, beans, soup and sometimes a pie. There was nearly always a shortage of milk so that breakfast was often Weetabix with margarine, or jam if there was any in the cupboard. We had porridge and ate a lot of jam sandwiches, sugar sandwiches and dripping sandwiches.

I went to Crag Road Junior School, a walk of about a mile and a half, while Danny went to a school nearer the town. By then I was the scruffiest kid in the class, maybe the school. For nearly all of the time I went to that school all I had to wear on my feet were a pair of cut-down wellington boots. Being so poor and scruffy never bothered me until our class were due to go on a school trip to the east coast fishing town of Whitby. On the morning of the trip all the kids had brought packed lunches except me. We were all milling around by the front door of the school waiting for the coach while the teacher ticked our names off her list. When she got to me she asked me where my packed lunch was. I gave her a blank look. I had no idea what a packed lunch was.

'You must have brought something to eat, Erwin,' she said. 'It's going to be a long day. Hasn't your mum made you anything?'

I felt embarrassed. She meant sandwiches. I had no sandwiches and no mum. 'No, miss,' I said, 'she forgot.'

I thought the teacher was going to be angry with me. She stared down at me and then turned and called to the other kids. 'Everyone. Gather round, everyone.' The kids approached and then the teacher lowered her head slightly, and almost in a whisper said, 'Erwin's mum is poorly and hasn't been able to make him any lunch. Who's got a spare sandwich for him, please?'

I squirmed. I didn't really know any of the kids very well. I was too quiet to make friends. Within seconds hands were being thrust in front of me holding every type of sandwich imaginable. I'd never seen brown bread before and began tucking in immediately. The kids were laughing as I pushed the food into my mouth, a feast of tomatoes and egg, lettuce and bacon, corned beef and pickle.

The teacher had to step in and stop me eating. She gave me a carrier bag. 'Put those in here and wrap them up, Erwin. You can eat them when we get to Whitby.'

My embarrassment had given way to excitement at having so many interesting and delightful things to eat.

On the day trip to Whitby we visited the ruined abbey and the teacher showed us how to make rubbings on the gravestones in the cemetery and on the brass etchings in a nearby church. Later she took us to the beach where we searched for fossils – the teacher said we were looking for ammonites; small spiral-shaped petrified creatures of various sizes. As we poked about in the sand and the rocks the salty smell of the sea filled my nostrils. It was such a fresh and unusual smell. A couple of my classmates found a tiny ammonite which made us all squeal with delight. After the beach we walked through the narrow streets of the town, looking in the shops and inspecting fishing nets and dried sea urchins hanging from the windows and the doors as the sea air wafted around every corner. On the coach back to school I felt a part of the class at last. I took the paper with the brass-rubbing patterns home but nobody took any notice. I didn't mind. It would have been strange if a fuss had been made about anything I did at school.

One of our classes was needlework. We were encouraged to make something for our families. I decided to make an apron for Aunt Stella. I picked the material, bright red with white polka dots, and spent for ever hand-sewing hems around the edges. It was my first ever go at sewing. Aunt Stella was scary in one sense, but there was also a comeliness about her that in an odd way I liked. I really wanted her to be pleased with the apron I was making for her but before I finished it I had a catastrophe.

Because of the distance he had to travel, Danny left home for school a good twenty minutes before I did. Aunt Stella was always still in bed when we left. For some reason I was running late. I finished my toast and jam and headed fast out of the door, only to trip over the two pints of milk that were delivered every other morning. The bottles smashed against the floor sending a crescendo of echoes around the empty stairwell of the flats. I froze. Milk spread through the shattered glass all over the floor and started dripping down the stairs. I heard a shout from upstairs. 'No, Aunt Stella,' I called back – no was my default answer whenever I thought I was being accused of something. I heard her footsteps as she got out of bed and stamped along the bedroom floor. The terror was growing inside me and I tried not to cry as she hurtled down the stairs in her dressing gown.

Instinctively I began to duck and cower, preparing for blows. She walked past me and retrieved the broom from the kitchen. I shrank further into the corner. The hallway was so narrow that she couldn't get a good swing at me with the broom handle. Instead she poked me with it, in my sides and in my chest.

I started to shout, 'I'm sorry, Aunt Stella!' and then I felt warm liquid filling my shorts and running into my wellingtons. I squeezed hard to stop the pee flowing and began crying out loud at the same time.

'Thick!' she shouted as she jabbed me hard with the broom. 'Thick, thick, thick . . .' She stopped to catch her breath and I got up, still sobbing. 'Now get to school or you'll be late,' she said. As I headed down the stairs she called after me, 'And stop crying. It's no good crying over spilt milk.'

I'd stopped crying by the time I got to the bottom of the stairs, but I could feel a hot, stinging sensation on my throat which was distracting me. When I put my hand to the spot I felt something moving, then I heard a buzzing noise. I grabbed whatever it was between finger and thumb and discovered it was a wasp and it had stung me. I threw it to the floor and stamped on it over and over again in a raging fit of temper.

I was so miserable on my way to school I stopped by a small copse that had long grass between the trees and cheered myself up by catching some grasshoppers. I rummaged in a dustbin for a jam jar. Soon I was bouncing all over the grass chasing the little critters and cramming them into my jar. The time spent grasshopper hunting helped my shorts to dry. When my jar was full I trundled along to school, only to arrive a good twenty minutes late. Assembly was already taking place, so I sneaked in at the back hoping nobody would notice me. A few heads turned, and then a voice boomed out my name. 'To the front!' I stayed put. 'To the front! Now!'

I took a deep breath and walked slowly to the front of the hall where the deputy headmaster was standing by the stage. He had a cane in his hand. 'Up,' he ordered, pointing to the middle of the stage with the cane. I climbed the few wooden steps and waited at the side while he made a speech about the importance of punctuality. Lateness was no longer going to be tolerated. I looked out at the sea of faces all staring up at me. I felt so small and ashamed. My shorts still felt a little damp and I was sure the whole school could see that I had pissed myself.

'You know the drill,' said the deputy head. He towered over me. I didn't know 'the drill' at all as I had never been caned before. 'Over you go, boy.'

I bent over awkwardly so that my head hung by my knees and immediately I became aware of the smell of drying pee coming from my wellies. My jar full of grasshoppers was half out of my pocket and I could feel tiny vibrations on the top of my thigh as the bouncy creatures hopped and sprang against the glass. I was just imagining what life for a grasshopper in my airless jar might be like when the first blow swished against my buttocks. It stung like hell, but though it was painful, I didn't feel hurt the way I did when Pam hit me with the broom handle. I squeezed my eyes shut and grasped my grasshopper jar tightly as the teacher whacked me another five times before telling me to stand up straight and 'get off to the back of the assembly'. I didn't even feel angry about what he had done to me. I was just glad to get out of the sight of all those staring eyes.

I had my head down most of the way home from school that afternoon, kicking stones and stamping my wellies in puddles. It seemed I could do nothing right. I missed my mother and I missed my father. I missed my Maw and my aunts and uncles who had always made me feel special and wanted and loved. And I missed my sister. When she first arrived I was as happy as could be. I loved her so much, loved pushing her pram, playing with her and making her smile. Since being at Stella's my sister and I had hardly spent any time together. I was so wrapped up in my own thoughts and feelings that I had almost stopped thinking about her. She was just one of the two toddlers in the house.

*　　　*　　　*

Alongside the path at the side of Moody Lane which led up to our block a row of huge trees hung their branches low and serpent-like over the heads of anyone walking below. When the wind blew the branches seemed to grumble and sneer. They reminded me of trees that appeared to have a life of their own in a sequence from a film I loved called *Great Expectations* where the boy Pip is running scared after an encounter on the marshes with an escaped convict. Pip was a good boy and just like me had lost his real family. The film delighted me, but the bit with the trees had scared the hell out of me, so much that even when there was just a slight breeze I always ran past the trees on Moody Lane. This time I was too unhappy to notice. As I sauntered underneath I dared them to hiss their usual whispers and see if I cared.

I still had my head down when I reached the clearing at the end of the path. And then I heard a voice shout out my name. It was a familiar, Scottish-sounding voice. I looked up to the bay window of what was our living room and saw a woman with a shawl draped over her head and shoulders. She shouted again. 'Erwin, it's me, your granny. Hurry up, son. I've come to see you.'

My granny? It must be my maw, I thought. I hadn't seen Maw for so long. I loved and missed her so much. I hadn't seen her since she left Thompson Street. Overwhelmed with excitement and relief I yelled back at the top of my voice, 'Maw!' I was sure she had come to rescue me. 'Maw!' I yelled again and then set off running as fast as my legs would carry me.

'Come on, Erwin, come on, son,' she called. I barged through the main entrance doors and climbed the stairs two at a time. My heart was bursting. It had been so long since I'd had a hug or a kiss. I knew Maw loved me, she used to always cover me with kisses, smother me with hugs. I remembered her smell and her fleshy arms and big soft breasts. Up the stairs I bounded. With every leap I became more determined to throw myself at Maw and hang on to her for ever. I pulled open the front door and hurled myself down the narrow corridor before bursting through the living-room door.

But there was no Maw. The only woman in the room was Aunt Stella. She was still wearing the shawl and grinning and I realised that it had been her calling out to me at the bay window. I was confused. Danny was standing near her. The moment they saw my big excited face they both erupted with laughter. My confusion intensified – and then it dawned on me they were playing a trick. I felt stupid. Then I felt hurt. So hurt. I had been keeping my feelings about how much I missed my family buried for such a long time. My face burned. I wanted to cry but the anger that was making my body tremble gave me the strength I needed to hold back the tears.

I longed for my father to return home. More than a year passed before he was released from prison. When he did finally turn up I was disappointed that he didn't seem to want to spend any special time with me or my sister. Aunt Stella threw a party for him. As a 'welcome home' present she bought him a guitar from the weekly payment catalogue. The guitar had the words 'The Big

Timer' written on it in fancy gold lettering. Lots of people came to the house to celebrate his release. They were all drinking heavily. Playing his guitar and singing his favourite songs my father was the centre of attention. People seemed to be drawn to him.

Danny and I hid under the stairs in the hallway watching all the comings and goings. When my father emerged from the living room on his way to the bathroom which was at the top of the hallway stairs we ducked back in the alcove. He had to wait at the bottom of the stairs for Aunt Stella's sister Mandy who was on her way down. Mandy started giggling. 'Hello, Big Timer,' she said. When she got to the bottom stair I saw her lift up her skirt and taking hold of my father's hand she thrust it down the front of her knickers. 'It's been a while since you felt one of these,' she said. My father left his hand there for some moments and at the same time kissed Mandy on the lips. Somebody shouted above the rowdy racket in the living room for more songs from my father and he pulled away from her. Mandy held on to his hand and then slowly stepped back staring after him as he climbed the stairs. When she walked past the alcove on her way to the living room, looking down and smiling to herself, I wanted to shout at her and tell her not to be rude with my dad – but I was too scared of what Aunt Stella might say if she found out. I was sure she would not be happy with Mandy and I didn't want her to think badly of my father, so I kept quiet.

My father got another job driving a big red lorry. It meant he was away from home again for days at a time. Sometimes he brought his wagon home with the trailer fully loaded ready for an early departure in the morning. After he parked up with a full load one afternoon I went to see what was tied down underneath the oily green tarpaulin. Unravelling a small corner of the canvas I loosened a cardboard box from the stack. When I opened it I saw it contained twelve bottles of brown sauce. Soon I was knocking on doors in the neighbourhood trying to sell it for sixpence a bottle. There were no takers.

With my stolen stock unsold I dumped the bottles and headed home to Moody Lane where a surprise was waiting for me. My father either saw me from the bay window taking the box off the trailer or somebody had told him what I had done. Maybe one of the neighbours to whom I'd been trying to sell the loot had snitched. As soon as I stepped inside the front door of the flat my father roared, 'Thief!' before punching me so hard on the back of the head that I launched into a series of forward rolls that took me all the way down the hallway and through the living-room door. As I tumbled my mind went black and I saw flashes of tiny sparks just like the ones I saw when Stella first hit me with the broom handle.

My father chased after me roaring again, 'Fucking wee thief!' I came to a halt in a heap and tried to shout out to him. Before I could get the words out he kicked me with such force that I was lifted off the ground and sent rolling back along the hallway. He punched me and kicked me again, and again I saw stars.

I felt the wind whoosh out of me, and barely able to breathe I croaked out a feeble half-shout, 'No, Dad . . .'

When I opened my eyes he was leaning over me panting and I could smell his beer breath. His hair was hanging down each side of his head giving him the wild-man look. 'Bed!' he shouted.

I dragged myself to my feet and limped up the stairs. I loved my father with all my heart. It was after that beating that I began to hate him too.

My father left Stella a couple of months after he got out of jail and took me and my sister with him. He never told me why we had to leave and I never asked him. In one sense I was glad to be leaving Moody Lane, but I knew I would miss Stella and Danny. With my mother gone and while my father was in prison they had been the only constants in my life. The longer I was with them the more I accepted them as family.

The Christmas before my father came home, Aunt Stella had got me and Danny a multi-action toy machine gun each from the weekly payment catalogue. The gun was called a 'Johnny Seven'. It fired plastic bullets, missiles and grenades and Danny and I had great fun playing soldiers. Before getting the Johnny Seven I made my own toys: spaceships out of clothes pegs and hair grips; and I used the same bits and pieces to play Cowboys and Indians. But the Johnny Seven was a real working, firing toy that needed no imagination. It was the best toy Danny and I ever had. I still missed my old life in Thompson Street, what I thought of as my real life – and I still missed Micky. But I'd been getting used to this new life and at school I had discovered books.

The teacher who taught reading and writing, Mrs Wagstaff, seemed to like me and praised the neatness of my writing which I practised diligently. One of my favourite books was called *Featherbedland*. It was about a little boy who lived between the springs of a huge feather bed. He was so safe and cosy and happy in his endless adventures and I loved imagining how wonderful it would be to live in such a place. The book I read that gave me the most comfort was *The Lion, the Witch and the Wardrobe*. I spent hours and hours reading and rereading about the four children who had been sent away from their home to live in a strange house in the country, where they discovered a mysterious wardrobe which led them into another world, a magical snowbound place called Narnia. I longed for such a wardrobe and would have done anything to have been able to join the four children on their amazing adventures in Narnia. I must have been a good reader as the teacher often asked me to stand up and read bits of the book to the rest of the class. I loved the story so much and I loved sharing it with my classmates. By then I also had a best friend at the school called Melvyn.

I was thinking about Melvyn as I sat in the cab of my father's lorry staring out of the windscreen at the long dark road in front of us. Melvyn and I were supposed to have been playing in a marbles competition. He had a couple of lovely coloured 'two-ers' and 'three-ers' I wanted to try and win off him. I'd been starting to get really good at marbles and was sure I was going to have at least one of his bigger marbles in my bag soon.

Oblivious to the constant rasping hum from the engine that separated the long passenger seat from the driver's seat my sister snuggled up next to me asleep, my arms wrapped tightly around her. When I plucked up the courage to ask my father where we were going he told me we were going to live in Scotland. 'Scotland!' I shouted. Scotland held only happy memories for me.

I pulled my sister closer and drifted off to sleep happily thinking about Riverbank and Maw and my aunts and uncles – and camp-fires and singing and laughter and great pans of lovely soup.

But the Scotland I woke up in was nothing like the Scotland I remembered. My father had brought us to his sister's house in a little town on the west coast called Stevenston and left us there. Before he climbed into his cab to go he told me not to worry. 'We'll all be together again soon, son,' he said. 'Make sure you take care of your sister.' I wanted to cry but was now used to keeping my tears in check. I was such a long way from anywhere and anyone I knew. Standing at the gate of the house on Caledonian Road I watched with a thudding heart as his lorry drove away. I stared after it, listening as it changed gears, all the way to end of the road and then it turned and disappeared.

Before Stevenston I had only ever met my mother's brothers and sisters – these were who I knew as my uncles and aunties. I had never thought about my father having brothers and sisters, other uncles and aunties who might care about me. My aunt Nettie and her husband, my uncle Soldier, had five children, three of whom were much older than me and one who was much younger. I shared a bed with the two youngest boys. The one who was closest to my age was my cousin Bobby. He became my new playmate.

Bobby and his family were very poor. Uncle Soldier had no job and so there was little food through the week – but then on 'Bru Day' when he got paid from the dole office he always brought home cakes and sweets for everybody. It must have been hard for them to suddenly have two extra mouths to feed. My aunt Nettie was good to us, but I think we were quite a burden.

The beach was only a ten- or fifteen-minute walk from Caledonian Road and often when my cousins were at school she told me to take my sister there to play. My sister and I spent hours playing in the sand or paddling in the shallow water when the tide was in. My sister was only three years old. I loved spending so much time with her, until one day we found a jellyfish stranded on the sand and my sister hit it with a spade and bits of its jelly body splattered into my eyes making them sting so much I thought I was going blind. I yelled in pain and terror. When I finally managed to open my eyes I saw that my sister had wandered into the sea. She was paddling almost up to her waist. I shouted at her and she turned and chuckled and then lost her footing as a small wave pushed her from behind. I raced towards her screaming her name, almost tripping as my feet splashed hard into the water. I reached her just before her head went under the water for a second time. Panicking I dragged her out on to the sand, both of us coughing and sputtering. Then she began to cry. I hugged her tight and kissed her on her forehead. I stroked her hair and hugged her again, but still she cried and continued all the way back home.

I was sent to the same school as my cousin Bobby. On my first day I got picked on by some of the other boys. They stood around me in the playground shouting, '*English, English, English . . .*' Even though when I was in England I had been trying to speak the same way as other children and like Aunt Stella and Danny I thought I was Scottish like my father. He had told me that I had 'Scottish blood'. So had my Maw. In Stevenston I had reverted to what I thought was my original Scottish accent – but it didn't convince my new schoolmates.

As the boys' chanting grew louder I was getting more and more frightened when I heard somebody shout out, '*Fucken' leave him alane!*' It was my cousin Bobby. Even though he was almost a year younger than me he was a lot tougher and had more presence. '*He's ma cousin fae England*', he told my tormentors. '*Anybody fucks wi' him fucks wi' me . . .*' I loved Bobby for that.

After Bobby's intervention I was accepted. I was even allowed to join his gang. There were around a dozen boys in the gang and after school we ran wild long into the night, exploring the railway yards, creeping into the back of the local Wonderloaf factory bakery when the night shift left the doors unlocked and we could snatch trays of cakes. Sometimes we sneaked into pub yards to steal crisps and lemonade. We looked for members of rival gangs, supposedly to challenge them to fight, though I was always secretly relieved that we never actually found any of our perceived enemies.

At weekends me and Bobby and a couple of his pals went down to the railway station to wait for passengers to alight before offering them our services as luggage porters. That was how we got pocket money for sweets. If there was a wedding the whole gang hung about waiting for the bride to emerge from the church. Local tradition was that all new brides carried bags of change to throw over their shoulders as a gift for any children present. This was called the 'scramble'. There was a scramble nearly every week. As well as supplementing the luggage-humping money, scrambles were exciting and fun. Afterwards we always ended up with cuts and bruises – but nobody seemed to care so long as we emerged with coins in our scuffed and grubby hands.

We were roughie-toughies who never cried – except I did once. One night six or seven of us raided a pub yard and stole a box of salt-and-vinegar crisps. We raced away to a den to share out the booty. In the excitement I had forgotten the trouble I had been having with a back tooth. It had a hole in it and every couple of days it began to throb and pulse with pain. I had been enjoying my first pain-free few days in almost a month, and forgetting all about the dodgy tooth I took a great handful of crisps from one of the bags in my share and crammed them into my mouth. I crunched down hard and suddenly it felt like somebody had thrust a red-hot electrified poker deep into the back of my jawbone. The edge of a jagged crisp had been forced into the hole in my rotten back tooth. As soon as it hit the nerve I screamed deathly screams over and over, collapsing and writhing in terrible agony.

My gang mates looked on in horror. Cousin Bobby tried to pick me up but I was going nowhere. Leaving me rolling around and screaming, my new pals scattered. Bobby didn't want to go, but finally he ran all the way home and returned with Uncle Soldier who carried me back to their house over his shoulder. I cried and sobbed through the night, keeping everyone awake, as the pain rattled unceasingly through the whole of my head. In the morning my uncle Soldier lifted me over his shoulder again and marched me to the dentist where he demanded immediate treatment, '*Or ah'll no be responsible for ma actions . . .*'

11

The day my father turned up in his lorry to collect us from Stevenston I ran away to hide. I loved him and missed him, but I was learning how to keep my feelings of love towards others buried. I raced to the back of a row of derelict garages a couple of streets away from Aunt Nettie's house and hid behind some large rubbish bins. Butterflies fluttered in my stomach. I could barely contain my panting. I heard raised voices getting closer and recognised my uncle Soldier's – then I heard my father's. 'Erwin! Erwin! C'mone, son. Ah'm taking you hame.' He shouted over and over and I could hear the anger building at my failure to respond. 'Erwin! For fuck's sake, son! C'mone. We're all going to be together again.' I squeezed my eyes tight shut. I so wanted that. I knew we could never have my mother with us again, but my sister, my father and me were my whole world.

I broke cover. 'I'm here, Dad!' I shouted, expecting to get a battering. Instead he scooped me up and hugged me tight.

It was already dark when my father set off in his lorry heading back to England with me and my sister once more huddled up on the long passenger seat. It was comforting to be so close to my sister again. I loved her but I was becoming fearful for her. Once I started school and joined the gang in Stevenston we had hardly spent any time together. She was only just learning to talk. Even though I was still only nine years old I was aware of how sad it was that she would never know our mother. She would never get to say 'Mammy' like I had.

We hadn't seen much of our father since our mother had been killed. It never bothered me that Aunt Stella didn't hug or kiss me, but I knew babies needed hugs and kisses and my sister got none. Aunt Stella looked after us in her own way, but nobody seemed to want to cuddle us and hold us close or say nice things to us about how special we were. The only one who was cuddling or kissing my sister was me and I didn't think that was enough for her.

The humming of the engine in the cab of the lorry was calming. Headlights from vehicles coming in the opposite direction were hypnotising. Occasionally I glanced up at my father. His face was set in a constant frown as he stared into the road ahead. I was too young to understand what was going on inside his head. I asked him where we were going. He said he was taking us 'hame'. I knew that 84 Thompson Street was smashed to pieces so it couldn't be there. I asked him if we were going back to Aunt Stella's. 'No, son,' he said. 'Forget about Aunt Stella.' She could be frightening – but I still missed her and Danny. They had been the main people in my life for the longest time after the crash. I missed their familiarity. It would be hard to just forget all about them. My father drove on in silence. My sister snuggled up to me and I wrapped my arms tight around her. Soon she was sleeping soundly in my arms and a little while later I too was deep in slumber.

When I woke up I was in bed. By then I was in the habit of sleeping curled up in a ball with my head under the covers. I lay for a while in the dark trying to get my bearings. I still thought I was in Stevenston, then I realised I was in bed alone – no cousins. My brain took some moments to clear before I remembered being in my father's lorry with my sister. Then I became aware of someone else in the bedroom. I could hear breathing. It sounded too heavy to be my sister and not heavy enough to be my father. Slowly I pushed the top of my head outside the covers just up to my eyes. I was in a single bed, one side of which was up against a wall. The room was huge. Diagonally across from me was another single bed below a large window. It was getting light outside and the curtains were letting in a dull glow. I could vaguely make out the shape of a long body under the covers of the other bed. The back of a head with long curly brown hair was poking out of the top. Alarmed, I gently pulled my covers around my face leaving just one eye free to keep watch on the stranger.

Eventually the head turned and I saw it was a man with a beard. He yawned and then pulled his arms free. I saw him squeeze his eyes shut as he whispered to himself, 'Fucking hell.' Then he noticed me. 'Hi,' he said. I ducked the whole of my head back under the covers. 'Come on, Erwin, you're not shy, are you?'

I had no idea where I was and couldn't understand how this stranger knew my name. I heard him make to get up and so eased my one eye back up to peeking position. He was sitting on the edge of his bed in his vest and underpants. He bent down to pick up his trousers. But there was something inside making them very heavy. As he lifted them I saw that one of the legs was already filled out with something long and rigid. He pushed his left leg into the empty trouser leg and then I noticed that where his right leg should have been there was just a stump. My one eye widened in wonder. I continued watching as he strapped and buckled the artificial leg to his stump and then stood up to fasten his trousers – then he turned and looked at me. 'Don't worry,' he said, 'I lost my leg when I crashed my motorbike.' He smiled and winked at me. 'But I can still play football.' My face reddened. I felt like I had been caught peeping at something I shouldn't have seen. I pulled my head back under the covers and heard his footsteps and the door opening. He spoke again. 'I'll see you downstairs for breakfast.'

My clothes were on a chair at the side of the bed. I got up and dressed and spent some minutes looking out of the window. I saw that the building was on the main road that ran along the bottom of Thompson Street, the one that Podge had chased me across. At least now I knew I was in Shipley. The window was on the left-hand side of the room and so high up I could see all the way to the bridge and crossroads and traffic lights above the river. The other side of the crossroads became Briggate and then Leeds Road.

Still puzzled by the house I was in I carefully made my way down two flights of stairs following the smell of frying bacon and the sound of a radio playing. I came across an open doorway where I stood in silence watching. The kitchen was big and bright with a wooden table that had a large bowl of fruit in the middle. It was the kind of kitchen I had only ever seen on television adverts. Standing in front of the cooker was a grey-haired woman wearing glasses and a striped apron. She had one hand on a large frying pan. The stranger with the false leg was sitting at the table.

I heard a sound behind me and then felt a hand on my shoulder. I jumped. 'Eey up,' said a deep voice. When I turned I saw a large man with a small head and a pointed nose. I turned back and the woman and the stranger were looking at me, smiling.

'Hello, Erwin. Come and sit down and I'll do you a nice bacon sandwich,' said the woman.

Over breakfast she told me I was in the Falcon pub. My father had brought me straight here from Scotland. My sister was being looked after by my uncle Frank and aunt Miriam. The stranger with the curly hair was called Donald. He was the youngest son of this elderly couple, landlord and landlady of the Falcon, Mr and Mrs Reynolds. 'Your dad will be here in a few days,' said Mrs Reynolds. 'He'll explain more then.'

I was allowed to come and go as I pleased in the Falcon and had great fun exploring all the empty rooms. The food Mrs Reynolds gave me was the best I had ever tasted. Pork chops and beef and great fat sausages. We had lovely creamy mashed potatoes and loads of vegetables and there was always a pudding with the evening meal.

I made friends with Donald. He showed me how to play table football in the saloon bar and we had some fierce matches. 'I told you I could still play footie,' he said smiling. He also showed me how to play the pinball machine and we challenged each other to get the highest score. I liked Donald a lot.

Mrs Reynolds was kind to me. She was always asking me if I was all right. 'Let me know if you need anything.' I didn't like to ask. Eventually I plucked up the courage to ask if I could have some lemonade, please. 'Of course,' she said – and brought back a packet of crisps to go with the fizzy drink. I opened the crisps and was just about to thank her when I caught the whiff of salt and vinegar. Immediately I had a flashback to the horror of the pain I'd suffered from the stolen pub crisps and I screamed, making Mrs Reynolds jump. 'Eey, lad,' she said, 'it's only a bag of crisps.'

At night I used to sneak downstairs and sit at the back of the saloon bar on a bench behind a small partition watching as the men and women came in to buy drinks and talk and play records on the jukebox. It was a busy pub. The air reeked of tobacco and alcohol. It was a smell I liked as it reminded me of my father. The customers bought me crisps and lemonade and sometimes when they looked a bit like my father when he was drunk they gave me money, threepenny bits and sixpences.

My favourite song on the jukebox was 'Release Me' by Engelbert Humperdinck. They played it over and over again. Another song I liked was 'Memphis' by Chuck Berry – I knew it as my father used to sing it to his Big Timer guitar when he was with Aunt Stella. They also played 'The Tennessee Waltz', which made me want to cry as I couldn't forget it had been my mother's favourite song.

It was nearly two weeks before my father showed up. By then I was settled in at the Falcon and would have been happy to stay there for ever. He told me I'd be leaving the Falcon soon. 'I've got us a new hame,' he said. 'We'll all be back together again soon.'

His news worried me and excited me at the same time. Him, me and my sister all being together again was my dearest wish. I hated the uncertainty of wondering where I would be living next. Where was this new 'hame' going to be? He stayed a while talking to Mrs Reynolds who gave him good reports of my behaviour, then he tousled my hair. 'I'll see you in a couple of days,' he said. As he walked out of the front door of the pub on to the main road I felt that horrible butterfly sensation in my stomach. I wanted to run after him and I wanted to cry. Instead I turned and ran upstairs before anyone could see I was upset.

Mrs Reynolds didn't mind if I went out for hours at a time. I wandered all over the place. I went through the tunnel at the back of the pub that went under the railway line, the one I'd been chased through by Podge. Out on the other side the stockyards were great to explore and I loved fishing for sticklebacks in the canal with a home-made net. I went looking for my friend Micky once. But when I got to his house I found that it was empty and broken like mine. I hung around for hours hoping I might bump into him, but I never did.

On a Saturday there was an open market in the town centre and I decided to try and get a job on the sweet stall. The man who ran it shouted how good his sweets were. I hovered about in front of him for a while until eventually he asked me if I wanted anything.

'Have you got any jobs?' I said. He told me to come back later and I could help him clear up. I duly appeared as the stallholders were starting to pack up.

'Hi,' he said, 'you can start by collecting all the empty boxes.'

I began picking up small boxes and putting them into the bigger boxes. I hoped for a bag of sweets for my wages. But as I cleared the underneath of the tables I came across two unopened cases each containing six boxes of fudge. I looked around to check that nobody was watching and then used my foot to slide them into one of the bigger empty boxes and then pushed them into my main pile. Slowly, while the Sweet Man loaded trays and half-full boxes into the back of his van I pushed my pile further and further away until it was safe to retrieve my plunder. Once out of sight I picked up the boxes of fudge and ran.

Stealing the fudge was my first major crime. I was so excited my face was glowing with anticipation. I'd never held such a quantity of sweets in my hands before. I got back to the Falcon and man-aged to smuggle the fudge upstairs in a carrier bag without being seen. Once in my room I opened the cases and counted out the boxes on Donald's bed. They looked magnificent. I heard a sound out on the stairs and panicked. I'd forgotten to figure out where I was going to hide my haul. Then I had a brainwave. Quickly I slid open the sash window above Donald's bed, pulling it up high. Leaning out I saw what I hoped I would see – the sill outside the window was about a foot wide. Carefully I began reaching over and placing the boxes of fudge neatly on top of each other. The sill took four boxes longways which gave me three neat stacks of four.

I'd just put the last one in place and pulled down the window when the bedroom door opened and Mrs Reynolds walked in. 'There you are, Erwin,' she said. 'Are you ready for your tea, love?'

I hadn't bargained for the fact that my treasured stacks of fudge were on full view to all the passing traffic coming from the left. Nobody walking on the pavement from the same direction could miss them either. Half the world could see the proceeds of my thievery – and eventually so did my father. He turned up a few days later. I hadn't been near the fudge. I had no urge to eat it. I was just comforted by the fact it was there.

I was around the back of the pub playing on my own with some chicken wire when I heard my father calling my name. I stopped what I was doing and listened. 'Erwin!' I felt joy at my father's return, but I also thought I detected a note of anger in his voice. 'Erwin!' I emerged from my play place with caution and made for the front door of the pub.

'Erwin!' He was definitely angry. I got ready for a battering. As soon as I turned the corner my father grabbed me by the back of the neck and marched me inside. He pushed me in front of him and forced me up the stairs. A couple of times I tripped and stumbled, but he kept pushing until we got to my room. He shoved me inside. There, laid out neatly on Donald's bed, was the evidence of my crime.

'Whit the fuck is that?' said my father, pointing at the boxes.

I was too frightened to respond. I closed my eyes when I saw his hand coming hard towards me and squeezed them tight when his half-closed fist caught my temple. I bent double and he roared, 'Whit the fuck is that? Are you deef?'

Trying not to cry I lifted my head up. 'It's fudge, Dad,' I said.

His eyes seemed to roll back in his head and he roared again. 'Fucken' fudge? Whit d'ye mean fucken' fudge?'

I thought I was going to get the beating of a lifetime. Instead he bawled and swore at me and then told me I had to take it back to wherever I had got it from. I told him the Sweet Man had given it to me. 'It was my wages for helping him,' I said.

He went to hit me again for being a 'fucken' liar' and I ducked. 'I'll take it back, Dad,' I said. 'I promise.'

After he had gone I gathered up the boxes of fudge in another carrier bag and dumped it in the big bin behind the pub.

I liked the freedom of living in the Falcon and I liked my own company. Every day I went out and about exploring. I spent time on the Delf remembering the fun I'd had with Micky, or wandered about the town centre, looking in shops or just sitting on the walls by the bus stops, watching the people. There were always crisps and lemonade waiting on my return, loads of fun on the machines when Donald was around and great meals in the kitchen.

One night I sneaked downstairs and was surprised to see my father. Nestling into my corner seat in the saloon bar I looked across to the lounge bar and there he was, standing holding a pint of beer. He had on a cowboy hat and a neckerchief tied loosely around his neck and he was talking in a very friendly way to a pretty blonde woman. I watched them both as they chatted and laughed. I hadn't seen him for days and I wondered why he hadn't been up to see me.

The saloon bar began to fill and soon my view was blocked. Mr Reynolds was behind the bar. He shouted for people to 'listen in, listen in', and then announced that 'Big Erwin' would be performing in a couple of minutes. Some people clapped and cheered and somebody whistled.

I heard my father thank everyone and then he laughed and said, 'Don't clap, just throw money.' This made people in the audience laugh and then he started singing. I recognised the song. It was 'It Wasn't God Who Made Honky Tonk Angels'. Through the crowd I kept catching glances of his friend the blonde woman. She was swaying and singing along and clapping, never taking her eyes off my father. It was another week before I was introduced to her.

My father came to the Falcon one morning and gave me some change. He told me to use it to catch a trolleybus at the stop just near the entrance to the pub and to tell the conductor to let me off at 'Little's shop in Foulfield'. I had heard of Foulfield. People said it was a rough place where there were tough boys who were always fighting and getting into trouble. I was scared. 'Can I come with you, Dad?' I said. He said he had to go to work, but that he would be waiting for me and gave me the address and directions to the house where he was going to be that night. It was just a two-minute walk from Little's shop. 'And don't get loast!' he said.

My father always gave me the impression that he thought I was stupid. Aunt Stella had said I was 'thick' and I believed her. The fact that I kept getting into trouble for reasons I couldn't explain made me certain that I was less intelligent than other children. I was going to do my best to get to the address my father had given me so he could see that sometimes I had brains.

As soon as Mrs Reynolds had cleared up after tea I set off for Foulfield. I was nervous as I stood at the bus stop. I jumped on the trolleybus and zipped up to the top deck hoping to stay out of the conductor's way so I could keep the money my father had given me – before remembering that I had to ask him where 'Little's shop' was so I would know when to get off. Reluctantly I handed over my fare and he said he would shout me.

My nervousness increased as we travelled along Leeds Road. We passed the Carnegie Library and the Blue Bell pub on the right at the bottom of Carr Lane. The Traveller's Rest pub was a few dozen yards after the Blue Bell on the same side and as we drew level to it I looked down to my left at the lamp-post into which Charlie Rogers's van had crashed. I hated that lamp-post. 'Bastard lamp-post,' I whispered. I stared at the pavement where my mother had landed on her head and had to hold down a surge of boiling hurt. 'Bastard pavement.'

So much had happened since the crash. It felt like a distant and a recent event at the same time. A sense of gloom cast a shadow over all my thoughts. Sometimes it felt like there were two mes – the one everyone could see and a secretly angry me that lived inside my head and which for the most part I kept to myself. I wanted to be good and kind and helpful and make people around me smile and laugh like before. But it was a desire that conflicted with the furtive part of me that told lies, stole and trusted nobody. Now I was in the habit of pretending to be whoever I thought I needed to be, depending on who I was with.

As I looked away from the scene of the crash I remembered that the night my mother was killed was the last time I ever said prayers. Every evening after my wash I would spend ages on my knees at the side of my bed asking God to look after all the people

I loved. My mother would sit on the bed beside me, patiently stroking my hair. I used to think God was the kindest man in the world – then he let the most important person in my life get killed in a stupid fucking car crash. I knew lots of swear words, though I rarely said any out loud. But I was so angry at God – I wanted to call him the worst swear word that I knew; the one my father used when he was at his most angry – I wanted to call Him a cunt. Instead I squeezed my eyes shut and wiped away my tears.

It was nightfall when I got off the trolleybus. On the other side of the road Little's off-licence was at the end of a short row of shops. A group of boys slightly older and bigger than me were playing around outside it. Nervously I crossed over and hurried past them with my head down. The road I was looking for was just around the corner. Minutes later I was outside the address my father had given me. I stood for a while and then knocked on the door. I heard voices and through the glass panel on the door I saw the outline of a woman.

The door opened and there stood the blonde woman I had seen with my father in the Falcon. 'Hello, Erwin,' she said. 'Come in, love, come on, come in.' I stepped inside directly into the small kitchen. 'Go through,' she said. 'Your dad's waiting.'

In the living room my father was sitting on a sofa with his guitar. There were beer bottles by his feet and he was drinking from a pint mug. 'Erwin son,' he said. 'C'mone in, son.' I could tell by his half-closed eyes and his slow talking that he had drunk a lot of beer. 'Carlene,' he called. 'Come in here.' Carlene was laughing. She came in and sat next to my father on the sofa. I could smell her perfume. 'Erwin,' he said and snorted, 'meet your new mammy.'

Carlene looked uncomfortable, closing her eyes and shaking her head. 'Ignore him,' she said. 'He's just a bit merry.'

Carlene turned out to be the youngest daughter of Mr and Mrs Reynolds. She was kind to me and good fun to be with. I travelled up to her house a few times over the next couple of weeks and stayed overnight sleeping at the bottom of her eldest son's bed. He was three years younger than me and had a two-year-old brother. My father told me that this was to be our new 'hame' and my sister would be joining us soon. I only saw him once or twice during my visits but I was relieved that each time he was sober. He and Carlene seemed very happy. She asked him once to play a Beatles song on his guitar. He started strumming and then began to sing, 'Beetles, worms, centipedes, woodlice . . .' and we all fell about laughing. I loved him when he was like that – like he was when we lived at Thompson Street and my mother was alive.

Soon I moved into Carlene's permanently. My father had a long-distance lorry-driver's job and was often away for two or three weeks at a time. Carlene made me feel welcome. Unlike Aunt Stella she was gentle. She never shouted or hit her children and she never even threatened to hit me. She was mad about Elvis Presley and had all his records. She played them for me and told me all about him. She loved dancing to his songs. One of her favourite Elvis albums was called *Flaming Star*. She played it so often it became my favourite too.

12

For a while after moving into Carlene's house I went back to the school I'd attended before my father took me and my sister Alison to Scotland. Alison had long since disappeared. She'd been living with my uncle Frank and aunt Miriam and their six children for a few weeks but then she'd vanished and I had no idea where she was. My school was more than two miles away and was a long walk in the mornings. More often than not I'd wander off and go and play by the canal or roam about the town. A couple of times a school inspector came to the house to see why I was missing but Carlene always made excuses for me.

When my friend Micky from Thompson Street and his family moved into a street nearby I all but gave up on school. Carlene never tried to control me. She fed me and put clothes on my back given by her friends or relatives or bought from a second-hand shop. I was happy in jeans and boots. With my father away for long periods I used to hook up with Micky and he and I ran wild together. We made rafts which we sailed on a lake in a nearby quarry and built our own go-carts using old pram wheels and bits of wooden boxes. We fished in the canal, hunted for tadpoles and threw stones through the windows of run-down factories.

One day the steam train the *Flying Scotsman* was due to pass through the town and we waited for hours with the crowd on the railway bridge at Briggate just yards from the town centre. When the train's whistle signalled its imminent arrival we screamed and yelled with everyone else and whooped with delight when the big train barrelled underneath us enveloping us in clouds of smoky steam so thick we could barely breathe or see each other.

Each time my father returned I was forced to stay around for a while and have a go at school again. By then I had mixed feelings about my father being home. It was great to see him, but his behaviour towards Carlene when he was drunk was terrifying. When he attacked her he kicked and punched her, paying no heed to her screaming and her obvious pain and distress. Sometimes the pitch of Carlene's screaming and my father's roaring prompted the neighbours to call the police but when they arrived my father reassured them that 'everything was all right'. They called him 'Jock', and seemed to be friendly with him. 'Just try and keep it down a bit, Jock,' was their strongest admonishment.

Carlene was too frightened of my father to tell on him. Whenever the violence erupted, me and the other kids scarpered and hid in an empty rabbit hutch in the back garden. Once when Carlene spotted my father from the front window weaving his way up the road she shepherded us together, quickly made a pile of jam sandwiches and then led the way to the rabbit hutch before my father came through the door. There we stayed until we were sure he was asleep and I agreed to sneak into the house to get us something to drink.

I poked my head around the living-room door to check my father was unconscious just as he opened one eye. 'Erwin son, c'm'ere,' he said. I moved towards him slowly. 'Do me a favour, son, and iron my cavalry twill trousers.'

I'd never used the iron before but I had seen Carlene use it. His cavalry twill trousers were his favourites. I felt a huge sense of responsibility and pride that he trusted me with them. I went in the kitchen, got the ironing board out and plugged in the iron. When I thought it was hot enough I pressed it on to an inside trouser leg but to my horror there was a hiss of smoke and an acrid smell of burning. I gasped and pulled the iron off quickly. But it was too late. The damage had been done. There, near the crotch, was a complete iron-shaped dark-brown singe mark. I gulped and opened the kitchen window to get rid of the smell. I turned the iron down and rapidly ran it lightly over the rest of the trousers before hanging them neatly over a chair in the living room.

'They're done, Dad,' I called.

'Good boy,' he grunted, and then turned over on the sofa so his back was facing me.

I scuttled back outside and told Carlene I thought he was still drunk. 'I've ironed his cavalry twills,' I said, keeping quiet about the burn mark. But I was keen to make myself scarce. 'I've got to go,' I said, 'I'll see you later.' And off I sped.

After wandering about aimlessly I ended up by some flats on a hill that overlooked Leeds Road. I could see the exact spot where the crash happened. Whenever I found myself close to where Charlie and my mother were killed I went into daydream mode, imagining what might have been happening during the moments just before the collision. Were my mother and father arguing?

Were the dogs barking? Charlie must have taken his eyes off the road. Was he trying to stop the argument? There would only have been a half-second between the van starting to veer and the impact with the lamp-post. Did Charlie see it? Did he shout? Did my mother scream? Did my father try to protect my mother? I hoped he did. I would have.

Suddenly I was shaken out of my trance by the sight of my father marching unsteadily down Leeds Road towards the town centre. Cavalry twills! My heart batted against my ribcage. Even from fifty yards away I could see the dark-brown pattern of the iron on his inside leg. I was about to turn and run when he looked up in my direction. Recognition sparked in his face. He shouted, 'Erwin! Erwin! C'm'ere, son.' Fear paralysed me. 'Erwin, c'mone doon here.'

I took a deep guilty breath and set off down towards him. Standing in front of him I braced myself for blows. Instead he thrust his hand deep in his pocket and pulled out half a crown. 'Here, son,' he said, swaying slightly. 'That's for doing a good job on my trousers.'

At first I thought he was playing a trick – then it dawned that he really hadn't seen the scorch mark. I took the money and ran. Once I was at a safe distance I looked back and I could still see him walking to town, the burnt brown iron patch flashing with every step he took.

Whenever my father was home the first thing he did in the morning when he woke up was shout, 'Erwin! Tea!' I'd dive out of bed and scurry about making the tea which I'd take up to him in his big chipped and cracked pint mug. One morning I woke early and heard the sound of a strange man talking to Carlene in her bedroom. The man was swearing a lot, speaking in a loud, croaky, lisping whisper. As I listened I could make out an accent that was similar to my father's and I wondered if he had left and Carlene had brought someone else home. Whoever it was suddenly shouted, 'Erwin! Tea!' I was shocked that he knew that I was the tea-maker. Automatically I jumped out of bed and got on with my chore. I'd soon see who the stranger was.

I took the tea up in an ordinary cup as the pint mug was reserved only for my father. I knocked on the door and the stranger told me to come in. Immediately I saw that there was no stranger. Carlene had the covers pulled up and my father was sitting on the edge of the bed. He was dressed in the clothes he'd had on the night before, but now they were covered in blood. 'Thanks, thon,' he said as I passed him his tea. His face was swollen, his lips burst. It looked like he had no teeth. I wanted to ask him what had happened. I wanted to snuggle up to him and make sure he was all right, but I daren't.

Eavesdropping on various adult conversations over the next few days I learned that my father had been in Shipley town centre that night walking with my uncle Frank and aunt Miriam after a heavy drinking session. Aunt Miriam and Uncle Frank were arguing. Aunt Miriam reached into her handbag and pulled out a big bottle of beer which she swung at my uncle Frank's head. He ducked and the bottle hit my father full in the mouth. It was almost a month before he got his false teeth and could speak and sound like himself again.

My father told me one day that Carlene was going to have a baby, 'another baby sister for you, or maybe a new baby brother'. It was exciting to think that a new baby was on its way. The baby turned out to be a new baby sister. On the day my father went to the hospital to bring Carlene and the baby home I was left to look after Carlene's two boys. While he was gone I picked up his guitar and tried strumming it like he did. Then I put on his cowboy hat. I was singing and strumming trying to be like him when a taxi pulled up outside the house. I put down the guitar and still wearing the hat I raced outside to greet the new baby.

My father got out of the front passenger seat and then, ignoring me, helped Carlene and the baby out of the back seat. The baby was a beautiful little blonde-haired, fair-skinned thing. I was dying to hold her and hovered impatiently around the three of them as my father helped Carlene indoors. Once inside he turned to me, snatched the hat off my head and hit me hard across the mouth with the back of his hand, bursting my lips and sending me flying into the living-room doorpost. I staggered and slumped on the settee, the taste of blood filling my mouth. 'And don't let me see you wearing that fucking hat again,' shouted my father. I cried inside. I waited until he was preoccupied with Carlene and the baby and skulked out of the house to play.

The gas meter took shilling pieces but few real shillings ever ended up paying for gas. Most mornings my father crouched at the open back door and rubbed the edge of a halfpenny furiously on the stone step, filing it down so it would fit in the shilling slot of the meter. The violent rasping sound he created was familiar to people who passed by the house on their way to work or to school. Once I came in late in the afternoon and found my father and my uncle Frank stretched out across the kitchen floor with their heads underneath the sink attacking the gas meter with forks and a hammer.

'Harder, Ged,' said my uncle Frank.

'Fuck it, Ged, I'm doing my best,' said my father.

They were both drunk and looking for more money for beer. Finally the padlock snapped open and my father pulled out the little money drawer, only to find that it was full of filed-down halfpennies. He went mad. 'For fuck's sake!' he yelled, throwing the box across the kitchen, scattering misshapen halfpennies everywhere. I did a rapid about-turn and joined Carlene, the boys and the baby in the rabbit hutch.

I hated it when my father hit Carlene. Unlike Aunt Stella she never tried to hit him back. Seeing her being battered was frightening and heart-breaking. When he was away working I spent more and more time out of the house – sometimes I'd stay out for two or three nights in a row, sleeping on the concrete ledge above the back door, or under a pile of old blankets in a redundant air-raid shelter on waste ground close to Micky's house.

Sometimes Micky and I caught the train to Leeds and back, hiding from the ticket collector in the toilets. We never got off the train, just travelled and looked out of the windows and then late at night we headed back to the air-raid shelter which had become our headquarters. During one of my father's absences I'd already been out for a couple of nights when Micky and I went exploring around the back of a nearby television factory shortly after all the workers had left. We were rootling through the bins when we noticed that one of the windows was broken. The glass had been replaced with a makeshift piece of board. Micky kicked out the board and climbed in. I clambered after him.

Inside the factory there is a strong smell of all things electrical. Dozens of televisions in varying stages of completion line the rows of workbenches. Micky and I run around marvelling at all the interesting things and then I spot a cigarette machine on a wall. 'Micky . . . look!' I call in a loud whisper. Using a big screwdriver from a bench I lever off the front of the machine. Micky finds a bag and we fill it with all the packets of cigarettes. In the money box there's a fortune in two-shilling pieces and half-crowns. With the money stuffed in our trouser pockets we make our getaway back through the broken window. In the air-raid shelter we stash the cigarettes under an old carpet and share out the money before heading off to Bradford where we know a fairground has been set up in Lister Park.

At the fair we buy candyfloss and toffee apples and have multiple goes on all the rides, paying for go after go on the dodgems. We laugh and run and spend the money as fast as we can. It's one of the most magical nights of my life. By the end of it we're skint and have to walk back to Shipley. By the time we make the town centre it's the early hours of the morning. Then we get a shock. Just as we are about to turn the corner on to Briggate and head towards Leeds Road my father and Carlene appear from the other direction.

'Erwin!' shouts my father.

Micky and I jump in fright and then he scarpers. Expecting a beating, I back away from my father, but fear stops me running. I've been away from the house for three whole days.

He grabs hold of me and instead of hitting me he hugs me close to him. 'Thank fuck you're OK,' he says. 'We've been looking for you everywhere.'

The night they found us my father and Carlene were really kind to me. My father had seemed genuinely worried. Even though it was gone two o'clock in the morning when he got me home he made me a big plate of eggs, beans and chips and promised to take me to the swimming baths the following weekend. But before he had the chance the police found Micky and me in the air-raid shelter sorting out the stolen cigarettes and getting ready to try and sell them around the houses.

Locked in the police car I began to cry with terror at what my father was going to do to me. 'Please don't tell my dad,' I begged the two policemen in the front. 'He'll kill me.'

The driver looked at me in his rear-view mirror. 'You deserve to be killed,' he said, and I cried even more. I didn't stop crying until we arrived at Shipley Police Station.

The car drove into the compound at the back of the station and I was marched in through a heavy blue-steel door. Inside my fear increased when I recognised the corridor with the cells either side from the night my father brought my sister and me after he'd left

Aunt Stella. A policeman opened a cell door and motioned for me to go in. This time the door was slammed shut behind me making me jump and shiver. I sat on the wooden bed and thought about the night I slept here with my father and my sister and wished they were here now.

13

It was a couple of months after I had been charged with breaking and entering the television factory that I appeared in front of Bingley Magistrates' Court, just a few weeks after my eleventh birthday. My father had been back a few times since it happened but had never mentioned my crime. Carlene never told him I had to go to court and neither did I. He was away again when the day for my court attendance arrived. Carlene came with me and sat at the back as various officials spoke to the three magistrates about my behaviour. Carlene seemed almost as frightened as me.

Finally the magistrate in charge asked me if I had anything to say for myself.

'I'm very sorry, sir,' I said. In truth I was only sorry I had been caught and had the secret, darker part of me exposed. The night at the fair had been wonderful.

'You will be on a probation order for three years,' said the magistrate, 'and if we see you here again you will be in very serious trouble.'

Being on probation meant I had to visit a man called Mr Jackson every Wednesday night at an office in the town near to Norman's Café where my aunt Sheila used to work. I liked Mr Jackson. I bounded up the wooden stairs to his office on the top floor and then knocked and waited while I got my breath back.

'Come in!' he shouted. He always seemed pleased to see me. 'Hello, Erwin. How is everything?' He asked me about school and about how things were at home. I always told him everything was fine. 'Don't forget, let me know if you have any problems.' I smiled and made things up in reply to his questions so he would be pleased about how I was doing. 'Well done.' He smiled approvingly. 'See you next week.' After a while I just stopped going.

The field at the back of Carlene's house was a great playing area. Digging with a stick one afternoon I came across an odd-shaped stone. I dug deeper until the stone was unearthed. There on one side of it was the image of a face. It looked like some kind of carved head. I picked it up and loaded it on to my home-made go-cart before deciding to take it to Cartwright Hall Museum in Bradford's Lister Park, where the fair that had given me and Micky so much pleasure had been. It was a trek, perhaps four miles or more. When I presented my find to the receptionist, she called more people to come and look. Finally a tall man in a suit and wearing silver-rimmed spectacles told me that he would like to accept my stone head and put it on public display. I was thrilled, though a little disappointed that no money was offered for what I had considered might be precious treasure.

I waited for more than a week before hiking back to the museum to see if they really had put my find on display. Before I could present myself to the receptionist again she smiled and stopped me. 'Hello,' she said, getting up from behind her desk. 'We were expecting you. Come with me.'

I followed her through corridors lined with paintings and big rooms full of sculptures and finally she stopped in front of a glass cabinet. 'There you are,' she said. I stood transfixed. On the middle shelf, sandwiched between a copper bowl and what looked like a sheath for a large knife, was my stone head. Beside it a small plaque explained where the head had been found and there, in bold capital letters, was my name.

I skipped and jumped as I made my way back through Lister Park, thrilled at the idea of lots of people looking at the stone head and seeing my name. Swans and ducks on the boating lake were being fed by visitors. Rowing boats were out on the water. The sun was shining and there were happy smiling people everywhere. I felt like one of them. I couldn't get the plaque with my name on it out of my mind. I imagined visitors discussing the head and saying my name out loud and skipped even higher.

Then I heard someone call me. 'Erwin!' I was miles from Shipley. Who would know me here? 'Erwin!' I stopped and turned round and saw it was Aunt Stella's son Danny. He waved at me.

I shouted, 'Hey,' and waved back.

Danny explained that he, his little brother and his mother now lived in a house just behind Lister Park. 'Do you want to come and see it?' he said.

I felt really glad to see Danny again. For all the unhappy memories I had of living with his mother, she had looked after me when there was no one else. When I thought about it, living with them had been calmer than living with Carlene. Thoughts about the broom handle were long forgotten. I must have deserved it anyway. As Danny and I made our way to his house I told him all about my stone head in the museum. I couldn't wait to tell Aunt Stella about it.

Their house was on a long street that ran almost parallel to Lister Park, in an area called Heaton. It was a big house. The street was a bit run-down and there were lots of dark-skinned children playing out. Some of the boys and girls wore brightly coloured silky trousers and tops – it looked like they were wearing pyjamas. 'They're Pakis,' explained Danny.

Aunt Stella was cooking their evening meal when we arrived. She seemed pleased to see me and invited me to stay to eat. It was good to be with them again. It felt almost like I had come back home. As we ate our eggs and chips I told Aunt Stella about my stone head and that my name was next to it in the museum. 'Better to have your name in a museum than in a prison,' she said.

Suddenly I thought about my crime and my appearance at the Magistrates' Court. Now I was a criminal I wondered if I would ever have to go to prison. I remembered my father had been in prison. 'Is prison a bad place?' I asked.

'Yes,' she said, 'it's for bad people.'

I knew my father had behaved badly to me and to Aunt Stella and Carlene – and he may or may not have hit the man called Larry with a glass – but I didn't believe he was really a bad person. I never forgot how much he once loved my mother and my sister and me. Before my mother was killed I never saw my father behaving badly. I wondered if now that I was a criminal it meant I was a bad person.

My father's absences from Carlene's house had been getting longer and longer. When he did turn up and park his big lorry outside, he only stayed a few days at a time – then he was gone for another few weeks. I liked Carlene but recently I'd been feeling lonely and a bit lost so before leaving Aunt Stella's place I asked if I could come back to live with her and Danny. 'Yes,' she said, 'of course you can.'

I never told Carlene I was leaving. I just stacked my few things on to my wooden go-cart and headed off for Heaton. Aunt Stella must have told my father that I was living with her again as he turned up in his lorry one day and asked me how I was doing. Me and Danny were happy playing again and Aunt Stella had got me into Heaton Junior High School where I had made friends and started learning things. People at the school seemed to like me and my father was pleased. He visited a few times over the months. I heard talk that he was seeing another woman 'down south', and wondered if he might take me and my sister there. Life with Aunt Stella this time around was better, but there were still arguments in the house when other adults visited.

One night there was shouting downstairs and me and Danny went to investigate. We crouched on the stairs and listened to the voices in the living room. We could hear Aunt Stella's sister Megan. 'You don't tell me what to fucking do!' she yelled. There was a loud thud and a scream and then Megan rushed out of the living room into the hallway. She was missing her skirt and we could see her legs all the way up to her knickers.

Her husband came out of the room to chase after her as she headed for the front door. Her skirt was in his hand. 'You're not fucking going!' he shouted. He caught her as she opened the front door and wrestled her back inside.

'He's fucking dead anyway,' she shouted.

Danny and I ran upstairs and crouched on the landing out of sight. We heard Aunt Stella talking, telling them to calm down. We continued listening as they all went back into the living room. There had been a fight and a man called Brian had been kicked to death in a pub in Bradford. Megan and her husband hadn't been involved, but it sounded terrible.

Aunt Stella had a friend called Norman who occasionally brought fish and chips for our supper. Whenever my father was due to visit Aunt Stella told Norman to stay away. My father turned up one day and said he was taking me and Danny on holiday. He took us in his lorry all the way to a bungalow in the countryside just outside Weston-super-Mare. This was Aunt Rena and Uncle Nelson's house where they lived with their five children. I found out then that this was where my sister was living too. It was here, my father told me, that I had been born, 'Just over the back of those fields, in Clevedon.'

Danny and I had a great time playing with my younger cousins and my sister, going for long walks in the fields, paddling in the brook behind the bungalow and exploring Uncle Nelson's scrap-yard. We stayed with them for two hot and sunny weeks. I loved being with my sister again. She was now five years old and her pretty face was framed with lovely thick long dark hair. She looked just like our mother. Aunt Rena worked in a bakery shop in Weston-super-Mare and brought back bags of cakes with her when she came home in the evenings. It was a magical time and I didn't want it to end. For a present before my father took us back to Heaton Aunt Rena bought me and Danny new shoes. His were brown lace-ups and mine were black slip-ons. I loved those shoes. When we got back to Aunt Stella's I polished them every day, sometimes three times a day, making sure they never ever lost their gleam.

I wasn't especially unhappy at Aunt Stella's house in Heaton, but I was missing something or somebody and I wasn't sure what or who. Needing familiar people and places, I woke up one morning and without telling anyone I headed back to Carlene's house in Shipley. All I took with me apart from what I was wearing were my black slip-on shoes. Carlene asked me if Aunt Stella knew I had come. 'Yes,' I lied.

As soon as I had moved back in with Carlene and her family I realised that what I had been missing was a sense of belonging. I didn't belong with Aunt Stella but I knew I didn't belong with Carlene either. At least at Carlene's I had a half-sister who was now a year old and prettier than ever. I loved her but I still missed my other little sister, even more now that I knew how much she looked like our mother.

Every now and then my father turned up at Carlene's and parked his lorry outside her front gate. He stayed for a few days at a time, drinking, playing his guitar and going out into town with Carlene. Then he'd leave. I fretted for a while when he'd gone but I was beginning to accept that we would never get back to living together again as a family.

After he left one morning I found a bottle of beer in a box under the sink. I opened it and sneaked off to the rabbit hutch to drink it and see what it was like. I took a big swig and waited. Then I took another: still nothing happened. I put the bottle to my lips a third time and gulped down more than half the contents. As I lay in the semi-darkness of the hutch a wonderful sense of peace came over me and I felt my face begin to glow. I finished off the bottle and drifted off to sleep.

Life at Carlene's continued in much the same way as it had before I'd left for Aunt Stella's. I rarely went to school and spent the days and occasional nights wandering, playing and searching for adventures, often with my friend Micky, but I also began playing with a group of older boys. Sometimes they stole sweets from Little's off-licence and regularly grabbed beer bottles from the yard at the back of the shop and then took them into the front where Mr Little handed over money as a refund on the empty bottles. Running with the older boys was exciting – we'd light a fire on the local recreation ground, the 'rec', and sit around it roasting potatoes. Sometimes they drank beer and often gave me a swig. Some of them smoked cigarettes and once somebody offered one to me. I took a drag on it which made me vomit. I never went near cigarettes ever again.

I went back to Carlene's late one afternoon and saw my father's lorry parked outside. I'd been away from the house for a couple of days and this was a great surprise. I hadn't seen him for weeks. I ran in excitedly only to find him asleep, drunk, lying along the length of the settee. 'Shhhhhh . . .' said Carlene. 'He's only just gone to sleep. Don't wake him up.'

It had been a cold week at the beginning of September and there was a roaring fire in the grate. I sat on the easy chair by the fire and looked at my father. He must have been hot. He still had on blue jeans and a jean jacket and tiny droplets of sweat had formed on his forehead. By the side of the settee was an empty beer bottle. Next to that was his pint mug half full of beer. I was happy to just sit quietly and be near him. Then he turned and grunted and opened one eye.

'Hello, Dad,' I said, smiling.

The deep frown lines on his forehead grew deeper and his eyes took on a hooded appearance. He reached for his pint mug and couldn't quite get his fingers around it. I smiled. I was about to offer to help him pick up the mug when he knocked it over and the beer spilled out and spread all over the lino. 'Fuck,' he said. Nervously I smiled again. Without warning he jumped up, grabbed me by my thick curly hair and screamed, 'Whit you laughing at?' At the same time he picked up the mug by the handle and smashed it on a little wooden pad on the end of the arm of the settee before making to push the jagged remains into my face. 'I'll fucking kill you!' he roared. I screwed my eyes shut in anticipation of severe pain, but barely a fraction of a second before it connected Carlene had grabbed hold of his arm. 'I'll fucking kill him!' he raged.

I gulped air fast and tried to shake my hair free from his grasp. Carlene managed to wrestle the remains of the mug from his hand, but then he back-handed her and she fell over. He began forcing my head towards the fire. I felt the heat from the flames getting more intense and gripped by terror I struggled like a wildcat. 'No,

Dad!' I shouted. Carlene jumped on his back and knocked him off balance. As he struggled to shake her off I broke free and ran.

I knew that I looked very much like my mother, especially when I smiled – and though this seemed often to please my father it also appeared to antagonise him, especially when he had been drinking. I knew I reminded him of her more than my sister because I had been a part of his and my mother's life for so long. I wondered sometimes if the fierceness of his anger towards me was because I had become a reminder of everything he had lost. As much as my undeveloped mind tried to understand what had happened to us from his point of view I decided I couldn't stay any longer. I'd had enough.

For the next few weeks I lived in the air-raid shelter. Initially I sneaked out and stole apples and rhubarb from people's gardens to eat. Then I broke into Mr Little's shop by throwing a brick through the glass panel at the bottom of the front door before climbing in. After filling my pockets with chocolate bars I picked up a couple of jars of boiled sweets and headed back to my den, almost making myself sick gorging on the stolen goodies.

Out on the rec I hooked up with the group of older boys I'd tagged on to earlier. Wanting to prove my worth and be accepted I willingly joined them when somebody suggested we break into Shipley Bowling Alley. Seven of us entered the bowling alley that night. We stole crisps and a crate of Babycham. I had already had a taste of how pleasurable and relaxing alcohol was and so didn't hesitate to drink several bottles when they were offered to me. Again I felt that lovely calm sense of peace. It didn't last. One of the boys in the gang blabbed to his parents who called the police. Another of the boys told the police that I was living in the air-raid shelter and they came and arrested me.

My father was now living in Weston-super-Mare permanently, I assumed with the woman I had heard rumours about, though nobody told me for sure. Carlene came to the court again; this time she had a man I didn't know with her. I thought he may have been her boyfriend but I didn't like to ask. I thought I was going to prison. The magistrate was annoyed with me. It was the same man who told me I'd be in serious trouble if I came to court again. He said I'd be going away somewhere, 'until you are eighteen years old'. Thinking I was going to jail I began sobbing and calling out for my father. In fact the magistrate had put me into care.

14

The children's home was a big black-stone mansion called Hill Top on the edge of Ilkley Moor and loomed over the town from the top of Wells Road. As the social worker's car pulled into the driveway and drove round to the front of the house I stopped crying. We passed a huge bay window with a crowd of boys' faces pressed up against the glass all staring in my direction. My heart thumped. Once I was signed in and had met Uncle Mike and Aunt Vera, the people who ran the place, I was told to 'go into the playroom and make some new friends'.

The boys at the home ranged in age from about six years old to fifteen. In the playroom a group gathered around me and asked me what I was 'in for'. I didn't understand what they meant at first. Then I realised they wanted to know what my crime was. I didn't like to say I had been caught stealing crisps and Babycham, so I said I was a robber.

'You fucking liar,' said the tallest boy. 'What's your name?'

'Erwin,' I said.

He pulled back his head and screwed up his face. 'Erwin? What kind of a fucking name is that?'

Another boy who looked a couple of years younger than the tall boy laughed out loud and shouted, 'Erwin, EARWIG! Erwin EARWIG!' He went on and on while my face burned.

The bigger boy stepped up close to me and said, 'On your knees, Earwig.'

I did as I was told and then he stepped back and swung his fist, punching me right in the middle of my stomach. As I rolled into a tight crouch the air whistled out of me in a great gasp. I hadn't been winded since my father beat me for stealing the sauce from his lorry and I'd forgotten how frightening it was. Unable to breathe I thought I was going to die. With a last strain I forced an intake of breath and slowly I began to recover. When I opened my eyes I could see through a teary haze that the boys were laughing at me. Later I found out that the boys who had ridiculed me were brothers. For the next year or so the younger boy had great fun goading and antagonising me, always threatening me with his brother if I even looked like I was going to retaliate.

It took me a while to find my feet in Hill Top. I felt so far away from anyone I knew. I didn't know where my father was or why he hadn't been around for so long. I wondered if I would ever see him again. I had no idea where my sister was although I knew that my half-sister was with Carlene. Now I was a proper criminal I wondered if anyone would ever want to see me again.

But life in the home was not all bad. The food was good. For breakfast we had 'cheese dreams', fried cheese sandwiches, or 'Marmite dreams' – and for tea they gave us toad in the hole, liver and onions, or egg, beans and chips. Every Friday we had fish and for pudding they gave us bananas and custard. The children ate together sitting at tables of four in the dining room. The staff, who we had to call 'Aunt' and 'Uncle', sat at a big table at one end of the room. After meals we each had chores to do, helping to clear the dishes or tidying up around the place.

Among the other children were some like me who had committed crimes, some who had been abused by their parents, some who were orphans and a couple who seemed to have mental problems. Generally we all got along. I made two best friends who like me had both been to court for burglary and when we talked about the future we never mentioned becoming train drivers or astronauts or doctors or lawyers. Instead we talked about being serious criminals, maybe even gangsters.

I liked the regularity of living at Hill Top. The best thing about it was we all had to go to school, and for many of us it was the first time we had attended school regularly for years. Though not a great student I did like school and despite my crippling shyness I made friends there too. Eventually the middle school I was at joined up with the local grammar school and became the first comprehensive in the town, but it was still called Ilkley Grammar School and most of the teachers were the original grammar-school teachers.

In the English class I was usually one of the first to put my hand up in spelling lessons and loved writing and comprehension. The English teacher always gave me good marks. It was the only class in which I shone, regularly achieving an A or an A plus on my report card. My favourite book was *My Family and Other Animals* by a man called Gerald Durrell. It was the story of his childhood on the island of Corfu. I loved that book almost as much as I had loved *The Lion, the Witch and the Wardrobe*. Just like all those years before at the junior school I always jumped at the chance to stand up and read for the rest of the class when the teacher asked for a volunteer. Otherwise I was an unusually quiet boy.

In the playground one morning a boy in the group I thought of as my friends had a loaf of bread under his arm and was tearing at it and eating bits at a time. I was kicking a lump of coal from a pile in a corner thinking about where my father might be when the boy shouted at me and told me to pick the coal up. I frowned at him and carried on kicking, then he threw a wad of his bread at me. 'Pick up that coal,' he ordered.

I felt anxious. I was missing my father and my sister and was feeling deeply sad. I thought the boy was going to hit me and I really wasn't in the mood to be hit by anyone. Ignoring him I gave the coal an almighty kick, which enraged the boy. He ran at me with a big scrunch of bread in his hand and pushed it in my face. Everything went dark and suddenly I was roaring at him. I barely recognised my own voice. Without thinking I jumped on him and began punching him and kicking him with all the force I could muster. 'I'll fucking kill you!' I shouted, repeating it over and over every time my knuckles or my shoe connected with his head and body.

Other children in the playground screamed, but I continued, becoming more and more out of control. A teacher appeared. 'Erwin!' she shouted. I carried on. The boy fell to his hands and knees, his half-eaten loaf of bread tumbled on to the tarmac beside him.

'I'll fucking kill you!' I raged. I had never outwardly expressed such anger or violence before. By the time the teacher pulled me off him I was breathless. I started to cry and then I ran. I ran from the playground and headed down the hill towards town. I kept running and crying and before I knew it I was on the main road out of Ilkley, heading towards Otley. I ran and walked for the rest of the day until I ended up back in Shipley.

What I didn't know was that my old maw was visiting Shipley that week. While I'd been away in the home my mother's sister, my aunt Bridie, had moved from Scotland to a house on the Foulfield Estate. Carlene was frightened when I turned up at her doorstep and didn't want me to stay in case she got into trouble with the police. She told me where my aunt Bridie's house was and said that Maw was staying with her and my uncle Jake. Bursting with excitement I sped off to find them. The house was at the top of the estate, the very roughest part where houses had windows missing and holes in front doors. When I arrived I banged on the door as loud as I could.

As soon as she saw me Aunt Bridie threw her arms around me and hugged me tight. 'Maw, look,' she called to the living room. 'It's wee Erwin!'

I cried with joy when I saw Maw and rushed to her, grabbing hold of her and sobbing into her arms. 'Oh, son,' she said, 'look at the size of you!' I hadn't seen her since a few weeks after the crash more than five years earlier. She looked very old and not at all well. She had a great blue and black bruise on the left side of her face. 'Don't worry, son,' she said when I stared. 'I just fell doon the stairs when I was tired.' I could smell alcohol on her breath. Around the room I saw empty beer and wine bottles and I realised that Maw, Aunt Bridie and Uncle Jake were all drunk.

The police picked me up in Shipley town centre two days later and after a couple of hours in the police station I was taken back to the home where I was made to stand outside the office door for the whole of the next day so everyone could see how bad I was. The hours stretched out, broken only by lunch in the dining room when I was forbidden to speak to anyone and everyone else was forbidden to speak to me. At the end of the day I thought I was in for some more admonishment when instead of being told to go to my room Uncle Mike summoned me into the office.

'Sit down,' he said. His tone had changed from angry to worryingly sympathetic. 'We've had a message from Carlene?' I nodded acknowledging I knew who Carlene was. 'It's about your grandmother. I'm sorry to have to tell you, Erwin, but she died yesterday.'

I didn't respond immediately. I didn't know how to. The maw I saw in Shipley earlier that week was not the same maw I'd been missing during all those in-between years. I still loved her, but when I saw her bruised and shaky I sensed that she had not been who I remembered for some time. I felt sad for her – and for me – but I surprised myself by not crying.

'And listen carefully,' he said. 'I know you love your dad, but you have to accept that all his talk of you and him and your sister being together again is never going to happen. I'm telling you this for your own good, Erwin.' I felt like I'd been slapped in the face. All thoughts of Maw disappeared as I burst into tears and ran out of his office.

My two pals from Hill Top, Mick and Kev, were popular in the school. Both even had girlfriends. Occasionally girls approached me and told me that their friends would like to 'go out' with me. As much as I was dying to say yes, my terror of not knowing what to say and making a complete fool of myself always made me say no. It had been drilled into me so often that I was 'thick' by Aunt Stella and my father I was convinced it was true.

Then I fell in love with a girl in my class called Angela. I don't know how it happened. One day I found myself in her presence and a tingling feeling I had never experienced before washed over me. My mouth went dry and my pulse raced. It wasn't just her loveliness, her flawless pale skin or her long fair hair that she kept tied in a neat ponytail. Her voice sounded like music and the way she walked left me breathless. I sat opposite her in class and whenever I could I stared into her eyes. Without flinching she stared right back. To me she was the prettiest girl in the school, maybe even the world. The fact that she looked back at me without complaining made me think she might like me too, but I just didn't dare talk to her.

After months of admiring her in silence I finally plucked up the courage to communicate with her. I didn't know exactly where she lived but I knew it was somewhere near the bottom of Wells Road, the long winding road that led up to Hill Top. Keeping a distance of about forty yards I walked home behind her and one of her friends one afternoon after school, all the while trying to think of something to say to her. I could feel panic rising as she drew closer to the point where she would be turning in the opposite direction to mine and I knew my moment would be lost.

Without a moment's thought I suddenly filled my lungs, opened my mouth and yelled at the top of my voice, '*Angela!*' I saw her flinch before she turned round. Her friend turned too and scowled at me. I saw Angela flick back her head as if to say, 'What?' So I shouted again, this time even louder. '*Will you go out with me?*'

She shook her head and smiled, before shouting back, '*Yes!*'

I couldn't believe it. Not knowing what to say next I ran off and almost got lost in side streets.

The next day her friend came over to me in the playground and said Angela would like to meet me at the Ilkley Lido, the big open-air swimming pool on the other side of town, the following Saturday. I couldn't wait. Saturday came and my whole body was tingling. I got into the lido and through the crowds of bathers saw her sitting on a towel on the grass in her swimsuit. She was with a couple of friends and her hair was hanging loose over her shoulders. The sun was shining on her and she looked glorious. I stood watching her for some minutes, making sure she couldn't see me, and then I turned and left. When it came down to it I was just too scared that if I spoke to her she would realise how stupid

I was. I couldn't bear the humiliation. On the walk back to Hill Top I cried with frustration.

Back in class I continued to stare at Angela and she stared at me, but thanks to my chronic shyness we never got close to having a conversation. Then Christmas came and Mick and Kev and I went carol singing to raise some cash. A posh house among a cluster at the bottom of Wells Road caught our eye. 'Whoever lives here must be rich,' said Mick. The three of us stood outside the glass-panelled front door and let rip with a rendition of 'We Three Kings'. After two verses we heard footsteps and through the glass saw the shape of somebody coming to open the door. As the shape drew closer recognition clicked. I'd stared at it for long enough at school and there was not the slightest doubt in my mind. It was Angela.

The moment she opened the door I turned my back. Mick held his hand out and took the money she offered. I was mortified. My face glowed hot. She closed the door and I breathed a big sigh. Outside her gate Mick asked me what was up.

'That was his bird,' said Kev.

'Fuck off,' I said, 'I haven't got a bird.'

Kev laughed and Mick then elbowed me in the ribs. 'Fucking hell,' he said, 'she's as fit as fuck!'

I was squirming. 'Fuck off,' I said again. She wasn't 'fit' – to me she was just lovely.

I avoided looking in her direction for most of the next day at school. But just as I was walking out of the school gates I heard her voice behind me. 'Not a very good singer, are you, Erwin?' and then a number of girls with her giggled, sniggered and squealed. My body tightened. I thought I was going to faint with shame. My first taste of love had died.

Ilkley Moor offered a great place of escape. Whilst I was at Hill Top I came to know the moor well. In the autumn kids from the home often got picked as beaters for the local shoot. Pay was half a crown and a feast of sausage rolls and hot soup. A favourite adventure was climbing the magnificent Cow and Calf Rocks – most of us had done the climb so many times with no ropes or any kind of safety gear we were all over them faster than the climbers who came with their helmets and their colourful rigs.

The old spa bath at White Wells Cottage was another source of fun and excitement. A little girl was said to have drowned in the spa bath and we often went looking for her ghost, scaring the hell out of each other in the process. On weekends we hiked all over the bracken following the ancient cup ring carvings on mysterious stones and looking for the tracks of the giant Rombald who, the story went, had been chased across the moor by his angry wife. Legend had it that the ghost of Dick Turpin could be seen on nights when there was a full moon galloping fast across the high ridge of the moor. I'd lost count of the nights I had spent at my bedroom window nervously looking out for him.

'If he ever sees you looking at him,' said Uncle Mike, 'he'll turn Black Bess and come for you!' All of us in the home knew the words to the ancient song 'On Ilkla Moor Baht 'at' and we all knew about the Brontë sisters who'd lived a few miles over the moor in Haworth. On dark rainy nights Hill Top could easily be a stand-in for Wuthering Heights.

Ilkley had a lot going for it as a place to grow up in a normal family. But though they looked after us as well as they could in Hill Top, none of us wanted to be there. Most of the kids ran away, or 'nicked off' as we called it at least once. I ran away often, sometimes staying on the run for a week or more. I was always looking for home. I slept in cars or outhouses, stole food from markets or sweet shops and walked and hitchhiked in no particular direction until I was picked up by the police and taken back.

Occasionally I ran away with other boys. Once me and Mick and Kev nicked off and hiked over the moor to Keighley where they were both from. I met Mick's mother and father and his big brother. They took me in and let me stay for a while. They seemed nice and I couldn't understand why Mick was in the home when he had such a close family. They were originally from Ireland and expressed approval when I told them I was from Scotland. 'We're all Celts together then,' said his father. I didn't know what a Celt was but I was happy if it meant I was like Mick and his family.

Another time a group of us nicked off and an older boy called Alfie who could drive stole a car, starting it up by crossing some wires under the dashboard. We piled into it and Alfie drove off. We stayed in the car until it ran out of petrol, ending up miles away in a place nobody knew, then we wandered through the night into the early hours until we came across a garage that was closed. Kev smashed a lower window with the heel of his shoe and we climbed in, ignoring the alarm bells that were ringing. We filled our pockets with whatever we could get our hands on but before we could make our getaway the garage was surrounded by a squad of police cars, blue lights flashing and sirens wailing.

Back at Hill Top we were made to stand outside the main office for days. 'You're all lucky you are not being sent up the road,' said Uncle Mike. 'Up the road', meant Moorland House, an 'approved school' a few hundred yards further up Wells Road where bad, criminal children were sent, we were told.

My pal Kev and I came closest to being sent up the road. When I was fourteen I got a paper round which I loved. I earned three shillings a week and started to save my money. I enjoyed seeing the nice houses where I delivered the papers, wondering about the people who lived there. I used to wish I could be one of them. Then I got another round on a Sunday.

One Saturday night Kev asked me if he could come and help me on the Sunday morning round. 'Sure,' I said.

But Kev had a plan. He was going to break in to a nearby guesthouse called Hollybrook. 'Are you game?' he said to me. I wanted to say no, I wasn't game, but I didn't want him to think I was chicken. Barely hesitating I agreed to join him.

We got up a little earlier than usual the next morning while the house was quiet and headed silently across the road and over the wall that surrounded the guesthouse. After a bit of sneaking

149

around in the grounds we found an unlocked ground-floor window and climbed in. Tiptoeing about we ended up in the kitchen where a huge Alsatian dog lay sleeping on a chair. A safe under the table still had the key in the lock. The dog stayed asleep as we opened the safe door. Inside on a shelf were neat piles of half-crowns which we shoved in our pockets quickly before scarpering.

Less than a week later we were caught when a shopkeeper telephoned the home to say two of their boys had been spending lots of half-crowns in his shop on sweets for a gang of their friends. This time the people in the home brought in the police and Kev and I were charged with burglary. A month later, head bowed, I stood in the dock at Otley Magistrates' Court.

The court solicitor tried to make excuses for me. 'Erwin has had a troubled life and is easily led, sir,' he told the magistrate. Poor Kev was getting all the blame.

I was given a 'conditional discharge' and told by Uncle Mike that I was on a final warning. 'Any more and you'll be up the road to Moorland House,' he said.

I loved my paper rounds and couldn't figure out why I had acted so stupidly and put myself so deeply in Uncle Mike and Aunt Vera's bad books. I hadn't needed or particularly wanted the money. The paper rounds had brought in more than enough. All I could think of was that it was simply because I was a criminal. A little while later my spirits were lifted by a wonderful surprise.

It was early morning and I was still half asleep when the housekeeper came into my bedroom and pulled back my blankets. She sounded agitated. 'Come on, hurry up and get up. Your father's outside.' She was a strange little woman with tight curly grey hair and large, dark-rimmed glasses. She wore a green overall and made no secret of her dislike of men. 'They sweat too much' appeared to be the main reason.

'It can't be,' I said groggily, lifting my head from the pillow. 'My dad's in Weston-super-Mare.'

I was sure she had made a mistake and that it was someone else's father she was talking about. Gripped by fear that she had got it wrong and that the rising joy in my chest would have to be buried again, I repeated, 'It can't be . . .'

But she was adamant. 'Come on,' she said, 'I've got the breakfasts to get on with. Get up and get down the stairs quick before he buggers off.'

My room was on the top floor and I shared it with four other boys roughly the same age as I was. They were still sleeping soundly as I wrapped my dressing gown around me and hurled myself down the stairs jumping two or three at a time. My heart raced faster and faster as I anticipated seeing my father for the first time in nearly three years. I'd only ever had one visit in the home and that was from Carlene, who brought me her favourite Elvis album, *Flaming Star*, as a present.

When I got to the bottom of the stairs I could hardly breathe I was so excited. I sprinted through the kitchen and pulled open the back door which led out on to the short driveway and sure enough there he was, standing by the gate with a cardboard box in his hand.

'Erwin son,' he called.

I couldn't hold back my tears any longer. 'Dad!' I yelled and ran to him.

He had come for me at last. Why else would he be there at that time in the morning, if not to take me home? Uncle Mike was so wrong. I charged into him and hugged him with all my strength, delirious with joy and blinded by floods of tears.

Then I heard the housekeeper's voice behind us. 'Right. You've got five minutes.'

I looked up at him disbelievingly. 'Aren't you taking me with you, Dad?'

He held my head close to him with his free hand. 'Here,' he said, pulling me away and handing me the cardboard box. 'I've got you some presents.'

I took the box and looked inside and saw a huge football rattle with its metal strike plate painted army green. Alongside it was a box containing a model aeroplane kit and a bag of boiled sweets. I couldn't remember getting a present from my father since we had lived at Thompson Street.

'Have you got to go, Dad?' I said.

'Aye, son,' he said. 'I've got to go to work. But don't worry, we'll all be together again soon.'

It was what he said in the letters he occasionally sent me, all the words spelt out in capital letters. Despite all that had happened I never stopped hoping that one day it might happen. I placed the cardboard box full of what had instantly become my most treasured possessions down on the ground.

'Please don't go yet, Dad,' I begged him and grabbed hold of him again around the waist.

'Son,' he said, 'I've got to go to work. I'll be back again soon. I promise.'

He gently prised me away and stepped back to the green van that he'd parked adjacent to the gate facing the hill. I sobbed as I watched him climb into the cab. He started the engine and turned the van round, shooting me a glance and a wave before gunning the engine and speeding off back down the hill. Stepping outside the gate I watched the van get smaller and smaller as it descended the long road. It had all happened so quickly. I stared hard after the van, willing it to turn round, wishing for my father to come back for me, until it disappeared around a bend in the distance and my longing was shattered by the shouted whisper of the housekeeper.

'Erwin! Erwin! Get back in here now!' Grasping the cardboard box tightly to my chest I skulked back up to the kitchen door, angry and hurt.

Several weeks after my father's visit one of the aunts told me I was wanted in the main office. I thought I was in trouble because of the constant racket I was making with the big foot-ball rattle. I'd already had a fight with a boy who said I was 'acting like a big kid with it'. I knocked on the office door and Uncle Mike called me in. He was sitting at his desk with Aunt Vera.

'Sit down, Erwin, we've got some news for you and it's not good news.'

My thoughts raced. I'd already had bad news when they told me Maw had died. I wondered who had died this time. I sat down and waited.

'It's your dad,' he said. He saw my eyes widen and blink rapidly with shock. 'He's all right at the moment,' he said. 'He's had an accident. He fell out of the cab of his lorry and is in a serious condition in hospital.' I burst into tears and sobbed. 'He's stable just now,' he continued, 'but he could get worse. The doctors are going to keep us informed and we'll keep you informed.'

I managed to stop crying before I left the office. But that night in bed I cried myself to sleep. My father had made life difficult for me in many ways, but I was sure I would not be able to bear it if he died.

My father wrote to me from his sick bed in Frenchay Hospital in Bristol. He sounded well in his letters and that cheered me up. He signed off 'Love Dad' and put lots of kisses which I counted to make sure there were at least ten. I wrote back to him, telling him I was doing well at school and keeping out of trouble – both of which were lies, but I didn't want him to be worrying about me.

Then I overheard a conversation between two of the home's aunts. 'You would never believe it, would you?' said one. 'A lesbian!' She sounded shocked.

I didn't know what a lesbian was and was about to walk on when I heard her mention my name. I stopped abruptly and listened.

She was talking about my father. 'She stabbed him, just missing his heart,' she said. 'The knife went right through him.'

My mind swam. He hadn't 'fallen out of his cab' after all. I listened intently. From what I could gather my father had been caught in bed with the girlfriend of the lesbian, who had grabbed a kitchen knife and stabbed him in the chest. I felt sick. I stumbled away trying to squeeze the image of what had really happened to my father out of my head. I walked outside and ambled around in the grounds kicking stones and spitting, never sharing what I had overheard with anyone.

In the end I achieved very little at school. My reports reflected a generally morose attitude. I continued to do well in English, but when I took the report cards back to the home the staff were more concerned about the negative remarks by other teachers. 'Erwin has a temper he must learn to control.' 'Erwin is a sullen child and needs to communicate more.' 'Erwin appears to have a chip on both shoulders.' Nobody at the home mentioned the fact that I was good at English. It was a subject that I came to think of as my 'secret good thing'. In time it faded into insignificance.

I was just a few weeks away from my fifteenth birthday when I ran away from the home for the last time. I was on the run for almost two months. I hitched lifts and jumped trains and somehow made my way to Scotland. I found my way to the home of my aunt Janet in Alyth, Perthshire. Pleased to see me she took me in and I worked on nearby farms alongside the casual labourers. Sometimes I went out into the hills poaching game or fish with my uncle David. I loved being with them, but one day I decided to leave. I was getting old enough to know that I was never going to find what I was searching for. I needed money so I broke into their gas meter while the house was empty and stole enough money for my bus fare to Perth where I stayed with another aunt and uncle until finally I accepted that I did not belong in Scotland. I telephoned the home from a public phone box and said I wanted to go back. 'Stay where you are,' I was told. Within an hour a police car had picked me up and taken me to a local children's home where I waited until a social worker was available to escort me back to Ilkley on the train.

At fifteen I could legally leave school. The summer of 1972 marked the end of my schooling and my pals Mick and Kev had left the home and gone back to Keighley. The time for me to leave Hill Top came in the autumn when I was one of the oldest kids in residence. It was no great wrench.

Aunt Vera told me that my father was living with another woman and her children and that they wanted me to go and live with them in Weston-super-Mare. 'As part of the family. The choice is yours,' she said. She didn't seem too happy about it.

My father did want me and we were all going to be together again after all. I didn't need to think twice. Weston-super-Mare was such a glamorous and exciting-sounding place.

'Yes please,' I said.

October came and the wind was blasting off the moor. I spent the first weekend saying my goodbyes and packing my bits and pieces of personal belongings, including three lots of still-wrapped Christmas presents that I had bought my father with my pocket money but never sent. They gave me some new clothes from the store on the top floor and two new pairs of shoes. Everything squeezed into a small plastic holdall. On the Monday morning I was issued with a travel warrant and had my journey explained to me. 'Everything clear?' asked Uncle Mike. I nodded. He took me to Ilkley train station in his shiny red Volkswagen car and waited with me on the platform until the Leeds train arrived.

'Don't forget,' he said, 'Leeds, then Bristol, then Weston-super-Mare. Your dad will be waiting for you at Weston.' I thanked him and he shook my hand. 'Take care,' he said, 'and good luck.'

I climbed on board the train and said goodbye to my childhood.

15

I should have guessed things were not going to go well when I stepped off the train at Weston-super-Mare Station and there was no sign of my father. I was only fifteen but whatever happened there was no way I was going back to the home if he didn't show. I wandered up and down the platform for a while, looking at faded posters advertising long-finished summer entertainments on the pier and browsing magazines on a small rack outside the platform kiosk before sitting down on a bench to wait. It was a long wait. I went to the kiosk and bought chocolate and crisps and a fizzy drink. Trains and passengers came and went. A couple of times one of the station staff approached me and asked me if I was all right. I said I was fine, thanks, 'just waiting for my dad'.

When he did finally turn up all my anxieties disappeared. It didn't matter that he was more than three hours late. 'Dad!' I shouted. I snatched my little holdall from the floor and ran to him.

'Right, pal,' he said, ruffling my hair and pulling me close to him. 'Let's go hame.'

It didn't matter either that he was reeking of booze.

My father's situation was pretty much the same as it had been when he was with Carlene in Shipley. This time he was living with a woman called Shirley and her kids on the same kind of run-down council estate as Foulfield. This one was called Bournville. On our block windows in houses where people were still living were broken and boarded. Old cars lay abandoned as playthings for wild kids. Late at night, especially at weekends, arguments in the streets turned into screaming matches and fights sometimes involving makeshift weapons.

My father's drunkenness and violence towards Shirley were the same as with Carlene. He punched and kicked her and dragged her around by her hair. Now I was old enough to see even more clearly just how wrong his behaviour was. Not that I could do anything about it. I had my own room at Shirley's which became my retreat from the chaos in the house whenever my father came home drunk.

I got a job as a trainee welder with a small engineering factory near the town centre and gave Shirley £3 from my £5 weekly wage. Being the youngest in the workplace I had to go to the shop each morning and afternoon for the cakes and sandwiches. It was the only time I really spoke to anyone. Because of how quiet I was the older workers constantly made fun of me, sending me for 'sky hooks', 'striped paint', and tins of 'elbow grease'. My gullibility compounded my belief that I was stupid.

One evening when I arrived home and opened the front door the noise coming from the living room sounded like there was a party going on. I stuck my head in and through a faint haze of tobacco smoke I could see there was a crowd of maybe a dozen people. Some were sitting on chairs and the sofa and couple of women were sitting on the floor by the fireplace. All had cups or glasses or beer cans in their hands. My father was sitting on a low stool in the corner with his guitar across his knee, a half-full plastic gallon container on the floor in front of him which looked to me like the cheap scrumpy cider I knew he often drank. In his hand was a mug from which he was taking a large swig. Shirley was snuggled up next to him. They all appeared to have been drinking for some time. Somebody laughed.

A long-haired bearded man shouted, 'Come on, Jock, give us another song, man.'

One of the women by the fireplace noticed me and smiled. 'Come in, love, come on.' Turning to my father she said, 'Is this your boy, Jock? He's a good-looking kid.' I blushed.

The man with the beard called, 'Come in, son, come in and have a drink with us.' He too turned to my father. 'Jock, he can join us, can't he?' He had a can in his hand and was offering it in my direction.

The women by the fireplace cheered approvingly. Feeling increasingly uncomfortable I was about to step back and close the door when my father strummed his guitar loudly. 'Not at all,' he said – and laughed out loud. He laughed again and then called me in. 'Erwin. C'm'ere, son.' I walked over to him nervously and stood in front of him. His drunken face was smiling broadly as he grabbed hold of my arm. 'This is my boy,' he said. 'He doesny drink, he doesny smoke and he doesny go with women . . .'

I couldn't believe what he was saying. Everyone laughed. A surge of explosive anger ran through me. I stepped away from him and then ran out of the door slamming it behind me. As I bounded up the stairs to my room I could still hear them laughing. I banged my door shut and threw myself on my bed, curling up in a ball and crying tears of humiliation.

I already felt I was a bit odd. I didn't smoke, that was true. I couldn't stand the smell of cigarettes and even the whiff of struck matches made me feel sick. I wasn't sure if I did drink. The odd times I'd tasted alcohol when I was younger I'd enjoyed the peaceful feeling it gave me and the momentary but unforgettable sensation of relief it provided from my constant state of anxiety. But it hadn't left me with any particular desire to drink more. As far as 'going with women' was concerned – I would have if I'd had the confidence and the opportunity.

There were a couple of sisters around the same age as me next door to Shirley's and they often giggled when they saw me coming in from work. One of them had caught my eye and if I'd had the nerve I'd have asked her out. Only the fear of having to go through again what I went through at school with Angela stopped me. I thought my father was a real bastard for doing that to me and I hated him more for it – but inexplicably, no matter how he behaved towards me, however bad he made me feel about myself, my love for him never diminished. It simply existed alongside my loathing for him.

What puzzled me about my father was why he was so popular – he always seemed to have friends. In spite of his violence and drunkenness everybody appeared to love 'Big Erwin'. After he'd shown me up in front of his friends I decided the answer was to try and be more like him. I waited until he was away driving for a few days and then went out one night with a plan. I caught a bus and rode it to the far side of town where I knew from my earlier wanderings there was a pub called the Hansom Cab. I wore my father's sheepskin coat over a couple of jumpers to bulk myself out. Now sixteen, I was big for my age but probably not big enough to convince a barman that I was old enough to buy drink.

The pub was deserted when I walked in. The barman was polishing a glass. The extra clothing and my nervousness were making me sweat. I wasn't sure what to ask for.

'Hi,' he said. 'What can I get you?'

'A pint of bitter, please,' I said. I knew that was what my father drank in pubs.

I drank the beer swiftly, relishing the increased sense of warmth and satisfaction it brought me with every swallow. I was surprised at how speedily it quelled my fears and made me feel secure, effortlessly lifting the weight of being me off my shoulders. I ordered another and before I knew it the barman and I were chatting away like old chums.

He asked me my name and offered me his hand.

'Eddie,' I said, shaking his hand confidently. 'I'm new in town, been living up north.' Eddie? That was never planned. It just came out of my mouth.

From then on any spare cash I had went on going out into Weston and drinking in pubs. I always drank the first two or three pints fast. Soon I'd be breezing from pub to pub. A pint here, a pint there – never staying long enough to get into conversation with anyone – until one night in a town centre pub called the Cardiff Arms. I was standing alone at the bar, occasionally glancing over enviously at a mixed group of young people about my age who were chatting and laughing by the jukebox. I finished my pint and was about to order another when I heard a girl's voice behind me.

'Hi there,' she said. It was a pretty voice, belonging to a very pretty blonde girl. 'You look sad,' she said. 'Would you like to join us?'

Minutes later I was by the jukebox with her and her friends swaying, laughing and singing along with them as Rod Stewart belted out 'Lost Paraguayos'.

'Eddie,' one of the boys said, 'you're one of us now!'

Pretending to be someone else wasn't the only thing that drinking beer allowed me to do. It also let loose a whole load of emotions that had been bubbling inside me for a long time. As I was standing at the bar in a place called the Bier Keller one night with several of my new friends and my first girl-friend, Anne, a curly-haired young man a few years older than us and reputed in the town to be 'hard' came alongside us and ordered a drink. I'd drunk several pints already and my mood had moved from timid, to pleasantly sociable, to an unfamiliar sense of recklessness. I could feel an urge building to unleash some energy, some anger.

I'd only known Anne for a couple of weeks. She was quiet and shy and had sent a friend over to me one night in the Cardiff Arms to ask if I would 'go out' with her. I'd had enough drink in me to say yes, but then I had been terrified of her finding out I was a pretender. This was our first night out together as a couple.

As the booze took away all my anxieties I felt my temper rising as I purposely stepped back and nudged into the curly-haired hard man.

'Oi! Fucking idiot!' he said.

It was all the impetus I needed. I banged my pint glass on the bar and without saying a word I drew my right arm across my left shoulder and swung it hard at him hitting him full in the face with the back of my hand. An explosion of violence erupted between us. Anne became hysterical. Other girls screamed and glass crashed and smashed. I was punching and kicking and so was he. I took a hard blow on the top of my head from his clenched knuckles which stunned me momentarily giving him the chance to beat me to the floor. Once down it was all I could do to cover my head as he kicked me over and over until he was pulled off me by bouncers and hustled away.

Anne had fled, but a couple of the people I'd been standing with helped me to my feet and took me to the toilets. In the mirror I saw my face was blotched red and swelling fast and my lips were bleeding. I began to sob and repeated over and over, 'Tell . . . him . . . I'm . . . sorry . . .' There was no rational reason behind my actions. In the morning I woke up with two black eyes, aching ribs and the taste of blood in my mouth.

Fighting in pubs at weekends became a bit of a habit and I quickly earned a reputation as a troublemaker. I never set out to be violent or angry. But I was always too embarrassed to just go out and 'meet friends' – first I would drink two or three pints in quiet, out-of-the-way pubs to get rid of my anxieties before heading into the centre of town. By then the alcohol had taken me past the rational stage. Beer ignited a peculiar fire in my belly that gave me a feeling of peace yet at the same time made me liable to unleash an uncontrollable rage. Getting barred from pubs around Weston and being talked about for causing aggro, even when I got a battering, gave me an identity among my new friends, but I knew it wasn't an identity I wanted. I just didn't know how to be any other way. At work I was still as quiet as a mouse. During the week I hid in my room. But on Friday nights I came to life with a bang. Several times the police were called to incidents I had instigated or been caught up in. The fact that I was never arrested was down to pure luck. That would soon change.

A knock on the door one mid-week evening brought more humiliation. My father answered it. I heard a boy's voice and recognised it immediately. 'Is Eddie in?'

My father must have given him a puzzled look. 'Eddie?' he said. 'There's nobody here called Eddie.'

The boy was from the group I'd first met in the Cardiff Arms. His family owned a seafront hotel and whenever I was near him I got the sense that he was suspicious of me. I heard him give my father a description.

'You mean Erwin?' said my father, who then shouted, 'Erwin! There's somebody here at the door for you.' How I squirmed.

The next time I went into town I was taunted about my 'real name'. Booze helped me to deal with that. I was aware that for some time my new associates thought I was 'a bit of a nutter'. I thought I was too.

I found out that we were moving house when I returned to work from the cake-shop run one afternoon and found my father staggering about in the entrance to the factory yard. He had a plastic gallon container of scrumpy cider in one hand and a tin of beer in the other.

'Dad!' I shouted. I thought he was looking for me.

'Erwin son,' he slurred. 'Geez a hand here.'

The window of the boss's office looked straight out on to the yard's front gate and I could see that somebody was watching us from behind the glass.

'Dad, what are you doing?'

He told me that he was trying to get into the flat that was in the building adjacent to our factory. He wanted me to climb over the wall that enclosed the flat's small courtyard and go and open the front door for him. Suddenly he swung the gallon container and let it fly over the wall. 'Hurry up, son, I'm dying for a pee,' he said.

I put the box of cakes on the ground and quickly scrambled up the wall and followed my father's cider over the top. I was amazed the container hadn't burst on the other side. I ran in the back door and through the corridor. I noticed a strong smell of infant piss in the air. I got to the front door, opened the latch and raced around to get my father. 'Dad, it's open,' I said. He stank of booze and tobacco smoke – he must have been at it all day.

'Good boy,' he said as I left him.

When I walked back into the factory the men berated me for being late with the cakes.

Then the boss arrived. 'Who was that?' he said.

'Some drunken bloke,' I said. 'He was locked out of his flat.'

The flat was rented by a woman called Jenny my father was seeing behind Shirley's back. Jenny lived there with her two young children. A couple of weeks after I'd let my father into her flat he told me that Jenny had been given a council house on our estate. 'Pack your bags,' he said, 'we're offski.'

I could never see that there was anything meaningful in his relationships and I couldn't figure out why the women my father lived with put up with his behaviour. I hadn't been at Jenny's long when I decided I'd had enough of my father's drunkenness and the frustration of my own growing misfit identity and decided to go back to Shipley for a while. One day with just a few pounds in my pocket I walked out of the door and instead of going to work took a bus out to the edge of town and alighted on the main Bristol road. I had slept rough before when I was younger and had no fear of doing it again. I made it to the outskirts of Bristol by late afternoon and walked the rest of the way to Avonmouth, following the signs for the M5 motorway. It was dark when I approached the slip road and turned and stuck out my thumb.

16

Shipley this time around was different. I stayed at my uncle Frank and aunt Miriam's place on Foulfield Road. Their six children were all still at school and I shared a bedroom with their two eldest boys. At the back of their house was a steep open field at the bottom of which was the little ginnel that ran alongside Carlene's house on Foulfield Avenue. Carlene still lived there but I rarely saw her. I got a job shifting stock around in a warehouse and my boozing continued. The weekend began on a Thursday and went on until Monday morning and for most of that time my aunt and uncle were drunk and violent. He cut her and bruised her at least once a month and she fought back with kicks and punches, but she always came off the worst.

I was making a name for myself in the town as a menace. It was never enough for me to just a have 'a couple of pints'. I drank until either I ended up fighting, or couldn't walk or speak properly.

In a pub one night somebody said to me, 'Erwin. I remember you when you were a kid. Where have you been?'

I gave him what I thought was a tough look and said, 'Been inside.'

Someone else who knew the truth chipped in, 'No you haven't – you've been in a children's home.'

I covered my embarrassment with more booze and aggression.

Two doors up from Aunt Miriam and Uncle Frank lived a family. There were a number of brothers and sisters in the house. The second youngest brother used to sit on the fence by his gate in the evening. 'Hi,' he said to me one day as I walked past his house. He was a tall thin boy with pale skin and a thick head of neatly combed straight dark hair.

'Hi,' I replied.

He said he remembered me from when I lived at Carlene's. 'Your old man was a lorry driver, always filing halfpennies for the gas meter,' he said.

I laughed. I'd forgotten all about the halfpennies. 'That's him,' I said.

We chatted for a while. He said his name was Dunwell and his father was dying of cancer. 'It's a bummer,' he said.

The idea of my father dying of anything terrified me and I felt for him. Dunwell and I became close after that. He worked in a warehouse in Bradford with his older brothers. We began hanging out together after work, either sitting on the fence by his gate, or going to the pubs around Shipley at the weekends.

Then I met a girl – Vicky. She worked in the same warehouse as me but I never spoke to her until I met her in a pub one weekend. We sort of 'went out' together for a while; until she twigged I was not quite what she expected. After she finished with me I went to her house drunk. A fight with her brother-in-law ensued as he tried to eject me. I pulled an open razor out of my back pocket and waved it in his face as he bundled me out of his front door, the glass panel of which was shattered in the process. The next morning I woke up in Shipley Police Station. The cell walls were all white brick tiles, the toilet pan fixed to the back wall had no lid and the bed was a block of hard wood with a thin, plastic-covered mattress – just as I remembered from my childhood visits. At Bingley Magistrates' Court I was fined £20 for having an offensive weapon and causing criminal damage. As soon as they let me out I went back on the booze.

That night I arrived home, walked into the living room and found my uncle with his hands around my aunt's throat. He had her against a wall. Blood trickled through her teeth and down her chin and one of her eyes was bruised and swollen. Her throttled breaths sounded like a death rattle. I raced to the kitchen, grabbed a knife from the cutlery drawer, dashed back and brandished it at my uncle.

'Get off her now!' I yelled. I loved them both, but I couldn't stand this.

'Fuck off!' he shouted back at me. He was roaring drunk. 'I'm your uncle,' he said. 'You're not going to stab me.'

I moved closer. Her eyes were glazing over. I jabbed the knife at him. 'Fucking let her go!' I shouted.

He pulled his hands away and she dropped like a stone. 'Come on then,' he said and edged towards me.

I waved the knife, slowly backing away out of the living room and into the downstairs toilet. He barged into the door but I managed to lock it, leaving him hammering and kicking on it as I climbed out of the window and with no idea of where I was going scurried away into the night.

For nearly a month I lived like a young hobo, hitching lifts, walking, scavenging food from the backs of cafés, drinking water and washing myself in public toilets. I slept in allotment sheds under tarpaulins; I slept in bus shelters, in a graveyard and in motorway service-station truck stops. It was rough and lonely living, yet I found that when I was on the move, even in such dire circumstances, I was less anxious about life than when I was static.

Eventually I landed back in Weston and went to see if my father was still at Jenny's. He was, so I moved back in. I got a job as a trainee welder with a company that made trailers, but within weeks I was back on the road, hitching the familiar paths to Shipley. And so the pattern developed. Every few weeks or months I was on the move. In between I committed more crimes. Drunk and running from a taxi without paying: fined £5; smashing a shop window when I was drunk, criminal damage: fined £10.

Back in Weston again I was thinking about staying at Jenny's for a while when my father came home one afternoon with a friend. They were both drunk.

'I've got you a surprise,' he said. 'It's outside.'

When I went to look, there by the gate was a brand-new bicycle. Immediately I took it out for a spin, cycling all the way into town and along the high street. As I pedalled past the bicycle shop I heard somebody shout, 'Stop thief!' I turned my head and saw the man who was shouting pointing at me and waving his fist. I pedalled faster. It turned out my father and his friend had taken the bike from outside the man's shop.

When the police caught up with me and took me into custody I pleaded innocence. 'I bought it from a man in a pub,' I said. At Weston-super-Mare Magistrates' Court three weeks later my father appeared as a character witness and backed up my story. 'He was pleased as he thought he had got a bargain,' he told the bench. For handling stolen goods I was fined £20.

I came back to the house late one night soon afterwards totally pissed. My father had a Vauxhall Cresta parked outside. He'd left his keys on the mantelpiece above the fireplace. Deciding it was time for me to be heading out again I took the keys and minutes later fired up the big car's engine. It had a column gear stick which I almost wrenched out of its socket in my attempts to get the thing moving. It shot off and swerved across to the other side of the road crashing through a gate and landing in a garden. Revving hard I found reverse gear and pulled back, somehow parking it in almost the same spot where my father had left it.

I took his keys into the house and replaced them on the mantel-piece before sneaking back outside. The front of the car was bent and crushed. My drunken reasoning was that he would probably think he had caused the damage without realising it, or someone else had crashed into his car in the night and sped off. I staggered up the street planning to leave the estate when I looked through the driver's window of a transit van and saw the keys were in the ignition. I slid open the door and climbed in.

By then lights were going on in houses all around. I heard somebody shout seconds before I gunned the van's engine and raced forward, bumping the car parked in front. With my foot hard down the van sped along for a couple of hundred yards clipping other parked vehicles before mounting the kerb and ending up in the middle of a large grass-covered roundabout. The engine stalled, but before I could climb out the van was surrounded by police cars. The next time I saw my father he was looking at me through the hatch in a cell door in Weston-super-Mare Police Station. 'Erwin son,' he said. 'What's wrong with you?' Weston-super-Mare Magistrates' Court fined me and placed me on probation for a couple of years but I was back on the road heading north before my first appointment.

My drifting up and down the country continued. I spent some time in Scotland at my aunt Janet's house in Alyth going out into the fields picking fruit and vegetables to earn casual money. When I had enough to live on for a time I was off, spending weeks getting back to Shipley. At my uncle Frank and aunt Miriam's place no mention was made of the stand-off between me and Uncle Frank. Whenever I turned up, they took me back. 'You've got to screw your nut,' Aunt Miriam said more than once. I knew what she meant, I just didn't know how to do it.

I hung around with Dunwell, drinking and sometimes fighting. Having a friend gave me more confidence but it didn't stop me getting drunk. Sometimes I got drunk and went and sat at the top of Thompson Street. Number 84, the house where I had lived with my mother and father and baby sister all those years earlier, had long been demolished and the space left grassed over. Half-a-dozen other houses across the street from ours remained just as I remembered them. On the horizon I could still make out the house with the high gables that I used to think was in Scotland.

One day I bumped into Aunt Stella in the Cricketers pub. 'Hello, you,' she said. I was seventeen and hadn't seen her for ages. She bought me a drink and smiling said, 'Do you remember the broom handle?' I smiled back and nodded. Then she took the silver necklace and crucifix she was wearing from around her neck and put it around mine. 'Here you are, love,' she said. 'I'm so sorry.' The necklace was too small and she struggled to close the fastener.

I left her after finishing my drink and as soon as I was outside I yanked the necklace off and threw it in the road.

I bought a tin of blue spray paint and sprayed my name on town walls. 'Erwin was here.' I sprayed bridges, bus stops, street signs and billboards. I never thought any more about it until I went for a job as a labourer with the local council. The foreman invited me into the yard office. He was a kindly-faced man with a thick moustache. He kept an unlit pipe between his gritted teeth which made him look like he had a constant smile.

'You're a big lad,' he said. 'You don't mind hard graft?'

I nodded. 'Not at all,' I said, 'I love it.'

He passed me a pen. 'We're always looking for good workers. Write down your name and address on this form and I'll see if I can get you a start for Monday morning.'

I couldn't believe my luck. I was desperate for some regularity in my life. My aunt Miriam said a job with the council was a job for life. I filled in his form and handed it back to him.

He looked at it and then lifted his head and stared at the wall, repeating under his breath, 'Erwin . . . Erwin . . .' Then he took his pipe out of his mouth and looked sharply at me. 'It's you, is it? Erwin was 'ere, there and every fucking where? Blue paint? Ring a bell?'

The colour drained rapidly from my face. I had never come across any other Erwins before and there was definitely only one in Shipley. I was caught bang to rights. He went to grab me but I turned and sprinted. He gave chase, yelling after me, 'Come back, you fucker. You've cost us a fucking fortune! We're going to get the police!'

Before the police had time to raid the house I told my aunt Miriam and uncle Frank I was moving on, packed a small bag and hitchhiked south. This time when I made it to Weston I found my father was no longer there. 'He's gone to live in Dover,' Jenny said. It took me almost a week to hitchhike to Dover. All Jenny could tell me was that she thought he had a flat on the high street. 'It could be anywhere,' she said.

From just outside Weston I got a lift on the A370 all the way to the start of the M4 in Bristol. My final lift was in a lorry that took me from the outskirts of London right into Dover town centre. During the ride I told the driver I was going to see my father. The miles shifted by in a blur until from scrubland way up high the little port town finally came into view. The driver asked me where I was meeting my father. 'Where do you want me to drop you?' I said I wasn't sure.

The traffic was heavy as the lorry eased its way through the narrow one-way main street. We stopped at a zebra crossing and when I saw the man halfway across I yelped in sudden recognition. 'That's my dad!' I thanked the driver for the lift and jumped out of the cab.

'Dad!' I shouted.

He turned calmly and as if only hours had passed since our last meeting instead of months he shouted back, 'Hello, pal. Ready for a beer?'

I stayed with my father and slept on the floor of his little flat for a few months. I got a job in another warehouse and worked part-time as a washer-up in a restaurant. When I wasn't working I was drinking with my father. We drank carry-outs back at his flat and argued like hell, a couple of times almost coming to blows. One night a Polish man we had been drinking with came back to the flat to share the carry-out. My father started having a go at him, accusing him of hogging the vodka bottle. Suddenly my father picked up the bottle and hit the man over the head with it. As blood spurted from his split scalp I decided it was time to go.

I hitchhiked north and ended up back in Shipley at my uncle Frank and aunt Miriam's place and hooked up again with Dunwell. It was his younger sister's birthday soon, he said, and he'd promised to provide booze for a party. He asked me if I was up for 'a smash-and-grab'. I'd never done anything like that before but agreed to help, 'So long as I can have a drink first.'

He showed me a piece of string with a load of worn car keys hanging from it. 'This will get us moving,' he said. We drank a bottle of his mother's fortified wine in his back garden and then went looking for a car to steal.

Stealing cars and smash-and-grabs on off-licences, clothes shops and food shops led me and Dunwell to Bingley Magistrates' Court shortly before my eighteenth birthday. One of our raids had been on a foreign-food warehouse. Another had been on a chicken farm from which we stole a couple of thousand eggs. When the egg theft was reported on Radio 1's *Newsbeat* we thought we had made the big time. To get rid of the stolen goods Dunwell and I borrowed a couple of prams and went round the houses of elderly folk selling the goods at doors for pennies.

In March 1975 we both got six months' in a detention centre, the so-called 'short sharp shock'. His shock ended up shorter than mine after he appealed and had his sentence cut to three months. I didn't know how to appeal so just got on and did my time in Redstone Detention Centre near Wakefield. It did nothing to halt my destructive behaviour. If anything it made me worse. Threats and violence were the main controlling tools used by those in charge. I expected a hard time. I'd been told about 'DC' by other boys I'd met in various police-station cells and communal holding cages. Apparently spontaneous punches and kicks were routine in all of them, especially at Redstone.

I found out how true this was one day in the gym. A PE instructor taking about twenty-five of us for a gym session told us to line up in four rows. I ended up in the row he decided to head.

'Put your hands on the hips of the person in front of you,' he said, 'and then crouch down in the bunny-hop position.'

We did as we were told. I was immediately behind him. The moment I placed my hands on his hips he sprang to full height, turned and swung the flat of his clenched fist, hitting me full on the left side of my face, almost toppling me. The stinging pain sent a wave of rage coursing through me, rushing from my legs and chest, through my shoulders and into my taut and bulging arms. The breath I sucked in sent so much energy into my own clenched fists I thought they were going to explode. I could feel the veins in my neck pulsing with the blood rush.

The PEI then screamed at me, 'What are you doing? Are you fucking queer? Do you fancy me?'

In my peripheral vision I was aware of the other boys standing gaping but my eyes were pinned directly on the officer. I wanted to lash out at him, to beat him to a pulp. Tears of furious ignominy began to well in my eyes. 'No, sir,' I managed to squeeze out between gritted teeth.

He hit me again and yelled, 'Why? What's wrong with me?' His fists were drawn back and raised, daring me to move on him.

Through tightly squinting eyes I stared hard into his face. The stand-off lasted just a few seconds before he abandoned the exercise and ordered us to start running around the gym. My anger drove me to the front of the group. Running and stomping with pent-up fury and indignation, I dared anyone to try and pass me. Nobody did.

Later, during my final weeks at Redstone, the same PEI and one of his colleagues had themselves a great giggle by getting me to dress in a leotard, heavy leather weightlifting belt and work boots and then barging into the cubicles of new arrivals waving a rounders bat and issuing graphic threats about what was going to happen to them once 'me and my mates' got hold of them in the dorms. In a book I once read about a boys' reformatory in the US the writer described his institution as a 'gladiator school'. If I had been writing a book about Redstone I could have described it in the same way.

After I was released I went back to live with Uncle Frank and Aunt Miriam and took to hanging around with Dunwell again. I met Sally, his ex-girlfriend, at his sister's house one day and she and I hit it off. Sometimes she came out with me and Dunwell when we stole cars. I thought I loved her. She said she loved me. But it wasn't long before a boozing, fighting, burglary and car-stealing spree led me and Dunwell straight to Bradford Crown Court to be remanded in custody just a couple of months later. Sally visited me in Thorp Arch Remand Prison. 'I'll wait for you,' she said. She wrote me love letters that smelled of her perfume.

In January 1976 Dunwell and I were both convicted of five offences and had twenty-five other offences 'taken into consideration'. The judge sent us both down for 'borstal training'. After a few weeks first in Leeds Prison and then Strangeways Prison in Manchester we were allocated to different borstals. Dunwell went to an institution in the Midlands while I managed to persuade the allocating governor in Strangeways to send me to an open borstal rather than a closed one. 'I just want to get my head down and pay for my crimes,' I told him. They sent me to the open borstal at Wetherby in North Yorkshire.

I hadn't been there a week when me and two other boys climbed over the low perimeter fence one night and went on the run for eleven days. We stole cars, raided shops and eventually got split up after a police chase in Leeds. I got away and headed for the Yorkshire Moors in a stolen Ford. I made it to the moors but with a police helicopter following overhead I crashed the car into a drystone wall before limping off, bruised and bloodied, over the scrubland. Police cars, vans and jeeps came after me. I heard tracker dogs barking. My left leg was bleeding badly from a gash on my knee. An hour or so later I gave in to the pain and exhaustion and, illuminated by the headlights of half-a-dozen police vehicles and the helicopter's searchlight, I flopped on to a rock and held up my hands.

After giving me a good hiding in Leeds Bridewell Police Station the police drove me back to Wetherby. On the door of the police station cell I'd been kept in somebody had scratched: 'Life is a song that goes on for ever.' I thought it was a lovely phrase to contemplate and kept saying it over and over in my head as the prison officers at Wetherby gave me another beating in the punishment block before putting me on the van back to Strangeways for reallocation. On my arrival the governor who'd recommended Wetherby was none too pleased to see me.

'Do you take me for a cunt?' he said when I stood in front of him again.

'No, sir,' I said.

'Well you're not going to like it where I'm sending you now.'

A week later I was in the van on my way to Stoke Heath Borstal near Market Drayton – another gladiator school for the damaged and the wayward. In the gym I lifted weights and in the workshops I learned how to weld cell doors. Sally wrote to me saying she would still wait for me. She told me she would visit me, but on the day she said she was coming she never turned up. Then I had word that she had started sleeping with the local milkman. I sent an angry letter issuing threats to the man. But by the time they released me in October that year I'd forgotten all about her. The downside was that I was bigger, stronger and probably more dangerous than I had ever been.

During my last few weeks in the borstal my aunt Miriam and uncle Frank wrote to me and offered me a home again. Uncle Frank was working as a ganger with a tarmacking gang and said he'd get me a job. I started as a rake hand the Monday after I got out. Dunwell had been released before me and had got a job as a bus conductor. We still went around drinking in Shipley pubs together.

One night we were sitting in a pub called the Alma when Sally's milkman walked in with his elder brother, a burly, red-faced man with tight curly hair. He looked about thirty.

I hadn't even taken a sip of my beer when the brother walked straight over to our table and asked angrily, 'Which one's mine?' The milkman thought I was after him and had brought his brother to sort me out.

He wanted a fight and since Dunwell had never been a fighting man and I supposedly was, I said, 'You'd better have me.'

Followed by most of the lounge bar's clientele we walked out to the courtyard at the back of the building. Sober, I was uncomfortable and unsure of how to initiate such a scrap, so like an old-time pugilist I took a step back and squared up to the older man. He looked a little puzzled at first but after just a moment's hesitation he did the same to me. We circled each other like bare-knuckle boxers for a minute or two – and then he suddenly lunged at me. I was nineteen years old and fresh out of a rigorous closed penal institution. For the thirteen months I was inside I used the gym three or four times a week, weightlifting, circuit training, skipping and bag-punching, yet fear was still making my heart pound. As the milkman's brother made his move I stepped to one side and countered with a right hook that hit him bang in the middle of his chest. He gasped and wide-eyed with shock he swore loudly. I was surprised by my own coolness. I'd never had a sober fight before with none of my usual threatening and roaring at the top of my voice or my typically hysterical wild arm-swinging, kicking, kneeing, gouging, or head-butting.

He came at me again and in a split second I made the decision not to punch him in the face in case I seriously hurt him. Instead I dodged him and whacked him quickly several times again in the chest until he fell backwards and crumpled in a heap against a wall.

I stood over him and said, 'Enough?'

He looked up at me and said, 'Enough.'

I helped him up and when he had composed himself he went back into the bar and bought the four of us a drink. Violence was never more civilised.

Just a few weeks later I was back in the same pub. This time I was drunk and maudlin when a man the same age as me walked in and started giving me what I thought was the 'evil eye'. There was no gentlemanly conduct this time. I had a few more beers and then confronted the man.

'What you looking at, you prick,' I said.

'You, you prick,' he said.

I went berserk. He tried to grab my arms and immediately we went into a clinch. We rolled over the pool table and crashed on to the floor. Cursing, scratching and wrestling, we tumbled through into the lounge bar scattering drinkers, chairs, tables and glasses. Customers screamed and yelled. Eventually with neither of us getting the better of the other the landlord and some regulars intervened and dragged us both apart. Still struggling and swearing I was manhandled out to the front entrance. Before I got the final shove I managed to grab hold of the heavy door and slam it with as much force as my raging temper could muster. I wrenched it open and slammed it again and then opened it once more; taking hold of the top edge I pulled and twisted with all my weight and might. The door finally buckled and I slammed it again before staggering off down the street. Within half an hour I was picked up by the police, taken into custody and charged with causing criminal damage to the pub door.

The case was heard a month later in Bingley Magistrates' Court where my legally aided solicitor was a man called Desmond Joyce from Bradford who was well known for representing the worst of the local reprobates, thieves and hooligans. He was a flamboyant character.

While I sat shamefaced in the dock he launched into his mitigating defence speech. 'Sir,' he said to the chairman of the bench, 'this young man is as strong as an ox! The truth is he simply did not know his own strength. This was an accident!'

He didn't convince me and I was sure I was going back to borstal. Instead the magistrates gave me a fine. Along with the costs I was ordered to pay £161 in instalments and then released. The next day outside newsagents' shops all around the town billboards announced to the world: 'Strength Costs Man £161!' I should have been ashamed and embarrassed. I was when I was sober, but when I was drunk I preened.

By now I was spending all my spare time and money in pubs, clubs or illegal dives, usually in the company of Dunwell. I kept working at the tarmacking and loved it. All I really did was work and booze. The Falcon pub had been renamed the Feathers and one night I was in there pissed and on my own looking for trouble.

'Oi,' said a man standing at the bar when I nudged him out of the way.

'Fuck off,' I said.

He was about my size and a little older. He pushed me and I retaliated with a lumbering punch to his chest. He hit me back and I stumbled, grabbing hold of his jacket, taking him with me as I fell backwards on to the floor. I knew him vaguely, I knew his name was Dave and he worked in the building trade. We punched, kicked and battered each other for a good ten minutes before the landlord and one of the barmen pulled us apart.

'You're both fucking barred!' the landlord shouted as he pushed us out of the front door.

I felt bad for Dave as I knew I had started the fight. Now the angry moment had passed I felt pathetic. 'Sorry about that,' I said once we were outside on the pavement. I expected him to want to fight on, but instead he offered me his hand.

'You were out of order,' he said, 'but fuck it, let's go to the Cricks.'

I shook his hand and off we went to the Cricketers pub in the centre of town. Dave and I became good friends after that. He invited me to join a boxing club with him in Bradford. It was called the Farmyard and was where the then British heavy-weight champion Richard Dunn trained. Dave picked me up in his father's car from my uncle Frank and aunt Miriam's place once a week and drove us over to the club. After the training sessions we returned to Shipley and drank pints of orange squash. Dave was a civilised man, a self-employed builder, and someone I really wished I could have been like.

A drunken brawl with a man called Graham lasted over an hour and carried on from the centre of Shipley up a good stretch of Leeds Road. We wrestled, stamped and beat each other for more than half a mile, rolling in bushes, spilling into traffic and falling over pavements, until we were so exhausted it seemed easier for us both just to shake hands and call it a draw. Graham was a known hard man in the town and, unlike me, widely liked and respected. I'd been barred from most of the local pubs at least once, and even the town's nightclub, the Criterion, only gave me a job as a doorman to stop me from causing trouble in the place. My drunken antics got me sacked from there eventually.

17

Just before Christmas 1976 I met a girl and for the first time in my life fell seriously in love. Nadine was five months away from her sixteenth birthday and with her dark hair and big eyes she was the most beautiful girl I'd ever seen. I had no idea of the impact I was going to have on her life. I didn't know how to behave in a proper relationship. All I could do was guess. Being with Nadine made me feel like a king and a fool at the same time – and then there was booze.

Nadine's hobby was dancing and her family lived at the better end of the Foulfield council estate. I was still living with Aunt Miriam and Uncle Frank in Foulfield Road. Nadine's father, a skilled toolmaker in a local factory, was unhappy about her relationship with me. He called me 'the pub fighter'. He had brought up his family well and provided them with a comfortable, smartly furnished home. With the drink and six children to provide for from my uncle's modest wage as a tarmacker there was not much left for nice things in their home. Any spare money they had went on booze anyway. The carpets were threadbare, there was no telephone and the furniture had long seen better days. They were kind to me but it did not stop me from being reluctant to invite Nadine back to their house. Aunt Miriam did her best, but she was up against too many problems, not least of which was Uncle Frank's drunken violence towards her and some of my young cousins.

Nadine's family were different. But I felt uncomfortable and intimidated by their familial warmth. When I was in the company of Nadine and her family my secret sense of inferiority and inadequacy was magnified; I think I was jealous even. Once she was sixteen Nadine and I rented a room from another tenant on the same estate and moved in. It was basic and sparse, but at least we were together. I continued to work alongside my uncle Frank. But even though I hardly ever saw Dunwell, I still carried on boozing, which brought the kind of trouble into my relationship with Nadine that she could never have anticipated.

After just a few months I persuaded her that we should head out and see if we could start a new life elsewhere. 'I'll stop drinking and I'll be able to make you happy if I'm away from this town,' I said. She didn't know that I'd been drifting around the country since I was fifteen years old, sleeping rough and scavenging like a wild thing. Neither did she know too much about my problems with the law.

Nadine had never spent a night away from home. We had a little money saved, enough to make sure we could eat until we found work. A bus took us to the centre of Leeds from where we walked to a junction of the M1 and waited on the slip road heading south with all we possessed crammed into two holdalls. Once we were on our way I felt more relaxed about our relationship. Without realising it at the time I had managed to bring Nadine down to my level and ensured that we were now together on my terms. Her teenage heart was so much in love with me that she didn't even notice.

Drivers were kind to a young couple and we were soon picking up lifts. It took us almost two weeks to hitchhike to Newquay, sleeping in underpasses, car parks and transport cafés. It was the start of the summer season and we planned to work in restaurants. Nadine had never had a job before. I had worked over the years in factories, on building sites and in various other places that needed no special skills or qualifications. In Newquay there was work for waiting staff and cooks, but neither of us had the experience or the confidence to wing it in positions that needed real competence. Instead we got taken on in a fish bar and diner where we did the washing up. Without enough money to get proper digs we slept rough down by the harbour. It was hard seeing anglers volunteering to spend hours late into the night and the early morning patiently waiting for a bite from the black sea when they had perfectly good homes to go to while we huddled together under a lump of filthy tarpaulin trying to keep warm and sleep.

We spent the best part of that summer in Newquay. After a few weeks of bedding down in various skippers and hidey-holes, one of the restaurants we worked in let us have a tiny box room to sleep in. It was only just big enough to hold one small-sized single bed, but to us it was sheer luxury. We argued a lot when we were working – even over who should wash and who should dry. I was always promising better things – but never knew how to get them. All I could do was hang on and hope. By early autumn Nadine was desperate to go home. We had washed and dried and argued ourselves to a standstill and, fair play to me, I kept my promise not to drink. We had saved some money and in the second week in September we set off hitchhiking north.

The journey back to Shipley was quicker than the journey south had been. We slept rough again, in barns and outhouses, and she was so pleased when we came off the motorway at Leeds and caught a bus to Shipley. Her family were just relieved to see her safe again. I went back to my aunt Miriam and uncle Frank's for a couple of days but without Nadine there was nothing for me in the town. I decided to hitchhike to Scotland and try my luck there where I knew my relatives would put me up for a while.

I was in a pub having a last drink before leaving when Nadine walked into the bar. She stood looking at me. 'Hi,' I said.

She ran up to me and threw her arms around my neck, burying her face in my chest. 'I'm coming with you,' she said.

Scotland was another long trek – first the M1, then the A1. It took us a week and a half just to get to Edinburgh where we ended up stranded for two days. It was cold and wet and winter was coming in fast. We were about to look for shelter late on the second night when a long-wheelbase Land Rover pulled over and we were invited to climb in the back with the driver's two dogs. It stank of farmyard, but we were grateful – even more so when we told the driver where we were going and he said, 'That's lucky, that's where I'm going too.'

We stayed at my aunt Janet's in Alyth for a couple of weeks, working in the fields picking potatoes for a local farmer. We saved our wages and then moved to Perth, staying once again with my relatives. It was hard going. The Hunters council estate where my uncle Archie lived with his wife and gaggle of children was the roughest in the whole region. Houses and apartments with broken and boarded-up windows and smashed front doors appeared to be abandoned. If it wasn't for the people and the wrecks of cars, the gangs of children playing and dogs barking, the whole place would have looked like a demolition site.

My uncle Archie, one of my mother's three brothers, was a well-known hard man in the city. A fairground worker, he headed up a bunch of cronies who spent their spare time drinking Buckfast Tonic Wine in derelict buildings. Within a few days of our arrival Nadine was covered in flea bites – and I was scudding back the Buckie with my uncle Archie. Nadine became so distressed that we moved out after a couple of weeks and into another relative's place in a more respectable part of town, the home of one of my mother's six sisters, my aunt Sheila.

We were there for a couple of months, working with potato-picking gangs on the farms outside the city. It was back-breaking work. Nadine and I were arguing a lot. I knew she was regretting her decision to join me. I constantly tried to reassure her that all would be well, but made no effort to make her life better. I hit her a couple of times during arguments when I was drunk and once I kicked her. Another time, while I was tanked up after a Buckfast session with my uncle Archie and his pals, Nadine turned up looking for me. I swore at her and dragged her across the room by her hair. Somebody told me to stop. 'I'll fucking kill anybody who wants to get involved!' I roared.

Nadine was also getting bullied and abused by my aunt Sheila. She was stranded in what to her was a foreign country with people who showed her no care or respect. All she had was me and I was on the road to nowhere. When I was sober and begged her to forgive me she did. We found a tiny flat in the city and moved out of my aunt's place. I got a job labouring in a foundry and Nadine found work in a supermarket bakery. Christmas came and went. We lived in peace for a few months, until the day my uncle Archie started bragging to his wine drinking pals that not only did I spar and train in Richard Dunn's Bradford gym, but that I had 'fucken' knocked him oot.' Dunn was famous for surviving to the fifth round in a title match with the world heavyweight champion Muhammad Ali. I'd only ever seen him once, when he sparred for a paying audience one Sunday morning. 'So you knocked oot the British champ did ye?' Archie's pals were incredulous, and one, a hard-faced Glasgow man they called Big Dodge, started tapping my chin hard with his clenched knuckles. 'Think ye can take me?' he said. His eyes had the bulge of too much alcohol. I was full of wine and maybe ten years younger than Dodge. I looked down at his hand feeling the rage swell inside me and then attacked him with an explosion of head-butts, kicks and punches. When his brother stepped in to help him I went for him too, only stopping when my uncle Archie smashed me over the head with a half-full bottle of Buckfast, splitting my scalp and leaving me with a two-inch wound that pumped with blood.

Out of the blue one day in the spring of 1978 one of my father's two brothers, my uncle Rab, turned up at our flat in Perth. We let him stay. But Uncle Rab was a professional con man. Family legend had it that he once sold a Scottish mountain to some American tourists. He was the only other member of my family who had regular run-ins with the police and occasional stints in prison. I loved him but I knew that trouble always followed him. He had a reputation for doing whatever was necessary to make crooked money, even if it meant using those close to him and causing them to suffer.

He took me out with him one night to a bar used by prison officers from Perth Prison. After introducing me as his 'driver's mate', he told a couple of the off-duty officers, 'in confidence', that he was a lorry driver hauling whisky. 'I've got twelve cases buckshee,' he said. 'A hundred and forty-four bottles. I want £1 apiece for them.' This was his signature con – his modus operandi by which he had been fleecing pub and club owners across the country for years.

It was an offer the gullible officers could not refuse. He was so cool they never even had an inkling that he had once been a prisoner in their jail. Quickly they raised the money in a whip-round among colleagues and handed it over to my uncle Rab in fives and tens. They also gave him the keys to a car belonging to one of them into which my uncle was supposed to load the dodgy whisky after he told them, 'It's my way or no way. I'll leave the keys on top of the wheel on the driver's side.' Outside the pub he threw the car keys over a wall and whooped before we took off and ran all the way back to my flat.

By then Nadine was six months pregnant and wanted to go back to Shipley to be near her family to have our baby. My uncle Rab also needed to get out of town fast so he hired a car and Nadine and I loaded everything we owned into it and off we headed back down south. Nadine hadn't seen her family for almost a year. Their reunion was tearfully happy. Her parents were just relieved that she was home safe. She made no mention of the hardships I'd subjected her to. Instead of being angry with me for taking her daughter away, her mother welcomed me warmly and her father invited me to live in their home with Nadine. They gave us a room and treated me like one of their own.

I got a job in Bradford as a labourer in an engineering workshop. It wasn't well paid and travel took up a good proportion of the wages. But at least I was showing Nadine's parents I was a worker. I paid for our keep and we all got along fine for a while. But my sense of not being like them, of being less than them, caused me deep anxieties and I didn't know how to deal with them. Soon I turned again to drink.

I took another job in Shipley as an operative in an oil drum refurbishment factory. It was the dirtiest work I had ever done. I got home at night with a blackened face and grease-covered overalls. A hot bath and a good meal were always waiting. But it wasn't long before I started going into town on my own and returning home late and drunk. Sometimes I went drinking black-faced straight from work. When Nadine's mother started locking the door on me I had to throw stones at our bedroom window for Nadine to get up and let me in. She said my behaviour was making her worried about the baby. In a booze-fuelled rage one night I shouted so the whole family could hear me, 'It's not even fucking mine!'

I left for work the next morning and put in a ten-hour shift. When I returned home in the evening covered in grime as usual the front door was locked. I knocked and Nadine's mother opened the door. She had no bath or meal waiting this time. Instead she threw out my suitcase.

'I want to speak to Nadine,' I said. 'I need to tell her I'm sorry.'

It was too late for remorse. Nadine's mother slapped me hard across the face. 'If it was up to me you'd never see her again and you would never see that baby.'

I picked up my case and walked away with my head bowed in shame, wondering why the hell I kept being so vile.

That night I slept in a nearby park and in the morning, still wearing my overalls, I washed in the public toilets before heading off for work. I slept and washed in the park for several days and nights before a man I worked alongside in the factory, seeing how rough I was looking, offered me his sofa.

A week or so after that I walked into a pub after work and the barman said he had a message for me. 'A pretty girl was looking for you. She looked pregnant,' he said. I asked him what she said. 'Only that she needed to see you – she seemed really desperate. I told her you might be in the Cricketers,' he said. 'She only left here ten minutes ago.'

I raced out of the pub and ran up towards the centre of town. Nadine was walking out of the Cricketers pub as I arrived.

'Hi,' I said.

'Hi,' she replied.

'I'm sorry,' I said. I asked her if she wanted me back.

She rubbed her swollen belly. 'We both want you back,' she said.

I held her close and tight.

We decided to go to the council and declare ourselves homeless. The baby on the way put us at the top of the priority list and within a week we had the keys to a smart ground-floor council flat a quarter of a mile from Nadine's family home. Her family hated the fact that she had taken me back but they still helped us with carpets and furniture. We bought a cooker on hire purchase and rented a television and a telephone. I got another job working nights in a radiator factory as a press operator. The money was good and we began to build a home, getting ready for the baby. It was my first real home since Thompson Street – and when our baby Nadia was born in Bradford Royal Infirmary that August I felt that at last I had my own family. I was there at Nadia's birth and watched as first her beautiful head and then the rest of her emerged into the world. The nurse handed Nadia to Nadine and I lay on the bed beside them, happier than I had ever been in my life.

But instead of being spurred to succeed for my family I was convinced I was going to fail them both. I started drinking my wages and went into rages, smashing up the house while Nadine fled in terror with the baby to the safety of her family. One night I was in an Indian restaurant drunk when the father of one of Nadine's friends walked in and made a comment about my behaviour towards Nadine. I attacked him and he ran, but not before I'd landed a couple of punches. He reported me to the police who charged me with assault and remanded me on bail to appear at Bradford Crown Court later in the new year. Nadine was mortified, but it didn't stop me boozing.

She left me when I was drunk. When I was sober I begged and pleaded for forgiveness until she came home. Over and over I made promises to change. When I made the promises I believed I meant them with all my heart. I couldn't figure out why I kept trying to destroy what we had. Once we even planned our wedding, drawing up a guest list.

The night before Nadia's christening, I got drunk and smashed my arm through a window, cutting a deep gash down the length of my forearm. The sliced muscle that was exposed looked like a slab of raw liver hanging out of the skin. Someone called an ambulance and I spent the night and the next day in casualty, missing my baby daughter's first special day. A little while later, just before Christmas 1979, I got drunk again and came home in a violent mood. I started punching doors and walls. Nadine made to flee, but before she could pick up the baby I was between them. She pleaded, but I scooped up the little one in my arms and issued garbled threats before sitting down on the floor in the lounge.

Nadine was crying. 'Please let me take her,' she said. The baby smiled and gurgled. She was just sixteen months old. I swore at Nadine. She screamed at me. 'I'll get the police!' She was becoming more and more distressed.

'Fucking get who you want!' I shouted back at her. 'They'll have to kill me to get her.'

She screamed again and ran out of the house, slamming the door behind her. A little while later a team of uniformed police barged in and surrounded me and baby Nadia.

'Come on, Erwin,' said the policeman in charge. 'We don't want the baby to get hurt.'

I swore and threatened but as soon as Nadia began to cry I surrendered.

From behind the police Nadine screamed at me again. 'You fucking coward! You're just a fucking drunk!'

One of the policemen took the baby from my arms while another hauled me to my feet and pushed me into the middle of his colleagues who huddled tightly around me and escorted me outside to their van.

When I woke up in a cell in Shipley Police Station the next morning I knew I had to accept that I was ruining my family. I had to bring it to an end. Mid-morning I was released without charge and I walked back to the empty flat. It was dark inside. The curtains hanging in front of the part-open lounge window were flapping. I sat in the quiet and then picked up the phone and got the number of a second-hand furniture dealer from Directory Enquiries. I told the man what we had and he said he was interested. 'Just bring your van and a wad of cash,' I said. 'No offer will be refused.'

When the dealer turned up I gave him a hand to load the modest contents of our home into his van and thrust the money he gave me into my back pocket before locking the front door and pushing the keys through the letterbox. When I walked away I knew I was finished. The booze still in my system from the night before eased the wrenching emotional pain in my chest slightly but I knew it was going to get dangerously worse. Time and again Nadine had forgiven me. When in lucid, remorseful moments I had asked why she kept coming back she'd said, 'I love you and I want us to be happy.' This time I knew there was no going back.

I hung around Shipley until Christmas Eve when I headed down on the train south to see if my father would put me up for a while. When I arrived at his Reigate bedsit he was out. With my family's furniture money in my pocket I went on a pub crawl, finally waking up on Christmas morning in a car park behind a bar in the town centre. After dragging myself up and not even trying to brush myself down I made my way over to my father's place. I found him lying asleep surrounded by empty beer bottles and cans. I woke him up. He shook his head and said, 'Hello, son.'

My father had more booze in his fridge so I cracked open a couple of bottles while he got washed and dressed. I had walked away from our flat with nothing but the clothes I wore. My father gave me a clean shirt and after finishing off the beer we headed to the nearest pub. There were only a couple open and only for three or four hours. We sank a few pints which I paid for and bought a carry-out to take back to his room. For the rest of the day he played his Hank Williams tapes while we drank, then he got his guitar out and we sang his favourite songs together before we both fell into a drunken sleep – him on his bed and me on a camp bed under his bay window.

I woke up some hours later in the gloom with my father kicking my bed. 'Erwin,' he said, 'the cairy-oot is finished. Go and get us another drink, son. See if you can get us some Guinness.' I rolled off the camp bed and pulled on my shirt and jacket. I checked I had money and told him I wouldn't be long. There was an off-licence a couple of blocks away from his front door. Outside the streets were deserted. Tiny flakes of snow swirled in the sharp breeze. I pulled my collar up against the cold and strode along the pavement, noticing the Christmas lights flickering in the windows of houses on either side of the road. Very few houses I passed had living-room lights on. When I got to the shop it was closed. I checked my watch and saw it was half past two in the morning. Since it was Christmas night the off-licence had probably been closed all day anyway.

I stared in through the big front window and took in the display. There were plenty of bottles of wine and spirits – but no beer on show and no Guinness. I saw a couple of bottles of Bacardi rum. I knew my father liked Bacardi. I looked around on the ground for a stone or a brick I could throw through the window but there was nothing hefty enough to guarantee the glass would break. I checked under a hedge and glanced over into the garden of the house next to the shop. There was nothing.

Then my eyes settled on an old stone trough that was being used to display shrubs and winter flowers sitting just a few feet from the shopfront. I bent over and took hold of both ends of the trough. At first it didn't move. I took a couple of deep breaths and heaving and straining I tried again. This time I managed to get it a couple of feet off the ground. Roaring like a weightlifter attempting a new personal best I lurched towards the window and lunged forward launching the trough directly through the lower part of the centre. The glass exploded like a bomb going off, shattering the peace and silence of the night. When the crashing subsided I opened my eyes and saw that the whole of the shop window had disintegrated, leaving just a few jagged shards protruding from the edge of the frame. Debris covered the grass in front of the huge black hole that had replaced the plate-glass. I was breathing hard and starting to panic. I blindly reached into the hole and grabbed two bottles from the wreckage before turning swiftly and sprinting away.

When I reached my father's place I rushed into the communal hallway, quickly closing the big front door behind me. Pressing my back to the door I waited, working hard to get my breathing and my heartbeat under control before I went to my father's room. Some minutes passed and I heard the siren of a police car. I waited a little longer. When I finally opened my father's door I saw that he had fallen back to sleep and was snoring loudly. A street lamp outside his bay window cast a shadowy glow into the room.

'Dad,' I said, kicking his bed. I was still a little breathless. 'I've got us a drink.' He groaned and snorted and I kicked the bed again. 'Dad,' I said louder. 'Look. I've got us a carry-out.'

My father turned and sat up and I passed him a bottle. His eyes opened and closed slowly trying to focus as he took it from me. He yawned, bleary-eyed, and swayed. With his hair hanging down either side of his baldy patch he was the wild man again. He pushed his face close to the bottle in his hand and squinted. I hadn't yet checked what drink I had stolen. When I did I saw that instead of Bacardi or wine I had snatched a couple of bottles of Campari, something I had never tasted before. I didn't even know what it was.

'Whit the fuck is this?' asked my father.

'Er, it's Campari, Dad,' I said awkwardly. 'It's all they had.'

My father's face grew more puzzled as he stared at the bottle, squinting and scowling. Eventually he lifted his head slowly and looking at me disapprovingly he said, 'For fuck's sake, Erwin, nay fucken' Guinness?'

His disappointment didn't stop him or me guzzling down every last drop of the contents of both bottles. It was like drinking a pint and a half of neat cough mixture. In the morning on his cream-coloured carpet by the side of each of our beds lay large, puddle-patterned pats of syrupy, cherry-coloured vomit, which at first I thought were pools of coagulated blood – until the vile taste in my mouth reminded me of my outrageous attack on the off-licence.

18

The phone in the hall rang outside my father's room and he went out and answered it. 'Erwin son!' he shouted, 'it's for you.' When I asked him who it was he said it was Nadine. Since Christmas Day neither he nor I had been fully sober. Even near sobriety triggered agonising throbs inside my stomach and chest which felt like demons trying to claw their way out with multi-pronged meat hooks. The call must mean that Nadine wanted me back, I thought. Instantly my internal pain disappeared. As I rushed to the phone wild thoughts raced through my mind. I was going to tell her how much I loved her and Nadia. To convince her I would tell her that I would walk a thousand miles in my bare feet – I would climb five mountains – and I would even hack off one of my arms just to show her how important she and Nadia were to me. She wanted me back. Whatever it took I would prove to her that I was worth her love. I still had some of the furniture money left. I could get a bus and be home the next day.

These thoughts were bouncing around inside my head as I grabbed the phone from my father. I could feel the blood pulsing in my temples. Desperate to hear her voice again I pressed the phone hard to my ear. 'Hello?' I said. I heard her breathe and clear her throat. 'Hello?' I said again. 'Nadine?'

She answered with a trembling voice. 'Don't "hello" me, you bastard,' she said slowly. 'I'm going to murder you. How could you do that to us?'

Dizzy with guilt I squeezed my eyes shut. The demons were back. I mumbled that I didn't think she would return.

'I might have done,' she said. 'That was my home too, and Nadia's. You had no right.'

Shame burned inside me. My reasoning had been pathetic. I just could not get a grip on my insecurity. This time I knew I had tested her way past her limit.

'I'm sorry,' I whispered. 'I hope you'll remember the good times.'

A moment of silence passed and then just before she slammed down the phone she screamed, 'Good times? Are you kidding? There fucking weren't any!'

I knew I was sinking but I didn't know how low I would go. There were signs, there were warnings. My father and I saw in the new year, spending the last of the furniture money in the pubs around Reigate. He had a car he had been given the use of by one of his drinking buddies who had been disqualified for drink-driving – a turquoise Datsun Sunny 120Y with a black vinyl roof. He drove us around in the car sober or drunk.

One day around the middle of January he was driving us back to his place after an afternoon drinking session in Dorking, when I turned to him and asked him why he had behaved so badly to me when I was a little boy. 'Why, Dad?' I said. 'I really need to know. Surely I wasn't that bad?'

The booze was making me tearful and self-pitying – that was when I was at my most dangerous. My father and I never spoke about 'the past'. To me my life was what it was. But I so wanted to believe that much of my father's violence towards me as a child was undeserved.

'What do you mean?' he said.

'You know what I mean,' I said.

He pulled the car over to the side of the road and turned off the engine. His head lolled slightly over the steering wheel and he blew out a deep sigh. We sat in silence as the traffic sped by – and then he turned to me and said, 'All I did was love you.'

I couldn't remember my father telling me before then that he loved me. But hearing him say it now, in the car, both of us drunk, set something off inside me. I thought of the despair and anxiety I had been living with for so long and the misery I had inflicted on so many others, not least Nadine – and suddenly I snapped. 'You never fucking loved me!' I screamed. 'How could you treat me the way you did if you fucking loved me?' I started raging. My father turned the key in the ignition but the engine wouldn't fire. I had never hit him before, but I could feel the anger inside me building, ready to explode. He turned the key again and again but still the car would not start.

Bellowing threats, I pushed open the car door and jumped out. As he continued trying to start it up I began punching the car door. I punched dents in the passenger side then I started on the bonnet, battering down with my fists, all the while moving round towards the driver's door. Passing cars sounded their horns but I paid no heed. He was still vainly turning the key as I punched and kicked the driver's door. I grabbed the door handle but he locked the door before I could pull it open. I banged on the roof and punched the window and then the car fired up. He floored the gas pedal making the tyres screech and smoke as he sped away. I roared after him waving my fists, 'I'll fucking kill you!'

For the next couple of nights I slept rough in a bowling-green club house. I had no money and no plan. I drank water from the taps in public toilets, but the longer I went without food the more I began to panic. On the third night I decided to steal a car. I waited until the early hours and then walked along the road looking for houses with long drives. I knew from my youth that cars parked close to houses with long drives were more likely to have been left with the keys still in the ignition.

It only took half-a-dozen forays before I found a minivan with its keys hanging in a bunch from the dashboard. I opened the door ever so softly and then turned on the ignition lights, before releasing the handbrake and pushing it into a three-point turn so it ended up facing out. Slowly I shouldered the car all the way to the end of the drive before jumping in, starting her up and driving away. The tank was over half full so I headed west on a route that would lead me to the M4. Driving through the night I made Bristol as dawn was breaking. Less than an hour further on I pulled in to the centre of Weston-super-Mare, dumped the car and took off on foot, walking towards my aunt Rena's house, a seven-mile trek along the A370.

To me Aunt Rena's was like an oasis. There was always food and everyone seemed to have plenty of money. My uncle Nelson's scrapyard gave the family a good living. My two cousins Kevin and Nelson both had transit pick-ups and had been making decent money from collecting scrap and rags since their teens. When my uncle Nelson died in 1975 Kevin took over the scrapyard and began to make really serious money. By 1980 he was buying a new Rolls-Royce every year and all his clothes came from some of the best tailors in the country. Even his shoes were handmade.

Their home was still a modest bungalow, but everybody had gold jewellery, sovereign rings and thick rope bracelets. Owning gold was what was important. Sometimes when my aunt Rena was drunk she would get dresses from her wardrobe to show me and tell me how much they cost. She gave me a gold ring once that had worn extremely thin – it had two entwined initials on the front of the round panel and looked to me like a lady's signet ring. 'Your first bit of gold,' she said. It didn't feel like a genuine gift. It seemed like she was giving me something that was of no use to her, scrap or otherwise, and I wondered about the person whose initials were on the ring. The ring had no special meaning for me and I later sold it to a jeweller for £4.

I hadn't planned to stay long this time, maybe a few days, just to try and get my bearings. I never told my aunt Rena what had happened between me and my father. My cousin Kevin gave me some work in the scrapyard, paying me £10 a day cash in hand. I spent most of the time cutting up a big red London bus with an oxyacetylene cutting rig. I liked Kevin a lot, but I never really knew him. I didn't really know any of them. When I was desperate they didn't seem to mind too much if I landed on their doorstep, even in the middle of the night, so long as I didn't stay too long.

This time I managed two weeks. My first Crown Court appearance for the assault charge on the father of Nadine's friend some months earlier was due in February. I told my aunt Rena I had to leave. She didn't say anything but I could tell she was glad I wanted to be on my way. She made me some sandwiches and organised a little pack of toiletries. I always felt love towards members of my family, I just never trusted that any of them loved me back. My aunt Rena sorted out a few of my cousin Kevin's old clothes for me, a couple of pairs of jeans, two shirts and a jacket, before seeing me out of the front door with a brief hug. The bungalow was situated right on the edge of the A370, the main road to Bristol. It was a busy road and I knew it well. I walked away and as soon as the bungalow was out of sight I raised my arm and stuck up my thumb at the passing traffic.

It took me just a few hours to reach the slip road on Junction 8 of the M5 outside Bristol heading north. My court appearance wasn't due for another week. For two days I was stuck on the M5 and had barely had a sniff of more than a couple of lifts. I was getting nowhere fast. Another day passed and still making slow progress I walked off the motorway and looked for a car to steal. I walked into a village and found a convenience store where I bought a bottle of wine and waited for nightfall. After drinking the wine I crept up a few driveways but had no luck finding any cars with keys in. I came across a Mini and decided to 'hotwire' it, pulling wires from under the dashboard and crossing the ignition wire and the starter wire.

Soon I was tearing back up the motorway slip road and crossing over to the outside lane, eating up the miles. I hoped I might get as far as Altrincham where I could cross over to the M62. Dawn broke and the petrol gauge was showing empty. I made it to a service station and pulled into a deserted section of the car park. As I was wiping down the steering wheel, the gear stick and bits of the dashboard I may have touched I noticed a figure approaching. I still had the engine running and pretended to look for something in the door pocket, ready to pull away in an instant if there was trouble. After some minutes of being stared at through the door window by a solitary individual I looked up and saw a long-haired, unshaven youth wearing a denim jacket. He smiled and nodded. I wound down the window.

'What?' I said.

'I just wondered how far you were going and if there was any chance of a lift when you set off again,' he said.

My anxiety disappeared. I smiled too. 'I'll do better than that,' I said. 'You can have the car.'

I told him I was fed up with it: it was a banger and anyway I had lost the keys. I said I had planned to abandon it there. 'But if you want it, it's yours.'

'Are you serious?' he said.

I wound up the window and climbed out. 'Go ahead. It needs some fuel though, or you'll be walking again before the next junction.'

He looked a couple of years younger than me and wore wide flared jeans that matched his jacket and baseball boots. He opened the car door and hesitated.

'Go on,' I said. 'It's all yours.'

I turned away and as I walked towards the cafeteria I heard the Mini's engine revving and gears crunching. When I looked back I saw the little car speeding towards the gas pumps. After that I never saw the car or the hitchhiker again. For the rest of the journey I slept in hidden places in motorway service stations along the way. I had money and bought the occasional mug of hot tea – but I had to make the few pounds I had saved from the wages Kevin gave me last as long as I could, so I only ate what I found left over on the plates of other customers.

After being remanded on bail at Bradford Crown Court I walked back to Shipley and stayed at my uncle Frank and aunt Miriam's place for a couple of days. I was going to go and see Dunwell. 'Haven't you heard?' said my aunt Miriam. 'He's gone to London. He lives in a squat with his girlfriend.' I went round to his mother's house and got his address. I thought it might come in handy in an emergency.

I couldn't stay in Shipley in such close proximity to Nadine and I couldn't go back to my aunt Rena's so I asked my aunt Miriam if she could lend me the money for the bus fare to Leeds where I could pick up the M1. I decided to hitchhike back to Reigate and see if my father would give me a break. I was on and off the M1 for the best part of a day. The M25 had yet to be laid and the only way to bypass the city was to go around the South Circular. I slept rough under a flyover that night. The next couple of days were slow-going and by the early hours of my fourth day on the move I found myself on a dual carriageway in Surrey. Even with the heavy coat and the thick woollen jersey I was wearing underneath it the February wind was biting. The air was so cold that every time I took a breath the hairs in my nostrils froze. It felt like I had been walking for ever. For the previous ten miles or so there had barely been any traffic. I was exhausted.

Stranded and surrounded by open countryside I was just about to give up for the night and get my head down on the other side of the hedge that was running parallel to the road when I spotted a 'picnic area up ahead' sign. My pace quickened. There was bound be some shelter there. I followed the signs and soon I was off the road and walking along a winding gravel driveway. I warmed a little when I saw the low-level brick building shedding a dim light on to the concrete path from its open doorway. Never had a public lavatory looked so welcoming. I couldn't get inside quickly enough. I checked the stalls and picked the one in the corner furthest away from the entrance. After stepping in and locking the door firmly behind me I got down on the floor and wrapped myself around the toilet pan, pulling the collar of my coat up as high as I could. Sleep came quickly.

I had no idea how long I had been there when I woke with a start to the sound of shrill voices, laughing and shrieking. Momentarily disorientated, it took me some seconds to come round and remember where I was. Suddenly I realised the voices belonged to children. A touring coach on some sort of school or club outing must have pulled in to the rest area to allow the kids a toilet break. I felt growing pangs of embarrassment. It was no big deal for me to sleep in a toilet; I'd slept in stranger, less welcoming places. But I didn't want to be caught, especially not by a busload of children. I pulled my coat even higher until the collar was covering my head and squeezed my eyes shut, willing the intruders to leave.

Instead the high-pitched chatter seemed to intensify. There was a crash against the door and then a hush descended. The voices shrank to conspiratorial whispers. Somebody rattled the handle on my cubicle door – again and then again. The whispers grew louder, urging, 'Go on! Go on!' Someone must have peeped through the gap between the bottom of the door and the floor and seen me lying there. I heard the scuffing of climbing feet against wood and my heart began to pound. I buried my head even deeper inside my coat.

Then the noise stopped and a triumphant voice rang out high above me. 'A tramp! I've found a tramp!' The excitement in the boy's voice was barely containable, as was the chorus of delighted squeals in response. I squirmed, too ashamed to bring my head out from beneath my coat.

Tramps, I had always thought, were old broken men with ravaged, pleading faces. They walked stooped and defeated . . . and they smelled. Well, close up I probably stank. But a tramp? I was only twenty-three years old. Surely I couldn't be a tramp. A man's voice interjected, calming the children down and ordering them back to their bus. 'But, sir!' shouted my discoverer, 'we've found a tramp!' There was no doubt in the child's mind about what I was. When they left I lay awake for a long time, listening to the wind and wondering at what I had become.

My father let me back in to sleep on his camp bed and then a stroke of luck came in August 1980 when I was finally sentenced to a couple of hundred hours of community work at Bradford Crown Court for the assault on the father of Nadine's friend. I breached the community service order immediately by hitch-hiking back down south. But during the journey I was picked up on the M1 by a van driver who lived in a tiny village just a few miles west of Reigate. His grandmother had died and left him a house. He lived there with his girlfriend. 'We're looking for a lodger,' he said. 'Do you need digs?'

The village had won the county's 'best kept' competition several years in a row. It had two pubs and an ancient green. I moved in with the van driver and his girlfriend and got a job in a factory up the road in Leatherhead as a semi-skilled welder. Learning to weld cell doors in borstal had been worthwhile at last. I paid my rent and started to live again – but I couldn't stay off the booze. The village pubs sold the strong honey liquor mead and I started drinking it. Soon I was barred from both establishments and the van driver threw me out of his house when I made a drunken pass at his girlfriend. My father thought it was funny. 'They've been without a village idiot for over a hundred years,' he said, 'and then you turn up.'

I slept on his camp bed again for a while but without transport getting to Leatherhead in time for work was hit and miss. My nine-mile hitchhike every morning began at 4.30 a.m. so I'd be there for six to get in some early morning overtime. In the end I found it easier to sleep rough in a canvas-covered lean-to around the back of the factory and wash myself in the toilets in the mornings. I was earning decent money but still couldn't find any affordable accommodation.

I took another job as a washer-up in a restaurant in Epsom, mainly just to give me somewhere to spend the evenings after work instead of wallowing in pubs. The shift went on until 11 p.m. leaving me too tired to chance hitchhiking back to my little bolt-hole in Leatherhead. Instead I took to sleeping in the potato shed in the restaurant's back yard and then I'd hitch the five miles to Leatherhead in the mornings.

When I wasn't working I drank. In a nightclub in nearby Cheam one night I got talking to one of the owners who was impressed when I told him I'd worked before as a doorman. I never told him that the owner of the club in Shipley only gave me the job to stop me causing trouble in the place. I told him my new name. 'Pleased to meet you, Jimmy,' he said. 'I need a good man on this door. Want a job?'

I bought a dark jacket, a white shirt and an elasticated bow tie and the following weekend began manning his club's entrance. He should have known he had made a mistake when they had to break open the door to a toilet cubicle in which I had fallen asleep drunk on only my second night. But the owner seemed to like me. Somehow despite the boozing and sleeping rough in the potato shed I managed to keep the three jobs going for some weeks. Just before Christmas I even met another girl, a good-looking waitress at the club called Lana. She drove a Ford Capri and gave me lifts back to the restaurant at closing time where I told her I had a room. We kissed and cuddled in her car then I'd say goodnight and head round the back to the potato shed. She never guessed. Lana lived with her mother who invited me to stay for Christmas. Her mother bought me a pen as a present and Lana bought me a shirt. I didn't even buy either of them a Christmas card.

In January I saw an advert in the local paper asking for a 'professional' to share a flat. I phoned the number. 'I'm a chef at the Royal Park Restaurant,' I told the chap. His name was George. I wrote myself a reference and went to see him. It was a neat flat in a posh house in a leafy Epsom street. George was persuaded by my reference and my spiel. We had a good hour's chat over coffee and then he said, 'When can you move in?'

We agreed on a date a week later and shook hands. Mid-week I was in the restaurant kitchen up to my elbows in greasy dishes from the night before when I heard the front door open. It was half an hour before opening time.

A voice I recognised asked, 'Is James around?' It was George.

I already had on a white tunic. I snatched one of the chef's tall pleated hats, thrust it on my head and brazenly strolled out to the bar. 'George!' I said, drying my hands on a tea cloth. 'Looking for me?'

Raf the barman stared wide-eyed at the chef's hat. George wanted to know if we could change the date of me moving into the flat by a couple of days.

'Sure,' I said, 'no problem.' After he left I winked at Raf. 'Don't ask,' I said.

Life was comfortable in George's flat. My room was big and George let me use his hi-fi. I watched the chefs preparing and cooking food in the restaurant and learned enough to be able to put together the occasional meal for Lana when she came round. Sometimes she stayed over. We were getting close, but I could feel that it was not going to be long before I'd have to be moving on.

One day in the factory a welder I worked with told me about a scheme to get some real welding skills. 'The government pays for it,' he said. 'If you get coded as an ASME IX welder you can work all over the world.' There were always adverts for ASME IX coded welders in the daily papers, usually for jobs in Germany. I made enquiries and found that the training centre where you had to go to be assessed was in Sydenham, in London. I was so determined that this was going to be my ticket to a better life I applied for a passport in anticipation.

Lana came with me and waited outside the training centre while I did my test. My welds were X-rayed. They had to be of a good standard before you could go on the course. The factory welding work was very basic electric MiG welding. At Sydenham they asked me to do complicated vertical pipe welds. When the X-rays were checked the instructor told me they weren't good enough. 'Keep practising your vertical welding whenever you can and come back next year,' he said.

I couldn't see that far ahead. I could barely plan for more than a day or two at a time. My drinking went up a gear. I lost my job in the nightclub when I intervened in a minor argument between two men and threw one of them out, not realising he was the 'sleeping partner' – one of the owners of the club. When I was drunk I never stopped to ask who was who or to find out what exactly was going on. I just staggered in aggressively. The week before I'd had a fight with two men from London. I took a beating but not before I had put one man down and bloodied the second. Lana came running out to the front and screamed when she saw me on the ground getting a kicking. As the men walked away one of them turned and said, 'Next time you see your boyfriend he'll be floating down the Thames in a bag.'

The drink was taking me over. I lost my welding job for constantly arriving late in the mornings. I owed George rent and money for the telephone. As the bills mounted up I finally got sacked from the washing-up job for being drunk. With no savings and no income I knew it was time to go. I packed a small case and left the flat with no word to George. I hitchhiked to Brighton looking for work in restaurant kitchens. I slept under an old boat on the beach. After a week of rain-lashed loneliness I telephoned Lana. I was desperate to hear some kind words, perhaps some words of love.

She answered with news that stunned me. 'I'm pregnant,' she said. 'We need to get married.' My head spun. 'We can do it this week,' she said. 'I'll get a special licence.'

I thought about the boat and the beach and the rain. 'Fine,' I said, 'I'll get there as soon as I can.'

That night I drank a bottle of wine before hot-wiring an old Vauxhall Viva estate. The wedding was booked for the following Saturday, the 4th of April. I moved straight in with Lana and her mother who by then hated the sight of me. I called my father who bought me a pair of shoes. Lana's brother lent me a suit. After the ceremony we went to a town centre pub where Lana's family paid for drinks and food. We spent the weekend together and then Monday morning I was gone. I took the car I'd stolen in Brighton and drove to London making my way to Dunwell's squat. It was in the East End, in a part-derelict council block off the Mile End Road.

It took me a while to find it. When I did I was shocked at how he and his pregnant girlfriend Maggie were living. The flat had been boarded up when he came across it. There was mould on all the walls and it stank of sewage. Their bits of furniture had come from skips. 'We found the settee out on the pavement,' he said. It wasn't just that it was poor, it was filthy. There were half-bottles of mouldy sour milk lying around in the grimy kitchenette and rubbish piled in corners.

Dunwell was pleased to see me. 'I can't stand these fucking Cockneys,' he said. I wasn't sure I wanted to stay but I had nowhere else to go. 'You can stay as long as you like,' he said, 'and it's rent free!' It was just as well as I was totally broke.

He cooked on a two-ringed gas camping stove, mostly egg, chips and beans and soup. He and Maggie were getting social security money which was keeping them alive and they were on the list for a proper council flat, he said, which they would get when Maggie had the baby. He told me about a dole office where you could just turn up with ID and explain you were homeless and you'd get cash handouts. 'It's in Scarborough Street, not far from here, I'll show you.'

I slept on the old settee under a grubby eiderdown they'd got from a jumble sale. Dunwell took me to Scarborough Street and at last the passport came in useful. The waiting room in this place was horrendous. It was full of winos and down-and-outs and it stank of human waste. I fitted right in. Every week I turned up and waited, sometimes as long as six hours, to collect my £9 'emergency money'. It was enough to get a daily paper so I could look for labouring work and make phone calls.

Then Maggie's brother Billy turned up. Billy was running a couple of social security scams and had pockets full of money. I quickly accepted his invitation to go out with him and help him drink it. Billy was a lot smaller than me and skinny with a pointy, pockmarked face. The only thing I think we had in common was that we were both social failures. When his money ran out he and I went out after dark stealing from cars. Sometimes Dunwell came too. Soon the squat was a full of car radios, cassettes and cassette players, gloves, scarves – car blankets. We sold the electrical goods to second-hand shops around the East End with no questions asked. Then we did a burglary together.

Billy knew about a judge's London flat. 'He's never there at weekends,' he said. He never told us how he knew. Months had passed but the car I'd stolen in Brighton was still parked up in a multistorey car park. We used it for the burglary. I drove while

Billy gave directions. It was near a place called Ludgate Circus on the way to central London. I parked the car down a side street. The flat was along an alley and up some stairs. Billy had a giant screwdriver which he used to force the lock on the front door. We were inside in minutes.

It may have been a judge's flat but there was nothing of any real value in the place. My heart was pounding like hell – I rarely did anything illegal when I was sober. Billy got a pillowcase and filled it with the contents of the drinks cabinet, but not before I'd swigged long and hard from a bottle of brandy. I picked up the small television and an old railwayman's lamp that was on the hearth. Dunwell found a stash of pornographic magazines and stood flicking through them under a reading lamp on a desk. Then Billy shouted, making me and Dunwell jump. 'Fucking hell! Look at this!' He'd found a gun and some cartridges under a bed. Twenty minutes later we were in the car and heading back to the squat.

The gun turned out to be a starting pistol. We talked about using it for an armed robbery, maybe on a bank or a building society. The closest we got was a lame attempt one teatime at robbing a nearby off-licence. Billy had the gun in his waistband under his jumper while Dunwell and I stood behind him geeing him on. Before setting out we had each drunk a couple of cans of extra-strength lager. 'As soon as you've got control we'll come in and ransack the place,' I said.

It was raining and the wind was getting up. Customers were coming and going. It was the busiest off-licence I'd ever seen. We stood around like the three stooges getting soaked for nearly an hour until Dunwell said, 'Fuck this, let's go home.' Billy looked the most relieved. We never even had a mask between us.

I left Dunwell's place and tried my hand at begging outside busy pubs in the city. I'd walked all the way up to Ludgate Circus. But I wasn't any good at it. I was too embarrassed when I was sober and never made enough money to get drunk. I slept behind a rubbish bin pen by the river. By day I wandered around without any focus or purpose. My directionless strolling brought me to a road that had a market running along its whole length. It was called Leather Lane. By the time I got there the market traders were packing up so I hung around waiting for vans and lorries to leave so I could scrabble about in the left-behind debris after something to eat. I found plenty of discarded fruit and some cakes. I also gathered a couple of big cardboard boxes to sleep in and later that night I found a great little concrete alcove down a side street where I could make my bed. I stayed in Leather Lane for nearly two weeks, scavenging by day and curled up in my den at night.

I was getting more and more anxious with every day that passed and decided I'd have to mount a smash-and-grab on a wine shop. As I looked for a suitable target one day I walked past a betting shop and could hardly believe my luck when I saw on a low-level window ledge what looked like two four-packs of beer. I shuffled up to the cans and saw that they were all still intact, held together with plastic webbing. I could tell they had been there some time as rust had formed around the ring pulls from them having been rained on. I picked up both packs and marched quickly away.

Once I was a good way off I cracked open a can and greedily guzzled down the beer. It felt good so I guzzled down another and then another. The warm glow of impending drunkenness shooed away my anxieties and I headed out on a new mission. I needed to see my father, I decided, and I'd need a car to get me to Reigate. I started trying the door handles of older cars parked down deserted side streets or around the back of shops until I found an unlocked Ford Cortina. In I jumped, bold and brave thanks to the stupefying effect of the booze. It didn't take me long to cross the wires under the steering wheel and soon I was breezing through central London in excited anticipation of seeing my father. He would help me. He would get me sorted.

Then I noticed how low the fuel gauge was. I needed petrol fast. It would have to be a self-service station so I could fill up and then sprint without paying. I pulled into a busy forecourt and braked next to a pump. But when I went to open the petrol cap it was locked. I looked across at the payment booth and thought I was seeing things. The woman behind the glass looked like Aunt Stella. I walked over and sure enough it was her. She recognised me and came running out of the booth.

'Hello, love!' she cried. She threw her arms around me and hugged me tight, ignoring the fact that I must have been stinking. I hadn't shaved or washed for so long.

I started to cry. 'I'm not doing too good,' I blubbered, and began sobbing into her shoulder.

'What's up, love?' she said. 'What's the matter?'

I gave my head a shake and wiped my eyes. 'Nothing,' I said. 'I'm on my way to see my dad but the car's low on petrol and I've lost the key to the petrol cap.'

She led me to her booth and took down a number of packs which contained replacement petrol caps and keys. As she did so she told me she had left Shipley for good. 'I've got a flat here,' she said, 'and this job – it's a new start.'

I was too muddled with alcohol and anxiety and the shock of bumping into her to engage her in a proper conversation.

She opened a couple of the petrol-cap packs and passed me the keys. 'See if these are any good,' she said. I tried them but none fitted. I had a strong urge to drink more beer. I still had four cans left.

'I'll crack on,' I said. 'There's probably enough in the tank to get me there.'

She asked me if I was sure I was all right and I told her I was. 'Just a bit down,' I said.

She said to tell my father she was asking for him. As I climbed back in the car she said, 'Take care, love.'

That meeting was so unreal. Of all the coincidences that might have been possible, that one was unbelievable. I hated Stella so much, but I had been pleased to see her. It left me totally confused. I knew the car would be out of fuel soon so I pulled off the main road and parked up. After drinking another couple of cans I got out and looked for another car to steal. With my last two cans in my coat pocket I tried handle after handle until I found the door of an almost identical Ford Cortina unlocked. It took me only seconds to cross the wires and soon I was speeding south following the signs for the A217.

It was dark by the time I got to the top of Reigate Hill, a steep incline that ran for over a mile right into the town. I was about halfway down in nose-to-tail traffic when a thunderstorm erupted. The wipers could hardly clear the deluge of rain that coursed down the windscreen. That and the headlights from the cars coming up the hill made it almost impossible to see out. I pressed on the foot brake a little too hard and the car slewed across to the other side of the road smashing head on into a car coming up the hill. My face hit the steering wheel with a heavy thud.

Dazed and breathless from shock, I threw open the car door and dashed out over the pavement and through a gate. The traffic was at a standstill both ways. I ran up a path and found myself outside a hotel. I ducked inside and strolled up to the empty bar. A barman appeared. 'Excuse me,' I said, 'do you have a phone I could borrow?' The barman's eyes widened with alarm.

I glanced in the mirror behind the bar and saw my face was streaked with blood. As the barman turned and hurried away I rushed back outside and ran as fast as I could through the bushes and gardens along the side of Reigate Hill. The roadblock I had caused stretched for as far as I could see down the hill and up the hill. It would take for ever just to get a tow truck through to the mess I'd left. I kept on running, dodging from garden to garden. Then I crossed the road, hurrying between the blocked cars. I spotted a telephone kiosk down a side street and ran to it. Inside I picked up the receiver and called the operator. I told her my father's number and asked her to make a reverse-charge call. 'It's urgent,' I said. I was desperate to see him but I was in such a mess; I needed him to meet me in town and drive me back to his place.

I heard my father's voice. 'Hello? Erwin son, is that you?'

Before I could answer the kiosk door swung open and two policemen grabbed me and yanked me outside. Several police cars appeared and I was hustled into the back of one and ferried through the back streets to Reigate Police Station. Police enquiries revealed I'd stolen the second car in the Greenwich area. A few days later I was transferred to police cells in Greenwich and presented to Greenwich Magistrates' Court on the 19th of May where I was fined £150 and disqualified from driving for six months.

It was just a couple of weeks before Maggie went into labour when I landed back at their squat. Dunwell told me he'd got the keys to a council flat in Hackney. He hired a man and a van to transport the beds, the settee and the rest of their worldly belongings to the new place. At least it was clean to begin with. They had a baby boy and called him Mervyn. Dunwell said I could have the spare bedroom until the baby needed it.

'I'll pay you some rent when I get a job,' I said.

'Don't worry about it,' said Dunwell. It was kind of him as I was making no contribution to the food either.

Billy came and stayed occasionally and he always turned up with money. He gave some to Dunwell, and then took me out drinking with him. He took me up the West End one day when Scotland were playing England at football at Wembley. After the game drunken Scots were on every corner singing and chanting. We got talking to a couple of tartan-clad characters by Piccadilly Circus who were swigging from a bottle of vodka. They shared it with us. Then one of the men suddenly took off, shouting threats. I ran after him calling for him to calm down.

The next thing I knew a transit van screeched on to the pavement in front of me and a gang of men in jeans and bomber jackets jumped out. 'Stick him!' shouted one. I panicked and started lashing out, kicking and punching as if my life depended on it. I thought 'Stick him' meant I was going to get stabbed. The men fell on me with their truncheons, their 'sticks': they were plain-clothes cops on the lookout for football troublemakers. They threw me in the back of the van and drove me to Bow Street Police Station. I was charged with threatening, abusive, insulting behaviour and appeared in front of the bench the next morning, the 4th of August, where I was fined £5 and given a two-year suspended prison sentence.

As soon as I was out of the courthouse I went and got a handout from Scarborough Street, got drunk and headed to Epsom intent on seeing Lana. I jumped the train from Victoria, which I often did, leaping over the barrier and travelling without a ticket. On the train I was asked by an inspector to show my ticket. I was so pissed I couldn't think of anything plausible to tell him so I just said it was lost.

'Well you'll have to pay a penalty, sir,' he said.

'But my wife's having a fucking baby,' I said. How that was supposed to make any difference I had no idea.

He asked me to sign a form which I refused to do and he left me alone. When I got off the train at Epsom the transport police were waiting for me. They took me to Epsom Police Station and I was locked in the cells for two days before being charged with breaching the Community Order I'd been given at Bradford Crown Court. On the 7th of August, just three days after my appearance at Bow Street, I was taken in front of a judge at Kingston Crown Court and sentenced to three months' imprisonment for the breach and carted off to London's Pentonville Prison to serve it. It was while I was in there that Lana gave birth to my second daughter, Louise.

I wrote to Lana from Pentonville and she wrote back. She said the council had given her a flat and she wanted me to move in with her, 'so you can be a husband and a father'. I served six weeks and when I was released I used the discharge grant to pay my fare to Epsom. I got a job in a garage in Chessington doing welding repairs on cars. But soon, as it had with Nadine, my drunkenness included violence against Lana.

One day I came home drunk from work with four cans of lager in a bag and she stopped me at the door. 'You're not coming in here in that state,' she said.

I could hear the baby crying. 'But she needs her daddy,' I slurred.

Lana went to shut the door on me and I threw the bag of cans at her, hitting her on the head. She screamed and slammed the door.

Just like Nadine used to, Lana took me back. She kicked me out a number of times, but always took me back when I begged and promised I'd change. 'I love you, Jimmy,' she said, 'but you need help. I want you to leave and not come back till you've sorted yourself out.'

I thought I loved her too but she didn't really know who the hell I was and I wasn't sure either. I was still in emotional agony at the loss of Nadine and Nadia and I hadn't a clue how to sort myself out. Lana had a Mini estate. 'Can I borrow the car?' I said. I hadn't planned to go far. I thought I could live in her car for a while until I could figure out a plan. She gave me the keys without hesitating.

I still worked in the garage but the owner guessed that something wasn't right. I stopped washing myself and often went into work smelling stale and boozy. I had turned Lana's once neat little car into a tip on wheels. 'I don't know what's going on,' the boss said to me, 'but if you don't get a grip I'm going to have to let you go.'

I saw a job advert in the evening paper for a doorman in a nightclub in Battersea, south London. When I phoned up I gave myself such a glowing testimony that the posh-talking manager offered me the job there and then. 'We'll just have to have a short interview,' he said. The club was called Riots and it was located in an old, long-established oyster bar called Bennett's on Battersea High Street. After buying another cheap dark jacket and trousers, a white shirt and an elastic bow tie, I scrubbed myself up in some public toilets and drove to the club.

It turned out to be an upmarket venue often frequented by celebrities. The manager showed me around. He was especially proud of the dance floor made of coloured squares of reinforced glass, beneath which was a pool full of live piranha fish.

'You do have a driving licence?' he asked. Part of my job was going to be parking guests' cars.

'Of course, absolutely,' I lied.

He never asked to check and the following week I was on the door welcoming guests and parking their cars. I tried to keep the garage job going at the same time but the owner's attitude towards me became too negative. One pay day I picked up my wages and never went back.

The job in the club kept me going for a couple of months, until the night a celebrity hairdresser threw an early Christmas party for his staff. There were three bottles of wine on every table and I was told I could help myself to two glasses. 'We're all guests tonight,' said the manager. I don't think he meant it literally. But between welcoming greetings and parking cars I guzzled down glass after glass of red, white and rosé. Long before midnight I was smashed.

The manager came to the door and asked me how much I'd had to drink.

'Only a couple,' I mumbled.

'Right,' he said, 'let me have the car keys.' I had bunches of guests' car keys in the inside pockets of my jacket. I was supposed to tie on a little tag with the guest's name and car registration, but they were all unmarked and mixed up. 'Now, please,' he said angrily.

I started to protest my innocence when he thrust his hand inside my jacket making a grab for the keys. I pulled away and suddenly he and two of the barmen jumped me and we tumbled on to the floor in a heap. We wrestled until they managed to pull the jacket off my back and roll me out of the front door, banging it shut and locking it behind me. I staggered to Lana's car in a daze.

The next day even though I felt as rough as hell by mid-morning I was out looking for a job. I got a copy of the *Evening Standard* and checked the small ads for labouring work. I wandered through the city, made some phone calls but got nowhere. I didn't know London very well and was in danger of getting lost. It was raining hard and I sneaked into the foyer of a cinema for shelter. As I made to sit down I noticed a small black wallet at the back of the seat. My heart raced. I snatched the wallet and sprinted back outside, running as if my life depended on it. Expecting pursuit I ran and ran, dodging shoppers and cars, and eventually came to a halt in a shop doorway. High on hope I opened the wallet. But there was no cash, just bits of paper and business cards, which had on them what looked to me like Arabic writing. I sifted through the cards and found that one was in fact an American Express credit card. The signature on the card also appeared to be written in Arabic.

I had never used a credit card before and had no idea of the procedure. I soon found out how easy it was. The first place I used it was a West End steak house. Sweating with nerves I put on a heavy accent and ordered beer and wine to give me the confidence I needed to stay and eat. Then I ordered a couple of steaks and all the trimmings. Several hours later having feasted like a rich man I presented the card to the waiter and with a flourish I signed the receipt ticket in the style I thought resembled the Arabic-looking name on the card. If the waiter had suspicions he kept them to himself.

I staggered out of the restaurant and headed down to a shelter I'd found on the Embankment to get my head down for the night. Over the next few days I used the card in a number of restaurants and then hit on a plan to use it to get money. I was going to buy gold that I could later pawn or sell. After another fraudulent meal washed down with the usual few beers and a couple of bottles of wine for extra courage, I entered a jeweller's near Liverpool Street and still using the phoney accent asked to see some sovereign rings. Despite my drunken, swaying frame and slurred, ludicrously accented speech, the jeweller took the card from me and said, 'Yes of course, sir. Please, follow me.' I followed him to the back of the shop and into a lift. He then stepped out and the doors closed behind him, trapping me inside. An hour or so later the lift doors opened and I was greeted by two City of London policemen. Offering no resistance I lurched into their arms and shortly afterwards I was locked in a cell in Bishopsgate Police Station.

I declined legal representation and asked to be dealt with as speedily as possible. After a couple of days and nights in the cells I was put up in front of the City of London Magistrates' Court bench three days before Christmas 1981. The prosecuting lawyer read out the various charges relating to my use of the credit card. She described my visits to the restaurants and the laughable attempt to buy gold at the jeweller's. The chair of the bench was a grey-haired woman whose warm eyes looked on my sorry state with some sympathy, I thought. She had the long list of my previous criminal convictions in front of her and asked if any reports were available. Without a solicitor I had to speak up for myself. I explained that I did not have a stable address and then mumbled an apology for my stupidity and for the trouble I had caused my various victims. I didn't say it but I needed to be dealt with straight away because I knew that if they adjourned the case and let me out on bail there was no way I would be returning. I didn't want to go to prison but I was sure I needed locking up.

The chair chatted in whispers to her colleagues and after retiring for a twenty-minute recess she returned with her decision. 'We have considered a custodial sentence,' she said, 'but we don't think it will do you any good.' She said I needed to get my act together and advised me to seek help. I agreed that I would try and get some help, though from where I didn't know. I would have agreed to anything that was asked of me in order to get the proceedings over with and be back outside in the fresh air.

She then sentenced me to five lots of three months in prison suspended for two years and warned me that any further criminal behaviour would result in my immediate committal to jail. I was touched by her compassion and consideration and thanked her. When I exited the main doors of the court that lunchtime I had nowhere to go. I did not know whether to turn left or to turn right. I decided in the end to have another go at life with Lana.

19

The last time Lana threw me out I set off walking south along the A24. I had a suitcase with some changes of clothes and personal bits and pieces. In Leatherhead I came across a night shelter for homeless men. I had no money and hoped I might get a bed for the night. The woman who ran the place took pity on me. She said I was too young to warrant a bed there without an official sanction. I was twenty-four. 'You can stay tonight,' she said, 'but you should really get a referral.'

I slept in a bed in an open dormitory where a dozen other men all many years older than me were sleeping. It stank. In the morning I looked for my case, but it had gone, my few pathetic belongings stolen by somebody more desperate than me. After a quick splash of water on my face I walked out of that place with only the clothes I had on my back, no money and not a clue where I was going. It was the spring of 1982. I hitchhiked to south London and jumped a tube barrier heading to Hackney and Dunwell's place.

I hardly moved from the house for a month. Dunwell fed me on chips and beans. Each day he went to the betting shop and always brought me back a paper so I could look for jobs. One day he was out and Maggie came and sat next to me on the sofa. I was watching the television. Baby Mervyn was asleep in his pram.

'Can I tell you something?' she said.

'Sure,' I said.

'I've been fantasising about kissing somebody else,' she said.

I turned and looked at her and she reached across and kissed me full on the mouth. Seconds later we were having sex on the living-room floor. After that, sex with Maggie happened most days when Dunwell was at the betting shop.

I spotted a labouring job advertised in the *Evening Standard*. When I phoned up it turned out the job was in Epsom. I got a hand-out from Scarborough Street and took the tube all the way to Morden in south London and then a bus from Morden to Epsom. The building site was a huge new shopping centre in the middle of town.

'When can you start?' asked the foreman.

'Tomorrow if you want,' I said.

I started the next day. It meant I had to set off from Dunwell's before 5 a.m. every morning to catch the first tube train going west from Liverpool Street. It was a two-and-a-half-hour journey there and back. But I had nothing else to do and it was great to have money again. I gave Dunwell money for rent and bought food and booze. I bought clothes from jumble sales in Bethnal Green Road and then one Friday night I met a girl in a pub. She was a pretty Scot with bright eyes and long dark hair and her name was Julie. The friend she was with was English.

'I'm Scottish too,' I said.

They said they both worked as nannies for well-off people in west London.

'I'm a builder,' I said. They seemed impressed.

That night Julie took me back to her apartment in the huge house where she worked in Holland Park Avenue. All the houses nearby were just as big. We were both the worse for drink. 'The owners are away for a month,' she said.

I followed her in through the huge front door which opened into a magnificent hallway with a marble floor lit up by a giant shimmering chandelier. I'd only ever seen such places in films. A wide ornamental staircase led downstairs and Julie beckoned me to follow her. 'Wait till you see this,' she said. I followed her through a number of doors and down more stairs and along a corridor. 'Ta da,' she said finally, throwing open the door to an underground swimming pool. 'Come on,' she said, stripping off and jumping into the water.

We swam naked in the pool, had sex and then retired to her little self-contained pad. It was all so clean and smelled so fresh and good. I left her in the morning and caught the tube back to Dunwell's place. The contrast between the living conditions could not have been greater.

I kept up my job in Epsom, working all the overtime I could.

The next time I saw Julie she said to me, 'I've told my mother I've met "the one".'

I looked at her. '"The one"?' I said. 'Well what are you doing fucking about with me?'

She punched me playfully. 'Don't be daft,' she said. 'It's you – you're "the one".'

She called me 'Jimmy' but she didn't even know my surname. I knew I wasn't fit to be anybody's 'one', and I felt sorry for her as I knew it was going to end in tears.

I turned up drunk at her employer's house one afternoon. She opened the door and I staggered in. 'You can't stay,' she said, 'they're back tomorrow.'

Ignoring her I shouted, 'Come on, let's go for a swim.' Then I tripped and tumbled down the big staircase, crashing into an ornate table at the bottom. It shattered into pieces.

'Fucking hell!' Julie shouted. She grabbed hold of me and dragged me back up the stairs before manhandling me back outside.

I hung around for a while pressing the bell and demanding to be allowed a dip in the pool. 'Come on, Julie! We can have a pool party!' I shouted, before eventually giving up and heading back to Dunwell's.

Later that week I phoned the big house and a posh-sounding woman answered. I asked for Julie. 'Just a moment,' she said.

When Julie came to the phone she whispered angrily, 'That table was an antique. It cost £5,000. Please don't come back. You're a nutter.' My position as 'the one' was over.

I got fed up with travelling to Epsom to work and decided that instead of returning to Dunwell's at night I'd sleep on the building site. When work finished I spent my time boozing in pubs until closing, then I went back to the site and got my head down in the canteen hut. I managed it for a few weeks but gave the job up eventually and went back to stay at Dunwell's. By then Billy had moved in with them and had my bedroom so I slept on the sofa in the living room.

Billy and Dunwell had been going out at night stealing from cars and I started going with them. Billy could steal a car faster than anyone. Sometimes we drove around all night looking for targets and then slept all day. Then Billy came up with a master plan to make some easy cash. 'Parking meters,' he said. The plan was to cut the heads off parking meters and rifle the contents. He stole a van and in the early hours we mounted a smash-and-grab raid on a hardware store on Hackney Road, snatching an industrial-sized pipe cutter.

The next night the three of us went out tooled up. I was the strongest so I had to do the cutting. It was heavy labour for small rewards. We took up to ten meter-heads at a time and then spent hours during the day with a hammer and chisel trying to prise out the contents. There was rarely more than five or six pounds in each cash box. But it was enough to keep me in in cheap wine.

One night me and Billy went out on a serious drinking session and on the way home he jumped on a man who was walking in front of us. I joined in the scrap and it turned into a mugging. We rifled the man's pockets and in the fracas an arm of his sheepskin coat came off, before he struggled free from us and ran. That was at the beginning of September 1982. Three months later our robberies and muggings left two people dead.

Life for double killers who fled to Foreign Legion

By HEATHER MILLS Old Bailey Correspondent

TWO double killers who fled London for France and joined the Foreign Legion were tracked down and arrested two years later following a raid by Scotland Yard detectives on an East End flat where property stolen from one of their victims was recovered.

JAMES MONAHAN, 28, and WILLIAM ROSS, 25, were each sentenced to life imprisonment at the Old Bailey yesterday.

Monahan—arrested in the south of France last August a day after he deserted from the Legion — was recommended to serve a minimum of 14 years by Justice ORTON, who described him as " brutal, viciou and callous."

Ross, said the judge, had been dominated by Monaghan and he was therefore making no recommendation of a minimum sentence.

Monahan was convicted of the murders of Mr Greville Hallam, 48, a former actor turned theatrical agent, who was robbed and strangled at his home in Haverstock Hill, Chalk Farm in September, 1982, and Mr Angus Cochrane, 29, a National Coal Board solicitor who died four days after being mugged of a few pounds in the Mall, three months later.

Two attacks

Ross was cleared by the jury of murdering Mr Hallam but convicted of his manslaughter.

He was also found guilty of murdering Mr Cochrane, who worked in Doncaster and lived at Gringley on the Hill, Notts. Mr Cochrane had been visiting London on business.

Ross and Monahan were living at Old Market Square, Bethnal Green, at the time of the two attacks.

Ross, who admitted two other West End muggings, and Monahan, were questioned by detectives investigating four other unsolved murders in London.

Sprawled on floor

Miss ANN CURNOW, Q.C., prosecuting, said Mr Hallam, a homosexual, met Monahan in a Soho pub where Monahan was selling video films.

Mr Hallam, she said, had a "peculiar proclivity" for the "rough trade" homosexuals who were large, tattooed and rough in appearance.

He only looked for them when he was depressed. Otherwise he kept an elegant home,

William Ross: dominated by Monahan.

James Monahan: "Brutal, vicious and callous."

furnished with antiques and was well liked and respected by neighbours and friends.

Monahan and Ross raided his home and Monahan—6ft 2in and powerfully-built—strangled Mr Hallam with an arm lock. He left him naked, with his hands tied, sprawled on his bedroom floor. Television sets, video equipment and a music centre were stolen.

Three months later, the pair ambushed Mr Cochrane as he walked along the Mall to his hotel. He was punched, kicked and battered with a brick and died in hospital when a life support machine was switched off.

Police recovered Mr Hallam's music centre last August from the home of Ross's mother and inquiries revealed that both Ross and Monahan had "boasted" about the two killings and had left London for France at Christmas 1982.

237

20

I spent the Christmas of 1982 drinking with my father in pubs around Reigate and sharing carry-outs in his bedsit in a state of disbelief and suppressed fear. On Christmas night I slept on his camp bed in the alcove under his one bay window, but as soon as I woke up on Boxing Day morning I decided I had to run and keep on running. My father was still snoring away in a drunken slumber.

I dressed and then shook him. 'Dad,' I said, 'I'm in trouble.'

He snorted and wheezed. 'Whit is it, son?' he said, before breaking into a rasping cough.

'I'm in big trouble, Dad,' I said. 'I have to get away fast. I'm finished . . . I need some money.'

I was desperate to tell him what I'd done. I'd tried to tell him the night before but he wouldn't turn down his Hank Williams tape. Now it was pointless. He was still groggy from the booze and didn't even question my urgency.

'Pokits,' he said. 'Take it oot ma pokits.'

I walked the mile and a half to Redhill Station with £45 in my pocket and caught a train to London's Victoria. Earlier in the year I'd read in a magazine an extract from a book by Simon Murray about the French Foreign Legion. The book was titled simply *Legionnaire*. I remembered Murray describing a place where, so long as you could handle the rougher aspects of life, a man could get lost. At Victoria I bought a one-way bus ticket to Dover and after a night in the ferry terminal I took the first boat in the morning across the Channel to Calais.

On the ferry I told a barman that I planned to join the Foreign Legion but didn't know where to go. He told me that he had heard there was a recruitment post 'somewhere in Lille', a big industrial city in the north of France. After paying the train fare and the coach fare to Dover and buying booze and a ticket for the crossing I was running short of money. That night I slept rough in Calais railway station and in the morning I jumped a train to Lille.

I guessed that if I made it into the Legion it was going to be hard going and dangerous. I thought that with any luck I might get killed. Maybe I could do something good before I died. I spoke no French and had no real idea how to go about enlisting. After a bitterly cold day spent wandering aimlessly around Lille, looking in shop windows, sitting on benches, watching the traffic – I spent the last few francs I had left on a couple of bottles of cheap wine and then looked for an alley I could skulk down and hide in. I found a quiet street away from the bustle of the town and by the time I hunkered down between a fence and a concrete shed the roads were already covered with a hard frost. All I had to keep me warm was my big old jumble-sale coat. I drank the wine quickly and slipped away to oblivion.

Sometime during the night somebody must have seen me and taken pity on me, for when I woke up I found I had been covered with a piece of old carpet. When I tried to sit up I couldn't. At some point I had slumped over so that I lay with my head against the ground and my hair, then thick and curly, had become stuck to the frozen pavement. I pulled and pulled until I was free and then wrapped my arms around my knees and huddled under the carpet. I felt rough and wretched and I was sure that had whoever had thrown the carpet over me not done so I probably would not have woken up at all.

Dawn broke but I stayed put. I didn't want to go anywhere. As the streets around me began to hum with signs of life I knew I had to make a move. I dragged myself up and out of the alley and then walked until I was back to where there were shops. I needed to find someone who could tell me where to join the Foreign Legion. With no French all I could do when I entered the shops was to say, 'Legion? Legion?' People turned away from me, frightened by my appearance, or disgusted. I tried the shop where I had bought the wine. I approached two customers who immediately turned their backs. The woman behind the counter waved her hand at me and with a raised voice was obviously telling me to get out.

I entered a baker's shop. There were no customers, just an elderly man behind the counter.

'Legion?' I said to the old man.

His initial look of suspicion changed when he heard what I said. His face lit up. '*Ah oui . . . La Légion!*' he said.

He took off his apron, gathered a bunch of keys and came round the counter. Heading towards the door he beckoned me to follow him. Outside he locked up his shop and again beckoned me to go with him. Soon we were in his car, speeding through the city.

'Scottish. Me, Scottish,' I said when he spoke to me. 'No parley French.'

'*Ah bon*,' he said, repeating a number of times while nodding, '*Écossais . . .*'

The car pulled up outside what I thought looked like a castle. '*La citadelle*,' he said. A soldier wearing an oversized navy-blue beret stood guard by an archway. He couldn't have been more than eighteen years old and though he was armed with a rifle he didn't look too threatening. I found out later he was a conscript. '*Ici*,' said the baker as we got out of the car. He spoke briefly to the soldier who looked at me and nodded before signalling to me with an outstretched hand.

'Thank you,' I said. I tried it in French. 'Er, mercy, mercy.' The baker laughed and took my hand in both of his. Then patting me on the shoulder he rattled off something incomprehensible before getting into his car and pulling away. His cordial, sympathetic manner made me want to cry. I was sure he had just wished me good luck.

The young French soldier walked me through an archway and stopped outside a heavy wooden door. On the wall by the side of the door was a small plaque with words in large letters: '*Légion étrangère*' and in smaller letters, '*bureau d'engagement*'. If I'd been calm and at peace and making a rational decision I might have felt some sense of fear or anxiety or even excitement about what might be waiting for me on the other side of the door. But I felt nothing. All I knew was that I had to go through it or I was sure I would die on the streets.

The soldier rapped hard and the door was opened by another soldier dressed in immaculately pressed combat fatigues. He was tall, lean-faced and square-shouldered. Just a faint shadow of hair covered the top of his shaved head. The two soldiers spoke and then the younger one turned and left – he looked glad to be on his way. The big Legionnaire beckoned me inside.

The recruitment post was a small barracks. There was a section where the Legionnaire who manned the post slept and at the other end of the room a number of bunk beds. Half-a-dozen bed spaces were occupied. A couple of men were lying full length on their bunks and both stuck their unkempt heads up so they could have a look at the newcomer. Another two were sitting up on their bunks. A long-haired, swarthy, proud-faced man was sitting on the side of a bottom bunk. He was holding a guitar and plucking gently at the strings. He stopped when he saw me. A sixth man, boyish-faced and timid-looking, was kneeling on the floor by the side of his bunk with his hands clasped together apparently in prayer. His hair hung just below his ears and was cut in a basin style which gave him a fragile, almost angelic appearance. He too stopped what he was doing and turned to look at me. All the men wore green tracksuits.

While the Legionnaire got on the phone to somebody, I assumed about me, I stood in silence. Eventually the guitar player nodded at me. '*Hola,*' he said quietly. I nodded back. There was an odd atmosphere in the place. It reminded me of being in a police station, in a communal holding pen in the morning when the drunks have finally sobered up and everyone is wondering what is going to happen next.

The Legionnaire put down the phone and said something to me in French. I stared blankly at him. 'No parley,' I said. I was twenty-five years old and all I owned in the world were the shabby clothes I stood up in. I had no skills and could barely articulate in English never mind any other language. My hair was matted and my eyes sticky. I was unshaven and unwashed. My mouth was furred up and my breath stank so badly I could smell it myself. The Legionnaire's clean, confident manner smacked of efficiency and competence which made me feel even more ashamed and pathetic. I turned away from him, and then he spoke again and startled me.

'You're English?' he said. I recognised his accent instantly. He was from Liverpool – a Scouser.

'We get a lot of Brits through here,' he said, ignoring the state I was in. 'Where are you from?'

It was a question I hated. I told him I wasn't really from any-where. 'I've had a few problems and been homeless for a while,' I explained. I daren't think about what I was running from. 'I'm trying to make a fresh start,' I said.

He gave no sign of being concerned about my vagueness. He must have heard so many tales and suspect justifications. He asked me if I had any identification on me. I had my passport and handed it over. 'Is this real?' he said peering closely at my photo-graph. He said people rarely handed over passports. Usually it was

243

driving licences or medical cards. 'The Frenchie over there gave me a bus ticket,' he said, nodding towards the young man who had been praying.

The Legionnaire told me he was a corporal and his name was Richard. 'It's not my real name but everyone calls me Rick.' He said most people changed their name when they joined up but it wasn't obligatory. 'It's something you might like to think about when the time comes,' he said. He gave me a run-down on the routine of the barracks and said I'd be getting a quick medical check that day and if I passed I'd be here for a little while.

Later that afternoon he escorted me to the doctor's office located deep inside the *citadelle*. The doctor was an officer in the regular French Army. He took my blood pressure, listened to my heartbeat and that was it. Rick was back to collect me inside the hour. 'You'll know if you've got to the next stage if you are still here in three or four days,' he said. 'So long as you're not wanted for rape or murder you'll have nothing to worry about.'

I knew I had plenty to worry about. Back in the barracks Rick told me to take the bunk above the young Frenchman. Rick told me that 'Frenchie' was just seventeen and that he got down on his knees and prayed every night and every morning. 'The French can't officially join the Legion,' he said, 'so they join up as Swiss, or Belgian or any other French-speaking nationality.'

The guitar player's name was Garcia and he was from Chile. As well as the young Frenchman there were two brothers from Poland, a German and a Ukrainian. Despite the language barrier there was some stunted conversation between us all but it was hard going using mainly facial expressions, gesticulations and grunts. On New Year's Eve Rick brought us in some beers. It wasn't exactly a party, but Garcia played his guitar and sang us some songs. We shook hands at midnight and wished each other luck. A week later we were loaded on to a bus and shipped the hundred and forty miles to Paris.

2 1

What I did not know then was that the majority of those who tried to enlist in the French Foreign Legion were turned away. But after three weeks in the selection centre at Legion Headquarters in Aubagne, near Marseille, during which I was subjected to numerous medical, physical and psychological tests, they took me in. Along with three dozen other raw recruits from countries all over the world, I was sent to a specialist training regiment based in Castelnaudary, a small town in the south a couple of hours' drive from the Spanish border.

The culture shock was enormous. I went from chaos to a rigid, disciplined regime that offered no compromise. During basic training the thirty-six volunteers in my section all began on the same level. For the four months of *instruction* in the foothills of the Pyrenees Mountains we were tested to our physical and mental limits. My heavy build at first was a severe disadvantage. The fitness programme was relentless. There was so much running, in PE kit, in combat kit – I thought that alone was going to kill me. Every morning as dawn broke we had to do pull-ups on a chin bar out on the square. Despite my supposed toughness, at my first attempt I couldn't even complete a single repetition. The strengthening process was ruthless. We were trained to function at the highest level during the harshest conditions of warfare in order to inflict the greatest damage on enemy combatants. It made drunken fights in pubs look childish and pathetic.

Discipline could be brutal. Throughout the training period push-ups, *pompes*, were the standard instant punishment handed out for any minor infringement of the myriad rules and regulations that in the beginning none of us really understood. We soon learned, often with the help of a prod or two from a pickaxe handle. But even then for no discernible reason a *caporal* or *sergent* might order us down on to the floor and have us pumping out push-ups just because they could. There was so much emphasis on physical exertion that within a short time everyone in the section was capable of performing pull-ups, sit-ups and press-ups like there was no tomorrow. But they never got easier. The more we could do the more we were forced to do.

We had to learn French, to understand it, read it and speak it – and woe betide anyone caught speaking his own language. At 5 a.m. one morning we were standing at the end of our bunks waiting to be inspected when our Moroccan *sergent* Vasquez walked into the *chambre*. '*Gardez-vous!*' he screamed. In perfect unison we jumped to attention, hands slapping thighs with a mighty *CLACK*! He walked down the room slowly, scrutinising not our kit all neatly laid out with meticulous precision along our beds, but our chins.

I had been so focused on getting the various items of clothing neatly folded and boxed off that I had forgotten to shave. Vasquez stopped in front of me. A super-fit, wiry man of about five foot eight, he had to crane his neck back slightly to look me in the eye. '*Vous n'avez pas rasé ce matin?*' he said.

I was tired and on edge but that still did not explain why my brain decided that I should answer him in English. 'No, sir,' I said. I tensed my stomach ready for the punches I knew were coming, but instead he caught me by surprise with a solid rock-like head-butt bang in the centre of my sternum. I lurched back on my heels and groaned. It felt like a blow from a three-pound hammer.

'*Putain!*' he screamed. '*Vous ne parlez pas français?*'

The shock of pain in my chest made me relax my stomach muscles, so I was totally unprepared when he punched me a quick one-two deep in the solar plexus. It was the first time I had been winded for a while and I had to fight to control my rising panic as my lungs strained uncontrollably for breath. I buckled but managed to stay standing, even keeping my arms firmly down by my sides in an attempt to show him and everybody else I could take it. Being hit was not something that was new to me but it still hurt like hell. I thought that by showing I could handle a little one-sided violence I might earn some respect. What I hadn't anticipated was that my resolve might antagonise Vasquez even more. Glaring furiously he drew back to hit me again just as our *chef de section Adjudant* Piaget walked into the room. Somebody shouted, '*Gardez-vous!*' and everybody stiffened in an even more exaggerated stance of attention.

Piaget asked what was going on. Vasquez explained that I had been insolent and had refused to answer when he asked me why I hadn't shaved. He added that I also refused to speak French. Piaget was as tall as I was but broader. A battle-hardened veteran of a number of Legion campaigns and interventions including their most recent high-profile rescue mission to Kolwezi in Central Africa during which more than six hundred and fifty rebel soldiers had been killed with the loss of just five Legionnaires. Piaget was one of the most highly respected and decorated figures in the training regiment and held the speed record for completing the gruelling combat assault course, the *parcours de combatant.*

He walked up to me and pushed his face into mine, so close that the peak of his kepi brushed my forehead. '*C'est vrais?*' he asked. His breath smelled of spearmint.

'*Oui, mon adjudant,*' I replied. There was no use complaining. I knew I would only lose if I tried to argue with the sergeant's version of events. I knew also that though Piaget was genuinely as hard and tough as they come, he was a fair man who we all respected and would be unlikely to take the sergeant's report too seriously.

Piaget turned his head. '*Alors!*' he yelled. '*Allez! Tout le monde . . . En bas . . . Pompes!*'

In an instant everyone was down and frantically pushing out press-ups. Piaget then instructed the man nearest to him to gather up all our dress boots and hurl them out of the window on to the square below. Not for the first time did we miss breakfast as we chaotically sorted out the mess after the *sous-officiers* had gone for theirs.

*   *   *

Almost every day during training we spent time on the square being drilled over and over until we could march in precise formation. We were taught to sing old Legion songs while we marched, which was supposed to give us courage, honour and a connection to ancient Legion customs and rituals. As the weeks passed we all began to find things about ourselves that made us valuable to each other. My high tolerance of pain and discomfort and the efforts I made to earn and keep my place turned me into someone others looked to for encouragement and motivation. On manoeuvres we marched for days and nights through rivers and forests and all over the foothills of the Pyrenees Mountains. Marching turned out to be something I was good at. When a comrade struggled with his *sac à dos* I was happy to take it from him. Sometimes I carried two backpacks as well as my own. Gradually the language, the uniform and my positive response to the experience gave me a powerful means of stepping away from the uncertain identity that I had despised for so long. It allowed me to reinvent myself as a reliable, dependable member of a team.

The demands in the Legion were intense but I was so desperate not to fail that I met every challenge and quickly learned the French language. I buried the knowledge of my crimes somewhere deep inside me. My progress in basic training was exceptional. Each month the section pennant would be awarded to the best shot with the FAMAS F1 5.56 assault rifle, the French Army's standard-issue infantry weapon. One month there was no best shot, so *Adjudant* Piaget awarded me *le fanion*, a tiny green-and-red flag embossed with the motif of a flaming grenade – the emblem of the Legion – for my ability to march tirelessly.

The structured routine and philosophy of reward for effort brought something out in me that I never knew was there. The powerful sense of family among our ranks meant that for the first time in my life I felt that I had found somewhere I belonged. I did well enough in training to be assigned to the *2ème REP*, the Legion's only parachute regiment, based in Corsica, where I became a heavy-machine gunner. Over the following sixteen months I trained in the specialist commando school in Mont-Louis; marched down the Champs-Elysées with the regiment on Bastille Day, taking the salute from President François Mitterrand; took part in manoeuvres on the mainland, sometimes alongside regular French troops; and operated in various roles in Chad, including mounting guard duty for the general in charge of Operation Manta, the biggest French military intervention in Africa since the end of colonialism.

22

'You chose to come back. That was the right thing to do. That proves you have a conscience.' The young Wandsworth prison officer had been coming to my cell for weeks. The cells of Category A prisoners were only ever to be opened with a minimum of three prison officers present. So I was surprised when one day my cell door was unlocked and he walked in alone. At first I thought it was a bolts-and-bars check or a cell search. I had noticed him a few times before when he was supervising orderlies on the servery or standing in a corner of the yard overseeing exercise.

In his early twenties he was like a boy compared to most of the Wandsworth officers – and he was seriously overweight. I had never paid him any particular attention, but he had obviously taken some notice of me. The first time he came to my cell he said he had heard I was in the Legion and told me he had once thought about joining but had 'bottled out'. He asked me if I minded telling him what it was like. His trusting manner towards me was disconcerting at first and made me suspicious. In the prison culture it was totally out of order. He explained almost apologetically that he had only joined the Prison Service when he failed to get into the Army after being cajoled by his father, a former soldier. 'I think he just wanted to see me in uniform,' he said.

What really surprised me was the way he spoke about his fellow prison officers. 'They blank me most of the time,' he said. 'I've been told I've got to do at least a year before I've got any chance of being accepted.' For all my suspicions I couldn't see any harm in talking to him and it was good to have the cell door open when everyone else was behind theirs. Sometimes we chatted for an hour at a time. If nothing else his visits broke the boredom of bang-up. He was easy-going if a bit naïve, but I liked that about him. His neutrality was such a contrast to the attitude of the majority of his colleagues. I told him about my time in the Legion and about my life before that – but I never spoke about my crimes and he never asked me for any specific details. When he said that I must have had a conscience to have handed myself in when I could have kept on running I never tried to tell him I was innocent. I just nodded. He was the first prison official to treat me like a fellow human being.

When he was on landing duty he often let me out of my cell for an extra shower and made sure I got into the clean-laundry queue on Friday afternoons. The trouble was the familiarity between us did not go unnoticed by other prisoners on the wing. Soon I became aware of little snippets of gossip and I knew I was in danger of damaging whatever credibility I had on the landings. To try to nip the situation in the bud I brought it up myself in the exercise yard. Unfairly I commented on the officer's gullibility and made the others laugh at him. He became 'the fat wannabe'. Even though he would spring the lock before entering, he had become so trusting that sometimes he sat on the end of my bed, barely two paces from where I was sitting on my hard-backed chair.

Alex the Israeli knew about the young officer's visits to my cell. So did his co-accused Felix. One morning Alex sidled up behind me in the breakfast queue. 'Legionnaire,' he whispered, 'can we parley?' He said he wanted to put something to me and would elaborate later in the yard. I nodded and headed back to my cell with my porridge and my hard-boiled egg. We missed exercise that day due to the rain – the notorious 'inclement weather'. It was another two days before we got out to the yard again, by which time I'd forgotten all about Alex's supposed proposal.

I was walking fast as I always did. I heard footsteps jogging up behind me and turned to see Alex straining to catch me up. 'Legionnaire,' he said, '*hombre*, slow down.' It was then I remembered his asking for a chat earlier in the week. I guessed it would be something dodgy – maybe a request to conceal a weapon or to ask me to agree to receive a parcel from one of his associates on the outside.

'*Qu'est-ce qu'il y a?*' I said.

'*Doucement, doucement,*' he whispered.

There were only a dozen of us in the yard and half-a-dozen prison officers watching our every move. Alex was not a good man to be seen having whispered conversations with.

He walked alongside me for a while and then leaned his head a little closer to mine. 'Your friend,' he said.

I frowned. 'What fucking friend?' I said.

'Shhhh . . .' he said. 'Your friend, the fat one.' I still wasn't sure what he was on about. 'Your friend who comes to see you . . . in your cell.'

Instantly I understood – the young prison officer. He probably wanted me to try to corrupt him. There was no chance of me even considering it. If he wanted to corrupt prison officers he would have to do it himself. 'Fuck off,' I said. 'He ain't my fucking friend.'

We walked in silence for some minutes, overtaking a couple of the others, nodding our good mornings as we passed. Once we were out of earshot of anyone behind or in front he leaned his head in towards mine and spoke again. 'Me and Felix, we're going to make a break from this place. If you help us you can come too.'

For all his apparent flakiness I knew that Alex easily had the resources to make a break from Wandsworth. It had high walls and razor wire but it was far from the most secure prison in the country. The place was hardly more secure than it had been when the Great Train Robber Ronnie Biggs had escaped over the wall twenty years earlier. Alex's kidnap squad had had the means to have a 707 cargo aircraft on standby at Stansted Airport ready to spirit away their victim and one of their team had been a qualified anaesthetist. They denied being Mossad agents at their trial, but even if they were only mercenaries, they were far from amateurs.

Wandsworth was so lax that just a few weeks earlier a man had been caught digging out the ancient mortar in which the bars of his cell window had been embedded. The cement had been damp and crumbly and he'd raked it out with a plastic knife, hiding it in his toilet bucket and then emptying it bit by bit down the sluice in the recess. He had replaced the mortar with bread kneaded into putty-like lumps of dough and only got caught because one morning he forgot to pack the dough into the holes he had dug the night before. When he was taken out of his cell for a probation visit prison officers went in for a bolts-and-bars check. From then on he was made to wear a blue boiler suit with broad yellow stripes down the front and back and was classified as an 'E man' – a potential escapee – and as such he was grouped together with the Cat As. He was in the exercise yard that day as Alex and I spoke.

Until that conversation with Alex escaping had never crossed my mind. What would I do? Where would I go? I had just spent nearly two years on the run – I wasn't sure that I could face that again. On the other hand years and years on the landings of the likes of Wandsworth Prison was also a miserable prospect. The idea gave me a quick rush of adrenalin. I slowed the pace a little and said under my breath, 'Fucking hell . . .' I was definitely thinking about it.

Half a circuit later Alex spoke again. 'All you would have to do is grab him,' he said. 'He is a slob. You could have his keys in seconds. You open up me and Felix. We go out to the yard. My friends will be waiting on the other side of the wall. Within two hours we will be out of the country.'

So that was the plan. Its chances of success, in the initial stages at any rate, would depend massively on me. Back in my cell I thought long and hard about what Alex had suggested. Lying on my bed I played out the various scenarios in my head, were I to agree. If I made a move on the officer he might freeze, or he might struggle like hell. The thought of hurting him horrified me. But supposing he just froze and I was able to take his keys and lock him in the cell without using any serious violence? It would take only seconds to unlock Alex and Felix. We could be out in the yard in two or three minutes. The fence would be no great obstacle: just slip a couple of donkey jackets over the razor wire. Their associates would organise a rope ladder for the main wall.

But who would be waiting for us on the other side? Not friends of mine, that's for sure. It would be easier for whoever it was to put a bullet in my head and get on with their business – or maybe just leave me high and dry to fend for myself. Three Cat As breaking out of a central London prison would attract a huge amount of attention. It would be do or die stuff – and for what? If I was lucky maybe a few hours or days roaming around the streets like a desperate beast. It was a ridiculous proposition.

It was no fun wallowing in my self-inflicted misery in a shithole of a cell in a shithole of a jail. But I knew I deserved to be there – and I really had started to think. Over the weeks in my cell, with the innocent assistance of the young officer, I had begun to try and untangle my horrendous life. In the Legion I had considered that if I behaved in a certain way, as if I was a man with good morals and values, I might become that man. That plan never had a realistic chance of working out. I would have needed to have had a better character – and if that had been the case I would never have had to join the Legion in the first place. Now I just wanted to try to figure out how I had ended up being such a harm-causer. Perhaps if I could work that out it might be possible for me to find a better way to live – even in prison.

Over the preceding weeks I had come to like the young officer. I don't think he realised for a moment that he was making himself vulnerable by entering my cell alone. The fact that he didn't see any danger in visiting me made me feel a little more human. It was important that he didn't feel frightened of me. I had spent so many long nights thinking about how I had become what I had become outside. The conversations had helped me to examine my life in a way I had never done before. There was a definite therapeutic element for me in his visits to my cell and one thing that gave me some comfort was his approval of the fact that, when my father told me over the phone that I was wanted by the police, my instinctive reaction was to return and face justice. 'You didn't have to come back. You could have kept on running, kept hiding. But you chose to come back. That was the right thing to do. It proves you have a conscience.'

My decision to hand myself in was the only redeeming feature of the events that had led me to the Old Bailey dock and I hung on to it. It helped me believe that I hadn't been born bad. When the crunch came I pleaded not guilty, but that wasn't my plan in the beginning. There had been no need for me to leave Camp Raffalli when I did. Chances are the Legion would have covered for me, if only to protect its own reputation. The fact that in that instant I chose to return had to mean there was something about me that might be salvageable. I was grateful to the young officer for helping me to see that. And I knew that the right thing to do in this situation was to dismiss Alex's plan.

Out on the landings and in the yard I would need to keep up my front. But the officer's visits would have to come to an end. It was more than a week after Alex told me about his plan when the officer came to my cell again. It was mid-afternoon, the quietest time of the day. I heard the keys jangling outside my door and got ready. I'd have to wait until the door was fully opened to make sure it was him and not just a bolts-and-bars check. The key turned in the lock and the door swung open. The young officer's smiling face appeared as he sprung the lock.

'All right?' he said.

I jumped up, immediately kicking back my chair. 'No I'm not fucking all right!' I shouted at him. 'What do you think I am – some kind of twat?' I saw the colour drain from his face. I took a step towards him and roared, 'Get the fuck out and don't come back! I'm not here for your entertainment!'

I could see confusion and fear in his eyes as he fumbled with his keys, panicking to release the lock so he could shut the door. I felt so sorry for him. He would have had plenty of crap from his colleagues about the scum we all were: psychopaths and reprobates. With me he had always been pleasant and courteous. After he slammed the door closed on me and rushed off down the landing no doubt he would be thinking differently. It had been self-indulgent of me to allow our chats, but I hated having to make him think ill of me. He would never know how much of a favour I was doing him.

The weeks passed slowly for the rest of that year. I had another couple of strained visits from my father. We talked about the prison food, about how I was coping and what the other prisoners were like. If we talked about the case the topic was always its weakness. 'Somebody's got to look at this, Erwin,' he'd say. 'You'll be oot soon, son, don't make any mistake about that.' He never asked how my application to the appeal court judge was doing and I kept quiet about the rejection. I could have appealed against the rejection, but the fact that I'd written to the judge in the first place was only ever a token move on my part to give some credence to my not-guilty plea. I couldn't tell my father that getting out was the last thing on my mind.

I kept up my routine, reading, keeping myself clean and doing my exercises. It was a relief when Alex and Felix were shipped out to their long-term prisons at last. I'm pretty sure Alex was suspicious about why the young officer had stopped coming to see me. We still chatted in the yard before he left, in English with a little bit of French. He said they were still planning their escape and I was welcome to join them. But I felt it was only a matter of time before he would turn snide on me.

In my cell I began thinking. Listening to my little radio gave me a view of outside society that I'd never seen before. My father sent me a world atlas which I hadn't been allowed to keep in my cell. But before the reception officers put it into my 'stored prop'

I'd had to sign for it. Inside the front cover my father had written: 'Amigo! You can't visit the world, but the world can visit you!' I flicked through the pages before handing it back and realised that, though outside I had never managed to make it as a participant, at least now I could look out from the inside as a spectator, an observer and a contemplator of the world in a way that had been impossible when I was there in its midst.

I'd listened to the Live Aid concert in July that year on my radio and marvelled at the unity people had demonstrated. The Band Aid single had made number one for Christmas 1984 and had been played over and over again for weeks afterwards. Before Live Aid there had been a violent clash between a convoy of several hundred New Age Travellers and the police at Stonehenge. The police said that they had come under attack from missiles and other weapons wielded by the Travellers. It turned out that almost all the violence had been perpetrated by the police and had been unprovoked. I thought a lot about the national miners' strike which had begun in March 1984 and had been so much in the news when I returned from France and through into the new year until its formal end in March 1985. I had met the two miners who'd been remanded in Brixton charged with killing the taxi driver. They were convicted of his murder and sentenced to life imprisonment. (Later their convictions were reduced to manslaughter on appeal.)

Before I had fled to France I had never paid any attention to the news or current affairs. What was going on in wider society seemed to have no relevance to me. The miners and the

Travellers, the musicians and the people who supported their cause – these were all people from communities that seemed to have a stake in society; so much so that they were prepared to go to some lengths to assert their value as citizens. Outside I had never met people like that.

One of my neighbours in Wandsworth, a man serving fifteen years for armed robbery, used to have the *Telegraph* newspaper delivered every day. I got to know him and got on to the list of people who read his paper after he had finished it. There were around a dozen secondary readers before me and often the paper would be a week old or more by the time it was my turn. It was such a big paper. Reading the whole thing took me the best part of a day. Before that I had only ever read tabloids and even then I'd never taken much of the news seriously. The *Telegraph* on the other hand had great sheets of information and analysis – there was comment and debate and an interesting letters page. There was also great news coverage of events abroad. Because of my experience in Africa with the Legion I was still interested in what was happening in Libya and Chad.

A friend and former comrade in the Legion based in French Guiana sent me a book called *Prisoners of Honour*, by David L. Lewis. It was about Captain Dreyfus, an officer in the French Army who had been wrongly convicted of spying in 1894 and sentenced to life imprisonment in a tiny, specially built prison on Devil's Island, ten miles off the French Guianan coast. Dreyfus was an innocent man, a man of magnificent integrity and loyalty to France, but had been charged and convicted even though people of high rank knew he was innocent. They were prepared to let him rot and were happy for him to die a terrible death to cover up their mistakes. Dreyfus was scapegoated for no other reason than he was a Jew. This book had a profound effect on the way I thought about truth and courage. It made me even more aware and ashamed of my own failings.

As the year drew to an end I was managing the fear out on the landings and was coping with the anxiety that accompanied the routine slamming of the cell door. The unappetising diet, the indignities of the toilet bucket and the limited access to clean clothes and washing facilities were deprivations that went with the territory. I had no desire to complain. It was just the way it was and it had to be coped with. I never thought about how others serving time alongside me were coping until my first Christmas in Wandsworth. In Brixton's A SEG the previous Christmas there had been plenty of distractions to take fretful minds off what we were missing. Banter, booze and luxurious food organised by the prisoners with wealth made up for lack of access to more traditional festive celebrations. Despite our circumstances there was still Christmas in Brixton. In Wandsworth there was no Christmas. For one of my neighbours there was literally no Christmas and neither would there ever be again.

Every weekend throughout the year the 'evening meal' was served between 3 p.m. and 3.30 p.m. It was the same the weekend before Christmas Day, which that year was on a

Wednesday. The preceding Monday and Tuesday operated like a weekend – extra bang-up and fewer staff. By early evening I was in bed, listening to my radio and reading. By 9 p.m. my light was out and my head was under the covers. Christmas morning came and the cell doors opened. I took out my bucket, emptied it and then collected my bowl of water for my wash before heading down for breakfast. The landings were quieter than other days. Somebody barged past me. 'Hold up,' I said, 'what's the rush?' He told me that on Christmas morning we got cornflakes and fresh milk instead of porridge. I hadn't had fresh milk since Brixton. I shuffled along, listening to the chit-chat, looking forward to tasting milk again – and then I learned something awful.

Sometime in the early hours of one of the previous nights I'd been woken up by sounds on the landing above me. I'd heard gentle footsteps, keys jangling and whispered voices. I'd stuck my head up and strained my ears for a few minutes but couldn't make out what was going on. I thought it might have been a 'ghosting' – the slang term for an unannounced, unexpected transfer, at any time of the day or night. I shoved my head back under the covers and thought no more about it.

When I found out what had happened I couldn't believe it. 'Are you sure?' I said to the man in front of me.

'Yeah,' he said, 'he's gone, one off on the threes!'

The strange excitement in the queue was not just because of the Christmas treat at the servery – but because the man in the cell above mine had hanged himself. It was the first I'd heard of it. The chap who passed on the news to me had been grinning when he told me. 'One off' (on the ones, twos, three or fours) was what prison officers called to their colleagues whenever they took a prisoner off a particular landing. He was telling a joke. I didn't know what to say, so I too grinned inanely.

As we got closer to the servery the joker in front of me stuck his hand in the air and shouted to the supervising officer, 'The geezer off the threes, guv, I'll have his cornflakes.'

The dead man's job had been wing cleaner, meaning he was out of his cell for an hour in the morning and an hour in the afternoon to sweep and mop the landings.

Somebody else shouted, 'I'll have his mop and bucket!' A couple of people in the queue cheered and others sniggered.

I collected my Christmas breakfast, which included an unusually edible soft fried egg and scurried back to my cell. As I spooned down the cornflakes and milk the image of what the man in the cell above me had done filled my mind. He'd shredded one of his sheets, braided the strips and made a cord. After climbing on to his bed he had tied the cord to the bars of his cell window, made a noose on the other end which he pulled tight around his neck and then stepped out into space. I managed to finish my egg and my cornflakes, but when I put my tray on the floor outside my cell door there was no sensation that I had just enjoyed a treat.

Eleven and a half months after I arrived on Wandsworth's D2 landing, a couple of hours after the evening meal, my cell door opened and it was Mr Barker. 'Pack your kit, lad,' he said. 'You're on your way.'

My stomach jumped. 'What, a transfer?' Mr Barker nodded and smiled.

I didn't have much kit to pack and was ready to go within a couple of minutes of him opening the door. Mr Barker stayed outside on the landing waiting as I gathered up my toiletries and my radio.

Just before I came out he took a step inside. 'Good luck,' he said, and offered me his hand.

My excitement about the move negated any consideration of the appropriateness or otherwise of him and me shaking hands. My defences were down for a moment and I grasped his hand tightly. 'Thanks,' I said.

Cat As are never told where they are going when the time comes for a transfer. Two prison officers had escorted me from D2 landing back through the prison to the reception department. My 'prop box' was ready on the counter. On top of the box was a manila file with my name on it. Minutes after being handcuffed I was surrounded by prison officers and ushered to an external door outside of which a prison transit van was waiting with its back doors wide open and its engine running. It was dark as I climbed in. Five prison officers climbed in after me. We sat on the benches on either side of the van and waited. Loud voices outside called to each other. I heard the stop-start of the static from their walkie-talkies and then listened as instructions were given for the main gate to be opened. There were more checks as we waited under the big entrance arch. I couldn't see out as there were no windows in the van and the partition separating us from the driver's cab was blacked out. The van pulled away slowly and soon the driver was gunning through the gears and the journey was on. I hadn't seen the gate on the way in and never saw it when I left.

For most of the drive the prison officers guarding me barely spoke. A toilet break at a motorway service station gave some respite from the constant hum of the engine. The driver parked the van in a spot furthest away from the entrance to the café area. I was handcuffed to a rail on the van wall and the back doors were opened. The officers got out and one by one took it in turns to urinate into a plastic bucket that was kept under one of the benches. One of them shouted in to me, 'Do you need a piss?' I shook my head. I did need to go but there was no way I was going to go in that bucket with the five of them watching me. The officer who offered it to me emptied the bucket under a hedge and then stuck it back under the bench. The smell of it lingered in the back of the van until the final stop.

It took more than five hours to reach our destination. Until the van doors opened I had no idea which prison I was headed for. But as soon as we were in the reception area I heard prison officers speaking and recognised the Yorkshire accent immediately. The only place we could be was Her Majesty's Prison Wakefield – also known by the locals as 'Monster Mansion'.

At Wandsworth talk of where we Cat As might end up invariably led to comparisons. Because we were high-risk prisoners the only places that would take us were 'dispersal' prisons. These were maximum-security jails in the high-security estate. The sole jail that everybody agreed should be avoided at any cost was Her Majesty's Prison Wakefield. As a lifer I had no choice where I was sent. Prison was prison in any case.

In so many respects I was just glad to be away from Wandsworth. Not especially because it was such a dire place, but more because I wanted to start trying to be my own man. Inside I totally lacked confidence and had no sense of authenticity whatsoever. Having to act in prison like I was somebody I wasn't was making it even more unlikely that I would ever find out who I really was, or confront the truth of my crimes.

By the time I got to Wakefield much of the notoriety surrounding my trial and conviction had died down. There was nobody here who knew me. I hoped it would be a fresh start and the beginning of my journey to try and be real. I was hustled through reception and installed in a specially reinforced cell on A Wing inside an hour of my arrival. The prison was the same Victorian design as Wandsworth but the cells were noticeably smaller. The prison officers who banged me up that night joked about the remnant of a shackle ring on the cell wall and seemed to enjoy pointing it out to me. 'Those were the days,' one of them said. But there was none of the blatant intimidation that I had received from their colleagues at Wandsworth.

The next morning, escorted by two prison officers, I was taken for an interview with the Duty Governor. I was marched into his office and presented as if I was attending a court martial. The

Governor was a stocky man and looked to be in his mid to late forties. He had a dark beard and a weather-beaten face that made him look like a farmer. The older of the prison officers barked my name and prison number and ended with a loud, 'Sir!'

The Governor cleared his throat and said, 'Thank you,' before nodding at the chair on the other side of his desk and inviting me to sit. The two officers sat in chairs that they pulled up to just a few feet behind me.

The Governor looked at me, then at the file on his desk. He sucked in through his teeth and then said, 'All right?'

I shrugged. 'Yes thanks,' I said.

He asked me what sentence I was serving. Since I could see it was my file in front of him the question was obviously a pointless one.

'Life,' I said.

He asked me some other questions regarding my religion and my dietary requirements. 'It says here you're a Mormon,' he said, 'and a vegan.'

I squirmed. This was the moment to begin my attempt at authenticity. I explained about the dodges at Wandsworth, the little scams the cons in the know worked in order to make life a bit more bearable.

Without looking up he nodded and uttered a quiet, 'Hmm . . .' He seemed to accept that such minor dishonesty might be understandable in the circumstances. Then he said, 'You've got a bigger problem than that. You killed and then you went away and got yourself trained to kill professionally. That makes you twice as dangerous as most of the men in this prison.'

I didn't know what to say. I stared at his desk. I didn't feel dangerous. I felt pathetic.

Then he spoke again. 'Our job,' he said, 'is to get you back out and functioning well. The judge said you have to serve at least fourteen years, but I think we're going to struggle to get you back out at all.' He asked me why I had gone to join the Foreign Legion.

'Fear,' I said.

'But that doesn't make sense,' he said. 'Surely you would have been more afraid of what might be waiting for you in an army of foreigners with a reputation for brutality and hardship? Do you think that when you went to join up you had a subconscious desire to be punished?'

I was only aware that my motivation for joining up was to flee and hide from the enormity of what I had done, but I wasn't going to admit that to the Governor, especially since I had pleaded not guilty. I'd dug a deep hole for myself with that one.

He asked me what my experience in the Legion had been like. 'Do you think it did you any good?'

I said that I thought it did do me a lot of good. In fact the more I thought about it the more I was sure that it was the time I spent in the Legion that was helping me to cope as well as I was with life in prison. 'It taught me self-control,' I said.

I was in the Governor's office for a good hour or so. I spoke honestly and openly about my Legion service. It felt like I was putting something to rest. Finally he ticked some boxes on a form and then wrote some more notes down on a separate sheet of paper. He closed the file and placed it on top of several others on his desk. 'OK, that's all for now. Thanks for being so frank. These chaps will take you back to the wing,' he said, nodding at the two prison officers who had sat in silence behind me for the whole of the time. 'Get yourself settled in – and try not to get too involved in the bollocks on the wing.'

23

Though the design of Wakefield Prison was much the same as Wandsworth's here the regime was driven by a great bronze bell hanging in the centre where the four wings converged. It clanged to wake the jail up at 7.30 a.m. and then at rigid times throughout the day signalling unlock, slop-out, meals, work and bang-up – and like a pack of dogs trained by Pavlov prisoners and staff jumped, scampered and slavered to its tune. Category B prisoners who had jobs left the wings to go to their workplaces at 8.30 a.m. Cat As were unlocked at the same time as Cat Bs but we had to wait until the Cat Bs had left before we were allowed to go through our respective wing gates on to the centre where we congregated under the watchful eyes of a tight ring of prison officers. Once we were assembled and accounted for an officer called into his walkie-talkie, 'Line the route!' Outside his colleagues with dogs formed a gauntlet that snaked from outside an exit door on C Wing all the way to the workshops. As soon as they were in place the order was shouted and off we trooped in single file to our work.

Among our number was probably the largest concentration of men who had featured in the most lurid headlines of the nation's tabloid newspapers. Serial killers and torturers rubbed shoulders with child abductors and notorious rapists. There were IRA prisoners, including one of the men involved in the Balcombe Street siege of 1975 who was convicted of seven murders, and two men convicted of the Birmingham pub bombings of 1974 which left twenty-one people dead. (The latter two would later be cleared of all charges.) There was a man who had been convicted of murdering more than a dozen young men and whose crimes were only discovered when body parts of his victims turned up in the drainage system of his apartment block. Another two convicted separately of multiple serious crimes including rape and murder had each at different times been nicknamed 'the Fox' by the tabloid press. The two were constantly arguing about who was 'the real Fox'. One day on the exercise yard they had to be pulled apart when, egged on by other prisoners, they were about to exchange blows. The heavier-set of the two was dragged away by half-a-dozen prison officers still screaming at the top of his voice, 'I'm the fucking Fox!'

Somewhere in the bowels of the prison even more infamous Cat As were being held that nobody ever saw. One lived in a specially constructed glass-and-steel cage after killing three fellow prisoners, two of whom he had slain in his cell on my wing six years before I landed. Another who had been convicted of murdering several of his outside employers was located permanently in the prison hospital. The prison's nickname was no exaggeration. I had become one of the worst of the worst, a member of a grim club with barely a spoon of hope between us.

I was given a job in the so-called 'engineering fabrication' workshop, known as 'Engines Fab', where I spent two hours in the morning and two hours in the afternoon filing down bits of metal and filling little boxes with the filings for, as far as I could tell, no discernible reason. After lunch at 11.30 we were locked in our cells for two hours while the prison officers had theirs. As at Wandsworth Cat As were escorted everywhere inside the prison by at least two officers and at the end of each escort the times and locations of departure and arrival had to be noted in a small, passport-sized logbook that contained the prisoner's mugshot and prison number – hence the reason Cat As were also often referred to colloquially as being 'on the book'.

If for any reason I had to be taken through the prison grounds, say from an accommodation wing to the hospital wing, a distance of less than fifty yards, in the same way as the work detail operated, officers with dogs lined the route. This was the procedure that was orchestrated about a month and a half after I arrived in Wakefield when I was taken from my workshop back to the wing for my first 'psycho call-up'.

Each wing had its own dedicated psychologist. All were women whose offices were converted cells. On my wing the 'psycho's office' was situated on the right near the gated entrance next door to the wing governor's office. The prison officers escorting me hesitated outside her door for a couple of minutes while they logged the operational details in my Cat A book and then turned the handle and walked in without knocking. 'One on, ma'am,' said the lead officer. The room was sparse. Her desk took up almost the whole of the right-hand-side wall. In the far corner beneath the window was a tall filing cabinet. The walls were painted cream and the fluorescent light was bright, but apart from the faint scent of her perfume and the large red alarm button just inside the door the cell was hardly any different from the rest.

The woman was small and plain-looking with greying hair cut in a neat bob. She wore large pink-framed glasses. 'Thank you,' she said to the officer, who nodded and closed the door. Turning to me she said, 'Please, take a seat.' I sat down on the only other chair which was positioned at the right-hand end of her desk, bizarrely – given the strength of the security measures that had been deployed to get me to her office – in between her and the red alarm button.

She said her name was Joan and asked me how I would like to be addressed. I told her and then she asked me to wait a moment while she finished reading something from the open file in front of her. I recognised it immediately as my file. Apart from the cursory exchange I had with the psychiatrist when I arrived at Brixton Prison after my conviction I had never spoken to any mental or emotional health professional in my life so I had no idea of what Joan might be expecting from me. I tried to anticipate her first question. I guessed it would be concerning my claims of innocence. As my mind raced trying to figure out a strategy with which to keep control of our interaction she scribbled an asterisk next to something she was reading and then looked up.

'So,' she said, easing back slightly on her chair, 'how are you settling in?'

The gentleness in her voice was a surprise, as was the hint of a sympathetic smile on her face when she looked at me. It felt good to be in the company of a woman again, even one whose job was to assess my dangerousness. Her manner gave me the impression that she was kind and considerate – everything I and the hard prison environment were not.

'I'm fine,' I said – my usual response whenever I was asked how I was – and then I started talking. I told her I thought the food was OK, 'better than at Wandsworth', and that it was good not be locked in a cell for twenty-three hours a day and to have access to regular showers. I went on about the prison generally, recounted my journey in the back of the prison van, mentioned my meeting with the Governor. 'He seems like a decent bloke,' I said. 'The only real downside so far is the work I have to do in the workshop.' I hadn't realised that I'd been wittering on so much I'd barely given her the chance to say anything.

'What's the job they've given you?' she said eventually.

When I told her she shook her head in mock puzzlement. I didn't want her to think I was complaining. I really didn't mind the job. 'At least I'm out of the cell for a good part of the day,' I said.

She nodded and then said, 'There are better jobs in the prison once people here get to know you,' she said. 'You might want to keep your eye out for a job in the Braille unit.'

I had no idea what a Braille unit was, but didn't want to appear ignorant and nodded back. I wanted to keep talking, but suddenly she was closing my folder and signalling with her body language that the session was over.

'Thank you very much for your time,' she said finally. 'I'd like to see you again next month, if that's all right?'

I had to make an effort to conceal my disappointment that our conversation had come to an end. It seemed to me to have been such a short chat. Politely I said that of course that was fine and I looked forward to seeing her again when the time came. I left her office and made my own way back to my cell. When I sat down on my bed and looked at my watch I saw that I had been with Joan for nearly two hours and it was me who had done almost all of the talking.

Compared to Wandsworth life on the wing at Wakefield was not altogether disagreeable. Fewer hours banged up in my cell was a big relief. The gloom, misery and general sense of hopelessness that the regime in Wandsworth generated had been hard to deal with, but that year of virtual isolation had been fruitful in one sense. The life sentence had stopped me in my tracks. I'd never had the luxury of so much time to think, which I'm sure prepared me for the conversations I was to have with Joan. Though I didn't know it then being able to speak to her was going to be the key to finding a way to live again.

With its education department, chapel, gymnasium and work-shops and people like Joan who wanted to help people like me, I began to see that there might be possibilities in Wakefield. Like everyone else I fell in with the routine dictated by the bell and gradually developed a pattern of existence. Weekdays I went to the workshop mornings and afternoons. In the evenings I went to the library or the gym. On Friday evenings I watched the weekly video film that the prison showed on one of the wing televisions.

Weekends we were allowed out in the exercise yard for an hour in the mornings and on to the football field for an hour and a half in the afternoons. During bang-up I read my library books or listened to music, drama or current affairs on my little transistor radio. Though it was good to be out of the cell for so many hours on and off during the day the constant forced daily interaction with so many strangers with varying levels of dysfunction was exhausting. It was a relief to get back behind the door at night and know there would be no serious disturbances for the next eleven hours or so.

It was another six weeks before I saw Joan again. The procedure to get me to her office from the workshop was the same as before but with different escorting prison officers. Just like the first time, once the movement had been recorded in the Cat A book the lead officer simply opened Joan's office door without knocking, walked in and announced, 'One on, ma'am.'

This session included tests I recognised as similar to those I had undertaken during the early weeks of the French Foreign Legion selection process. After we'd exchanged some small talk about prison life Joan produced a couple of exercise books and some forms and asked me to fill them in and answer the questions, 'As honestly as you can, please.' I felt I could trust Joan, but I was nervous of her at the same time. She wasn't like a prison officer but she still carried keys.

I filled in the forms, answering the questions in the manner of the person I thought I wanted to be, rather than the amoral character I believed I had become. I noticed that some of the questions could be cross-referenced with others by whoever was checking them, I guessed in order to try to ascertain their level of reliability. It was hard to work out the most favourable answer with Joan sitting only a couple of feet away from me. She appeared to be attending to some paperwork as I sat quietly scribbling my responses, but for all I knew that was just a ploy. Maybe she was sitting there concentrating on what I was doing from the edge of her peripheral vision. Maybe we were both playing a game and trying our best not to let the other know.

I was over an hour completing Joan's assessment papers. When I finished I cleared my throat, sat up and placed the pen she had let me use on the desk.

She took a few moments before looking up from her paper-work. 'All done?' she said.

'Yes,' I said, 'thank you.'

She shuffled up my answer papers and the exercise books and put them in a folder. 'These will give us an idea of who you are,' she said.

I feigned nonchalance, but inside I winced. It seemed like I had been a phoney all my life. They would have a job on their hands finding out who I was when even I wasn't sure of the answer. Back in my cell I just hoped that the answers I had given would give them the impression that I was not the completely hopeless case I thought I was.

Trying to acclimatise to prison time meant getting used to living the same day over and over again. Real time moved slowly. Then I'd wake up and find that a week had passed, or a month. The monotony of the regime was broken only by occasional moments of high drama. An IRA man called Sean set off an incendiary device made from thousands of match-heads in a toilet recess on my wing. Everybody cheered him from behind their cell doors as he was dragged away by the control and restraint team – otherwise known as the MUFTI squad.

Out on the exercise yard one morning the sound of a commotion and raised voices made everyone look up. A number of cells on the top-floor landing, the 'fours', were being refurbished and scaffolding had been erected outside the windows. One of Sean's IRA colleagues, a man called Hughie, had climbed out of a cell window that had had its frame removed for repair and leapt on to the scaffold pursued by two prison officers who grabbed him by the arms. In one hand he had a hammer – his other hand was a clenched fist. As he wrestled with the officers he started shouting, 'Freedom! Freedom!' Seconds later men from the exercise yard began yelling abuse at the prison officers and soon it seemed that the whole yard was roaring. The sound was incredible. The officers on yard-guard duty started blowing their whistles in earnest bringing streams of their colleagues running from the wings and a few minutes later they had the yard surrounded. Still we roared. It was an invigorating moment and brought us all together for a little while. The Irishman was eventually overpowered when other prison officers arrived to assist their colleagues and dragged him back inside. Later on the wings the momentary prisoner camaraderie he had inspired quickly dissipated. That was one thing I was learning fast about prisoners – how suspicious we all were of each other and how fickle.

Despite the ever-present sense of mutual distrust on the landings I did make some new friendly associates. It was a relief to find that not everybody was deranged or psychopathic. Dave was a former postman serving two life sentences for shooting dead two men who had been harassing his mother over a debt. Short, several stones overweight and asthmatic when he was sentenced, Dave had taken up running around the prison yard, raising thousands of pounds in sponsorship for various charities while shedding the weight and virtually curing his asthma. Dave was a motivational character, determined and focused. When I asked him one night in between shots as we played a game of snooker how he was managing to stay so positive while serving a life sentence, he thought for a moment and then said, 'It was hard at first – and it still is. But I thought fuck it, I've been sentenced to life so I'm going to live.'

I was a long way from being convinced that it was possible to live in prison, but Dave's attitude helped me to fashion my thinking about how I was going to do my time. So much of it was going to be about attitude. George, a Scot, had killed a man he claimed had been an intruder in his house. He said he'd heard noises downstairs in the early hours and when he went down to investigate became involved in a fierce struggle. The weapon he'd used in the killing was an ornamental sword he had taken from his lounge wall in an effort to protect himself, he told the jury. When evidence emerged that his victim had been seeing George's wife behind his back the jury decided it was no coincidence and convicted him of murder. When we met he was in the process of applying for a transfer to the Scottish prison system. 'There's too many mind games down here,' he said. 'Up the road you know where you stand. Here they spend all their time trying to get into your head.' George had been brought up in Glasgow's tough Easterhouse Estate before, ironically, moving to England to get away from the violence of gang life. Despite his gruff manner he was a steadying influence on the wing and an easy man to be around.

Another pal was Howie. He had a battery-powered record player and was always playing his favourite Gerry Rafferty album *City to City*. We all loved that album. In his early twenties Howie had strangled his girlfriend after a minor tiff. He'd tried to plead manslaughter, citing 'diminished responsibility' as a result of the mood swings he experienced when his diabetes caused his blood-sugar levels to fluctuate. Unconvinced, his jury too found him guilty of murder. An educated young man before prison, Howie could not have been more of a gentleman. His dream, he said, was to continue his education in prison and train to be a teacher when he was eventually released.

Nobody said anything, but we all knew a teaching career for Howie would never be anything more than a fantasy. When his blood-sugar levels got low his temperament changed dramatically. He was forever having difficulties accessing his medication from health-care staff, which exacerbated his condition. You knew when he was having problems. A dark shadow fell over his face and he became sulky and petulant and impossible to speak to. We never saw him get overtly angry, but it wasn't hard to imagine what might happen in an intimate relationship if his mood suddenly turned black. It was apparent to anyone who got to know him on the landings that in all probability he had been telling the truth at his trial.

Finally there was inveterate smiler Fowzie. He was the only survivor of the hostage takers who had been overwhelmed by the SAS after seizing the Iranian Embassy in London in 1980. Aged twenty-eight when I met him, Fowzie still looked like a skinny boy and had only survived the SAS assault on the Embassy, he said, because some of the hostages had recognised his vulnerability and shielded him. Convicted of two murders, he was serving life with a minimum term of twenty-five years, yet a more gentle soul inside the prison would have been hard to find.

These were my associates on the wing, with whom I often played snooker, cards or backgammon. It brought some light relief to have people around that I felt reasonably safe with and with whom I could enjoy some easy conversation without having to put up any kind of front. We had all been convicted of terrible crimes – and all of us harboured significant faults and flaws – yet when we associated we shared humour and exchanged banter that would not have been out of place around a pool table in any local public house. We never talked about our crimes – or for that matter any of our failings – but we all knew each other's business. It's the way of prison to know who's who – to know the strengths and weaknesses of your neighbours and acquaintances. But even though I was finding a way to live on the wing and those that I tentatively trusted seemed to trust me, the only time I came close to feeling in any way authentic was during my interviews with Joan.

During the course of my early call-ups I had formed the view that Joan had a genuine interest in helping the disturbed, the damaged and the broken of society. A couple of times I was on the brink of opening up to her. But I had to be careful. Another neighbour, a man called Vic who was serving time for safe-breaking, had noticed my name on the board for a 'psycho call-up' one day and told me just before the lunchtime bang-up, 'Don't forget, they only know what you tell them.' I had convinced myself that my best chance of survival would be to maintain the line I had given them from the beginning. If I said I was innocent for long enough maybe they would start to believe me. Except the more I saw of Joan the more difficult planning to lie to her was becoming.

About a year after I landed in Wakefield I was on my sixth call-up in Joan's office when I let down my defences for the first time. As usual I sat quietly waiting for her to finish writing notes in my file on her desk. After all this time and through all our conversations she still hadn't asked me about my claims of innocence. In fact she had said nothing at all about my crimes. Finally she closed my file and looked up. 'Well,' she said, 'have you thought about what we talked about last time?'

We had discussed the way people become who they become. Joan had explained to me that this was a complicated process and that the way our lives turned out depended on many factors. Something she said that made me think about my life journey was that nobody chose the life they were born into, 'But we're all born lovable,' she said. I found that such an obvious truth, yet it was something I had never before considered. Now it sounded profound.

She talked about the way we make decisions and choices. She said that generally people reacted to the same circumstances in different ways. 'We are all individuals,' she said, 'and that's how we think, act and react – as individuals.' I had never tried to blame my problematic behaviour on anyone else. As far as I could see I was just who I was. I had made the choices that had led me through the prison gates. Although when Joan asked me if I had my time over again would I make similar choices I answered without hesitation, 'No.'

'Why not?' she said.

'Because they were so obviously the worst choices I could ever have made.'

When she asked me whether I believed that at the time, I said I didn't know. 'I don't actually remember making them,' I said.

Joan said that good choices and decisions depended on good circumstances and good information. She said that few of us sat and pondered the costs and benefits during everyday decision-making. 'Most decisions are made instinctively,' she said, 'on the spur of the moment. If you are in a good place in life, in yourself, the chances are they'll be good decisions, leading to good actions – bearing in mind that for every action there is a reaction.' She said it was important to think about the consequences of any actions that any of us might be contemplating. Ill-thought-out actions so often resulted in reactions which could not have been anticipated. In chaotic lives – however they had become that way – the reactions to actions made through bad choices and decision-making could be catastrophic, 'as in your case'.

Joan told me that nobody was born bad, and that whatever a person might have done to end up in prison, it did not define all of who that person was. These were notions I had already been exploring in my head during the long hours of bang-up in Wandsworth, but it was hard sitting in there with this kind, humane lady and for the first time inwardly confronting all my sins. I had behaved as badly towards others as it was possible to behave, yet I had to hang on to the idea that I wasn't inherently a bad person. For all my failings I never went out wilfully looking to harm anyone.

'I was trying to get you to see that we are all much more than the sum of the result of our actions, whether good or bad,' she said. 'Even though you are in here you still have choices to make – important choices. My job is to try and help you to make the right ones. I want you to move forward. But before you can do that you need to understand your past and the path that led you here. Just as importantly, I have to understand it. And we can only achieve that by talking.'

I was still determined to stick to my innocent line if the subject arose. I was sure in my heart that, no matter how long they kept me in jail and no matter how many times Joan or her colleagues interviewed me, so long as I was alive I was never going to acknowledge any guilt or face up to the truth. The hole I had dug myself with the not-guilty plea had got deeper and deeper with every week that passed. But I wanted to talk to her. I wanted to know how I had become what I had become. I wanted to believe I was redeemable. Joan's gentle, non-judgemental tone gave me hope. She made me feel safe and – despite all I had done – she made me feel that I might have some value.

In my cell at night and in the workshop during the day I had been thinking long and hard about my past. Joan was making me feel like an ordinary person. She was making me think that had certain things in my early life outside been different then I might have been able to have a life like any other right-thinking, normally functioning member of society. In some ways these thoughts were frightening. But in other ways they gave me hope. That was why I was keen to cooperate with her. Her office became another refuge – a place where we might both find the truth.

'So,' she said, 'you've been thinking. That's good. Can you tell me now then, when do you remember being happy?'

I took a deep breath. It wasn't even remotely a question I had anticipated. Happy? That was a tough one.

We sat in silence, me staring at my knees as my mind rummaged for a happy memory. All I could find was misery, strife and pain. Anything that looked like happiness I knew had only been play-acting. In company I always tried to smile for the camera. There were recollections aplenty of drunken revelry, almost all of which ended painfully for me and others – and a number of remembered intense floods of relief whenever I was released from police or prison custody. Those first few steps into the fresh free air were always heady and exhilarating. But how do you define happiness? A jolly picnic with friends or loved ones? I couldn't remember any of those. A family celebration – a wedding? A birthday? I couldn't recall a single one. A holiday perhaps? I'd never been on one. Sometimes it felt like I had always been searching for something. I was just never sure what it was. I doubted it was happiness. Peace, maybe. Love – I'd tasted that, I thought I had a lot to give and wanted it badly – I just couldn't trust that when I loved anyone could truly love me back.

Suddenly I remembered my moment of joy. I lifted my head quickly and looked at Joan's face. Her eyes opened wide in anticipation. 'Watching my first daughter being born,' I spluttered, gleeful at the memory. 'As she emerged into the world, all grey and wrinkled, I remember a huge surge of joyfulness,' I said. That was a lovely moment, beautiful, exquisite.

Her mother was so young and needed a strong, capable mate who could care for her and provide for a family. My behaviour was becoming more erratic – alcohol, violence and self-loathing were destroying any chance I had of being who I thought I wanted to be. It was only going to be a matter of time before I failed them both completely and I knew it even then. But for those few minutes when that vulnerable little thing took her first breaths and squeaked her first shrill cries of life I think I was happy.

I was just as happy when my second daughter was born, although for a much briefer time. She was born when I was in

Pentonville Prison; I'd asked the Governor if I might be allowed to be taken to be present for her arrival but he'd refused. A telephone message had been relayed to me by a prison officer who lifted the spyhole on the cell door and shouted, 'Congratulations, you've got a little girl!' For a brief while inside I felt elated. I now had two little girls. I should have been proud. Instead I felt pitiful. How much lower could a father get than to be lying on a bed in a prison cell being told such wonderful news through a hole in the door by a guard?

Now sitting quietly in Joan's office I thought about the disadvantages with which I had saddled those two new people, neither of whom had chosen the life they had been born into. I was just glad that, thanks to their mothers, both had been blessed with lives that hopefully would be much better than mine. Eventually I asked Joan if we could talk about something else. 'Take your time,' she said. 'Do you want to tell me about when you were a child?'

The next few call-ups were hard going.

24

For the best part of my second year at Wakefield the conversations I had during call-ups with Joan involved me reliving my childhood over and over while she offered some tentative interpretations of my 'drivers' and 'triggers' – the factors which pre-empted my deviant and criminal behaviour. Her assertions that much of what had happened to me when I was very young had not been my fault were bitter-sweet assurances. She said that I had absorbed a great deal of the negative judgements that had been levelled at me when I was a child. 'Children learn to be who they are going to be from those around them as they are developing,' she said. 'The infant psyche acts like a sponge, soaking up programming information from its surroundings.'

She said that in my case I was vulnerable on a number of fronts. Just the fact that my mother had disappeared from my life so unexpectedly was going to have an effect. But without any comforting explanations from other responsible adults and with no reassurance that I was still going to be safe and loved it was inevitable that I'd be left with severe and enduring insecurities. 'Being shuttled around from pillar to post after you were taken from your home in Thompson Street and then being subjected to violence, without any solace or comfort,' she said, 'was bound to have a detrimental effect on your development.'

She was clear about the impact of adult influence on a child's self-perception. 'If parents tell their children they are no good the likelihood is that the children will believe them,' she said. 'If it's beaten into them they will believe it for sure.' To me this made some sense. For such a long time I had thought of myself as unintelligent, unlikeable and not worth very much. I had no idea why – I thought it was just the way I was. Any time I managed to get people to like me, respect me or love me I thought it was because of my play-acting – that I had manipulated them with my ability to present a persona that hid my 'true' inferiority. Through talking to Joan I was beginning to understand that much of my harmful behaviour had been driven by a powerful subconscious need to reveal what I believed to be my true self – a twisted way of testing whether anyone would still like me or care about me if they knew the 'real' unpleasant, unlovable, stupid me. The danger came when my abusive use of alcohol took away my intense inhibitions and unlocked so much of my suppressed anger and hurt.

I had never spent so much time before thinking about my past and going over it in such detail. Who does? The most frightening and painful aspect of my discussions with Joan was the realisation that I might not have been as bereft of good qualities as I'd thought before my slide into regular criminal behaviour – and that even then I had still been redeemable. The internal agony that this caused me was indescribable. Hatred for those who had taken my courage when I was so young and when I needed it most burned inside me.

When I told Joan how angry I was at my father and Aunt Stella she said that this was natural. 'Natural?' I said. Christ, I was angry.

Joan said it was all right to be angry, 'But it might help you to forgive them,' she said.

Forgive them? How does anyone forgive someone who has caused them so much pain and confusion? I wasn't even sure how to go about forgiving anyone. Did it need prayers? Did I need to go to church? Joan said both of these might make it easier. 'But all you have to do is imagine the person in your mind and whisper, "I forgive you."' And that's what I did, in my cell, in the dark – and immediately I felt freed from their estimation of who I was.

During one call-up Joan presented me with the complete documented account of my failed life. My criminal record was laid out on her desk. It was the first time I had ever seen my criminal history on paper – my 'pre cons'. There were seven A4 pages. I counted fifty-one criminal convictions, ranging from burglary to theft, deception, receiving stolen goods, multiple driving offences, offensive-weapon possession, threatening behaviour, criminal damage, assault – and finally murder. I looked at the date of my first court appearance, for breaking into the television factory. It was just a month after my eleventh birthday. In hindsight and in the context of where I had ended up it looked so trivial. I understood that what I had done would not have been trivial to whoever was in charge of the factory. But had I been a criminal? Did I need punishment? If I had been looking at the history of someone else I was sure I would have seen a little boy who was no more than a troubled, bone-raggedy scamp in dire need of care, attention and, dare I say it, love.

I was young and perhaps not as well-adjusted as most children that age, but I had known the difference between right and wrong and I knew it was wrong to steal and tell lies. If anyone had pressed me at the time, however, I would have been at a loss to explain *why* I was expected to choose right over wrong. I had no learned appreciation of morality. My behaviour seemed to be driven by whatever I instinctively decided was necessary in any given set of circumstances to get me through a day safely. I'd been a thief and a liar since long before my first arrest and conviction. My father's punitive violence towards me had no remedial impact on my troublesome behaviour. If punishment had ever been going to deter me from behaving badly I would never have put a foot wrong in my life.

'How do you feel looking at your criminal record?'

I think Joan had a good idea how I was feeling. My past criminality was just so appalling. She had never asked me about the murders – my 'index offences' – and I'd never said anything. The distractions of the prison regime, my educational activities and my call-ups with her had, in a way, protected me from having to face up to them.

'Angry,' I said finally, 'angry, ashamed, guilty. I wish I'd never been born.'

'Understanding is not excusing' was one of Joan's catchphrases. I knew there were no excuses for any of my criminal actions, even the relatively petty, childish stuff. But since those long days and nights locked in my cell in Wandsworth Prison my need to understand had been growing. Joan was giving me the tools to try and work myself out.

'Most of the people in this prison have been hurt and damaged at some point in their formative years and the rest of us have had to pay for it,' she said. 'Unless we try to understand we'll have no chance of ever resolving what drives such harmful behaviour.'

Earlier that year Joan had persuaded me to enrol in education classes. I resisted. More than once I told her, 'Joan, I'm too thick for education,' which irritated the hell out of her. I suppose it was what I'd been told when I was young and had believed ever since.

Joan persisted. 'Nobody is "thick" as you put it. We are all born with potential and we owe it to ourselves to realise that potential – to become who we should be.'

'To become who we should be'. I loved that phrase. Joan's contention that early events and actions beyond our control have a profound effect on our development and behaviour sounded so rational. She also said that it was possible to rectify the impact of most damage done, almost no matter how long ago or how deep-rooted. 'If the desire is there, with effort, commitment and determination, self-realisation is achievable,' she said. 'Self-realisation' was another term she used that I had never heard before. What she meant was that now I had food, clothing, accommodation and a structured existence I should be able to break away from habitual impulsive and reactive behaviour and choose more effectively how to conduct myself. Even though my choices were limited in prison there were still plenty to be made.

'Get out of bed, don't get out of bed. Go to the workshops, don't go to the workshops. Read a book, don't read a book. Educate yourself . . . You see? Little choices and big choices – you have to make those choices when options are presented.'

Joan's calm rationality helped me to clarify my thinking. I would have loved to have had the values and integrity she had. When I thought about it there was no reason why I could not adopt her principles and learn to live a life that had meaning and purpose, a decent life – and maybe one day become 'who I should have been', even in prison. Her job was to assess my risk, my 'dangerousness' – but her underlying manner was very much that of a champion, something I had never had before. She inspired hope that it might be possible for me to find a better way to live and as the weeks and months edged by I became more determined that that would be my goal. I was still pretty convinced however that I was beyond being able to be educated. I was almost thirty years old. Sitting behind a desk like an overgrown schoolboy held very little appeal. But eventually and only as a means of acknowledging Joan's efforts I put my name down for evening classes.

Initially I wasn't sure what class to opt for and then I remembered my old 'secret good thing' – when all those years ago at school I'd regularly achieved good marks for English. And so, with some apprehension, I applied to join the English class and much to my surprise the ability still appeared to be there. Analysing texts was a joy, so were the discussions about the importance of using the right words when writing essays – and of course so was my old favourite – reading aloud to the rest of the class.

The teacher was a pretty young woman who by day worked in a local private school. Her prison job provided her with a supplementary income. She had two children, she told us, and it was for them that she and her husband worked all the hours they could. 'They deserve the best start in life we can give them,' she said. It made me think of my own mother and father and their endeavours to build a better life when they first left the poverty of their lives in Scotland. When my mother was cleaning and working in the mills and my father was labouring or driving – it must have been to try and give me and my sister a better start in life than they'd had. Instead the crash destroyed us all.

The teacher used to give me extra homework to be completed in my cell at night. I'd only been in her class a few months when she told me I was ready. 'For what?' I said.

'For an exam,' she said.

Two weeks later four of us sat the GCE O level exam. To her delight we all passed. I couldn't wait for my next session with Joan so I could show her my certificate. When she took it out of the large brown envelope and looked at my grade 'A' she said casually, 'I told you we all have abilities and potential.'

In the next session she gave me a book to read: *One Day in the Life of Ivan Denisovich*, the first published story by Alexander Solzhenitsyn, the Russian writer who had been imprisoned in the gulags. 'Read this and have a think about the nature of imprisonment and its place in society,' she said. Before that I had put little thought into my reading. It was a pleasure, sometimes I learned things, as I did when I read the powerful story of Alfred Dreyfus when I was in Wandsworth. But I'd never read specifically to learn or to enhance my thinking. Up until then I used reading to help me not to think.

This book was published in 1962 and covers just one day in the life of a prisoner in a Soviet labour camp who, similarly to Dreyfus, has been accused of spying. He's a political prisoner and he's innocent. Before the book was published the Soviet people had almost no knowledge of what life was like in a gulag. Though the physical hardships suffered by the Russian prisoners were incomparable to what I was experiencing, what surprised me were the similarities I recognised in the psychology of captivity. For the first time I realised that the effect of captivity on human beings and our reaction to it is universal. Feigning servility to authority and duplicitous interaction between prisoners were instinctive survival mechanisms and the only quality that commanded collective respect was moral strength. The book also made me realise that the experience for the prisoner whether guilty or innocent was the same.

Joan gave me other books by Solzhenitsyn, including *The Gulag Archipelago* and *Cancer Ward*. Then she gave me *Crime and Punishment* by Fyodor Dostoevsky – a dark, gripping story that haunted me for a long time and made me think deeply about the motivations behind every criminal action I ever made. The anti-hero, Raskolnikov, has committed murder and when, near the end of the book, he finally confesses to a woman friend she replies, '"What have you done to yourself?"' Until then I had only considered the damage my crimes had caused others. This book made me aware of how badly crime damages the perpetrator. There were days when I felt so low and empty that I wondered if living again was ever going to be possible. When I told Joan how I felt she said, 'There is always a way back . . . if you want it badly enough and are prepared to work hard enough.'

Deciding I wanted it, I joined other classes, history and geography. I did more homework in my cell, learning about how society worked and how the cultures of different countries had evolved over the centuries. Learning seemed to give me strength. The books that Joan lent me were as educational as any textbooks. Other than in a minimal way when I was in the Foreign Legion I had never thought about how other societies had emerged. I knew so little about my own country. The more I learned the more I wanted to learn. As my big empty head filled with knowledge it was as if somebody had switched on a light bulb and illuminated all the shadows. Education lifted me like I had never been lifted before.

One day a prison officer opened my cell door and asked me if I would like to work in the Braille unit. 'The tests indicate you have the aptitude for it,' he said. The tests had been those I had undertaken during my earliest sessions with Joan. Transcribing the written word into Braille took some mental skill and discipline and apparently my responses in the tests had indicated I might be good at it. He explained what the job entailed and said there was a place for me if I wanted it.

Working in the Braille unit was so far removed from the mindless purposelessness of working in the engineering workshop.

This had to be one of the best jobs in the prison. There were just fourteen of us, each with our own desk and Braille transcribing machine – a Perkins Brailler – which looked a little like a crude typewriter with just six keys. Pressing down hard on different combinations of the keys created raised dotted patterns in neat rows on large squares of heavy brown paper which blind people could run their fingers across to read. The technique was learned from a book called *The Braille Primer* which you had to work through stage by stage. There was a pattern for every letter and then there were patterns for letters that were regularly found together such as 'er', 'ed', or 'ing'. These were called 'contractions'.

It took a couple of months to get the hang of it. I had never done anything for other people before – never understood that giving could be more satisfying than taking. Being able to do this Braille work for ordinary souls who could not see was about as worthwhile a way imaginable of spending time in prison. It also helped me cope with the guilt of my crimes.

What surprised me in the Braille unit was the number of prisoners there who before their convictions had lived the kind of lives far removed from mine. There were three men who had been teachers. One had been a lawyer, another an executive for a large, well-known food-processing company and another had been an eminent surgeon. These were educated, capable men who'd had families and lived in the kind of houses I used to look at when I was on the streets wondering how anyone got to live in such a place. The surgeon had been to boarding school and often jokingly likened prison life to what he'd experienced there. I guess they could have been described as middle-class professionals – yet all had been convicted of murder.

It puzzled me on the one hand – on the other it reminded me of Joan's tenet that how we become who we become is a complicated process and there are no simple answers to why some people behave particularly badly towards others. It did seem relevant to me that the majority of the people I lived alongside in prison appeared to have had similar life experiences to mine – they had been in care, had limited education, had had family problems from a young age and had issues with alcohol, drugs or mental health. Yet as Joan said there were huge numbers of people who had had difficult and painful formative years but who did not grow up to cause harm and distress to others. 'Remember what I said, that we are all individuals and react in individual ways to similar situations. Damage sustained in childhood is still damage,' she explained, 'and will always manifest in adulthood in some form or other. Mental illness, difficulties in relationships, emotional insecurity, chronic guilt – deviant criminal behaviour is just one symptom.'

I was surprised to find that I could transcribe Braille as well as any of those I considered intellectually superior. At first and absurdly, considering we were all prisoners serving life for dreadful crimes, my instinctive response was to adopt a subservient manner towards them. But as I became more proficient – often being consulted when pictures or graphics needed to be described in detail alongside the Braille transcription – my confidence grew. When I discussed this with Joan she said, 'Well, you too could have been a teacher or a doctor or a lawyer if you'd grown up in the right kind of environment.' What was hard to get my head round was that the people I was talking about had grown up in that environment, had become teachers, doctors and lawyers – surgeons even – and still ended up in prison alongside me serving life.

Steadily as the weeks and months passed I was creating a pattern of living that was giving me a sense of purpose. My job during the day in the Braille unit and the various classes I was attending in the evening, alongside the books that Joan was giving me to read, were providing me with more fulfilment than I had ever before experienced. Having a handful of good associates on the wing coupled with my visits to the gym and my running around the exercise yard at weekends afforded me a sense that I was actually living rather than just existing.

When the head of the education department approached me one evening and asked me if I would consider embarking on a higher education programme I thought he was kidding. 'We think you are capable of studying for a degree,' he said.

Part of me believed deep down I could do it – but a bigger part of me needed reassurance. Hoping for just that I said, 'But I don't think I'm intelligent enough.'

The head looked at me as if I was teasing him, but I was being sincere. 'Well, it's up to you,' he said. 'If you want to try it we'll support you.'

Alongside this process of enlightenment I was also learning more about the unpredictability of prison life. I became friendly in the gym with a thickset chap called Chris from another wing – two or three times a week we would walk in the exercise yard together. He was a quiet man, a few years older than me and serving twelve years for an armed robbery on a betting shop. He talked a lot about his family and the break-up with his wife. He'd lost his job and ended up owing maintenance for his nine-year-old daughter. 'I wanted to give her better,' he said. 'I must have been crazy to think armed robbery was the solution.'

From what I gathered he had never been in trouble with the police before and was just a regular working man who seemed to have had some kind of breakdown. Fully expecting Chris to be joining me as I walked out on to the yard one day I spotted one of his associates dodging about in an agitated manner. When he saw me he ran towards me at full pelt. I stopped walking.

'It's Chris,' he said, before catching his breath. I thought he was going to pass on a message, that he'd been shipped out or something. It was worse. 'Chris is dead,' he said. 'He topped himself last night.'

I couldn't believe it. I'd seen him in the gym just two days earlier. There were no signs. He seemed such a stable character. I was stunned. 'You're kidding,' I said.

The man explained that Chris had made a rope from a shredded bed sheet and hanged himself from his cell-window bars. It was exactly what the man in the cell above mine had done that black Christmas at Wandsworth.

A few weeks later I returned to the wing from the Braille unit one day and found Dave the former postman waiting for me at the gate. He looked glum.

'What's up?' I said.

'It's Howie,' he said. 'He went into a diabetic coma last night with his face in his pillow and never woke up.'

Howie was just twenty-two. Diabetes wasn't supposed to be a killer at his age. The consensus among the men on the wing was that the difficulties he'd been having getting his medication from staff were as much to blame as his illness.

Soon after Howie died a tiny Indian chap I'd made pals with called Mr Patel, who made curries in a ground-floor cell that had been turned into a kitchenette by the installation of a two-ring electric cooker and a sink, began giving away his food stash. He sent a message for me to go to his cell. I pushed open his door and found him lying in the dark.

'Take,' he said, pointing to a bag of spices and some tins.

'Hang on a minute,' I said. 'What's happening?'

He said he wouldn't be here in the morning. 'Tomorrow I go. I done too long. Finished,' he said.

He too was a lifer and I knew he wasn't getting out any time soon and neither was he down for a transfer. To humour him I took the stuff but said I'd give it back to him if he didn't 'go'. When they opened his cell the next day they found him dead in bed. After more than ten years in jail his heart had given up.

In doing my time I tried to be a bit like Dave the former postie. He kept his head down and didn't appear to have any enemies.

Fear still loomed over every interaction but I combated mine by using the gym, keeping fit and staying alert. In my dealings with fellow prisoners I tried to be as courteous as was appropriate, without seeming too afraid. I was well aware by then that kindness and politeness in prison are routinely seen as a weakness. When the man on my wing who attended the weekly meetings to choose the two videos we got to see at the weekends said he was getting shipped out I agreed to take his place. One day I arrived at the library late and all that was left for us for our Saturday-night film show was *E. T.* It was essentially a children's film about a friendly alien. I took it back and wrote up the schedule on the wing noticeboard.

The next morning in the breakfast queue I bumped into a short, stocky character known to have a short temper. Before I could apologise he started shaking his fist and ranting. 'Fucking *E. T.*! We don't fucking want fucking *E. T.*!' I'd forgotten all about the film I'd brought back. In any case it never occurred to me that it was going to upset anyone.

People were staring in our direction. The louder he roared the more heads turned. He needed calming down. 'The screws will be on us in a minute,' I said.

Suggesting I make us a cup of tea I invited him to follow me into my cell. Once he was inside his tirade and fist-waving became hysterical. 'Fucking *E. T.*, you cunt!' he yelled. He was in danger of losing control and I knew we were microseconds from violence. Intending only to eject him from the cell I grabbed the front of his shirt. He sidestepped and pulled me round full circle. He must have seen over my head that my cutlery was standing in a plastic cup on a shelf that was now directly above his head. He reached up behind him with his right hand and grabbed hold of my knife, thrusting it down with huge force into the corner of my left eye. It happened so fast and unexpectedly that I still hadn't let go of his shirt. The knife was only plastic, but it was hard and rigid enough to cut meat. In the couple of seconds it took me to react properly he had raked it down my face and hammered it into my scalp more than half-a-dozen times before I managed to bring my head down fast and crash it hard against the bridge of his nose. I honestly didn't want to hurt him but I had to stop him stabbing me before he took out one of my eyes.

He slumped on to the end of my bed, blood gushing from his nose. I went to help him up. 'Are you OK?' I said.

Suddenly he sprang back to life and rushed out of the cell leaving me alone and dazed. The whole incident had been so ridiculous. I needed to see what I looked like and took out my shaving mirror. The only ones we had were small Perspex squares that had been painted on one side with reflective paint. The image you saw when you shaved was like something you would expect to see staring back at you in a fairground hall of mirrors. The face that I was looking at now was even more grotesque. My left eye was closing fast and blood from the wounds in my scalp trickled down alongside the swollen dark tracks the knife had left on my forehead and cheeks. I was a mess. The toilet recess was just a few yards down the landing from my cell so I darted out with my wash bowl and filled it with cold water. Back in my cell I soaked my towel and pressed it hard against my face in an effort to reduce the swelling.

I missed breakfast but there was no way I could avoid going to work in the Braille unit. When I was asked what had happened I said I'd collided with a footballer the day before as I jogged around the football pitch. I told Joan the same thing when I turned up for a session with her a few days later. I think she knew I was lying.

'There was nothing I could do to avoid what happened. But I did all I could to make sure I didn't seriously harm anyone,' I said.

'I believe you,' she said. I so needed her to trust that I was telling the truth.

25

Joan and I talked about the various convictions on my record and I told her as much as I could remember about the circumstances. Every serious conviction had resulted from a crime committed whilst I was under the influence of alcohol. I hated myself for being so weak. By the time she brought me to the point where I decided to confess to my part in the murders I was sure there was no hope left of my ever being able to live in any meaningful way. Then she asked me if I knew what empathy was.

'Is it like sympathy?' I said.

'Sympathy is when you feel for someone who is suffering in some way,' she said. 'Empathy is when you imagine what it might be like to be in that person's shoes, looking at the world through their eyes and identifying with them in order to understand their experience.'

I wasn't sure of the point she was making.

'When you pleaded not guilty at your trial, did you consider the effect that would have on the people affected by your crimes?' I lowered my eyes and shook my head. This was the first time she had ever been so specific. 'You could have made it a little easier for them. Do you understand that?'

I did now. I hadn't considered it at the time. All I had been thinking about was myself. It didn't matter what my co-accused was saying. There could be no justification for my lies. I should have told the truth.

'Yes,' I said. I couldn't look at her.

'Can you imagine what it must have been like for them? You have to take responsibility for all the consequences of your actions, as well as the actions themselves. Do you understand that?'

I still couldn't look at her. I was so ashamed of myself. 'Yes,' I said.

I was relieved when the session came to an end before I could make my confession. I wasn't sure that I would ever be able to put it into words. But Joan had brought me to this point with incredible skill and care and I knew I had to. I decided to write it down. After bang-up I spent all night in my cell writing every detail I could remember. It was a long and painful night. After breakfast the next morning I slid the twenty odd pages of truth under her office door. I went to work in the Braille unit as usual and tried not to think about what she would be thinking when she read what I had given her.

By the end of the day I had made up my mind to pack in all my educational activities. Who was I trying to kid? I just could not justify my 'self-improvement', my 'personal development', my 'rehabilitation'. I'd been in denial for too long. Now that I had come clean about my crimes I couldn't face anyone, especially not myself. I still went to the gym, but my workouts became acts of contrition as I hammered myself to sheer exhaustion. In the meantime I'd handed all my educational coursework back to the various teachers. I contemplated putting myself 'down the block' for a few years – having myself located in the punishment block. The shame I felt was overwhelming: the pain I had inflicted on my victims and their families and friends was unforgivable. I kept imagining the funerals. I raged at myself. How could I have behaved like that? How could I? And the biggest question of all: Why?

I didn't know.

During a lunchtime bang-up period almost three weeks after I delivered my confession to Joan I heard the key turn in the cell door and looked up. When the door opened Joan was standing next to the landing officer.

'What are you doing?' she said.

I was lying on my bed reading. 'Nothing,' I said.

She stepped into the cell and I sat up.

'They tell me you've given up your education.' I nodded. She looked right into my eyes. 'For what reason?'

She had never spoken to me so firmly before.

'I can't see the point,' I said.

'You can't see the point?' she said.

I felt stupid. She knew I was hiding from something. The truth was that I couldn't bear to feel good about myself. Feeling good about myself was mental torture.

'Look,' she said. 'You've worked hard with me since you've been here. Working through your issues has not been easy, I know. You said it had helped you and I think it has. You owe it to yourself to try to understand your life so you can come to terms with all that has happened, so that you can live again. And you will live again if you want to. You've made good progress. But you need to have a rethink on this,' she said. 'You can give up. As we discussed before, you have a choice. My view is that you should use your time in prison to do the best you can – and I want you to think about this: you owe it to your victims.' She turned and left the cell and the landing officer banged the door shut.

'You owe it to your victims.' For days Joan's words reverberated in my head. I couldn't sleep. I barely ate. All the stresses and strains of prison life paled in contrast to this idea. It seemed rational but at the same time so distorted. What I owed my victims could never be paid. For the first time I thought seriously about making a little rope and a noose from my bed sheets. I looked at the bars on the window. I could be free within minutes. Why not? Joan's words kept me alive. 'You have a choice. You owe it to your victims.'

I saw Joan another half-a-dozen times before she retired. Those sessions were the most difficult of all. While she gently coaxed and cajoled we talked about the contents of my confession in forensic detail. I cried – in Joan's office, in my cell. Understanding how I had become what I had become before prison was central to my agreeing that it was possible for me to live again. But the more I found out about myself that was positive and the more I came to understand the importance of moral values the deeper became my shame, guilt, regret and sorrow when I thought of my victims. In my drunken criminal thinking I had become so selfish and psychologically detached from other human beings. Every crisis I'd had, from adolescence to adulthood, had been of my own making, and every one pushed me further away from the path to authenticity. Even when I loved, it was only in order to benefit me, to satisfy my needs and no one else's. I couldn't remember one truly authentic relationship.

I chose to live in the end. By choosing to live I was choosing to serve my life sentence, however challenging it got and wherever it was going to take me. Nobody was forcing me to stay incarcerated. It was my choice, to stay alive and serve my time – and I would do it the best way I could, whatever it took. I owed it to my victims. Before she left Joan gave me a postcard. 'I want you to keep this with you and look at it whenever you think you have had enough,' she said. Printed in large letters the inscription on the front of the card read: 'Today is the First Day of the Rest of Your Life.'

The optimum time for a lifer to spend in any one prison was three to five years. I was taken off the Category A list in 1989 and that summer I was transferred to high-security Long Lartin Prison near Evesham in Worcestershire. I'd read about Long Lartin in an article in the *Observer* magazine some months before. There was an interview with a prisoner called Eddie 'Teddy Bear' Watkins. A poem Watkins had written was reproduced in the article, the first line of which was: 'I have sipped from the well of bitterness'.

I landed on B Wing that August and was allocated the cell opposite Watkins's. The design of Long Lartin could not have been more different to that of Wakefield, Wandsworth or Brixton. It was built in 1971 with accommodation specifications that were much more limited than those of the Victorian prisons. There were six wings holding around seventy prisoners each. The cells were tiny, maybe six and a half feet long and seven feet wide. The low ceilings and dull fluorescent light intensified the sense of confinement. The cells were on either side of a narrow corridor called a 'spur', and since there was no space for personal property inside, kit and other items were stored in laundry bags which hung on the wall outside the cell doors.

The claustrophobia down a spur was almost tangible. Watkins was serving a minimum tariff of twenty-five years. My neighbour on one side was Brian Keenan, at the time the highest-ranking IRA officer in custody. On the other side my neighbour was a man serving a minimum of thirty-five years for the murders of five people. I was no longer a Cat A prisoner, but many of my neighbours were and the sentences being served were among the longest I had come across, even back in Monster Mansion.

I soon found out why the nickname for Long Lartin among the prisoners was 'Paranoia City'. Suspicion and distrust were the common ground. Moods could turn from jovial to savage in an instant. Barely a day passed when the alarm bell did not ring on more than one occasion. Half-a-dozen alarms a day was not unusual. I was offered a job in the gym as a cleaner, a 'gym orderly'. It meant I could keep fit and strong and able to handle any trouble that came my way. But how anyone was supposed to become a better human being in that violently unpleasant place was a mystery to me.

As well as my gym job I did some part-time work in a tiny Braille unit a teacher had set up in the education department. That gave me a sense that I was doing something meaningful. In my cell I focused on my books and on my Open University studies – and I started going to chapel. The chapel at Long Lartin was an oasis of peace in a community riven with conflict. I'd learned to play the guitar in Wakefield and took it with me to the chapel on Sundays. I played hymns and joined in concerts organised by the chaplain. The chapel was a refuge for anyone who wanted a bit of respite from the paranoia and violence of the wings.

Encouraged by the chaplain I tried believing in God and went through a religious phase for a while, reading my Bible, saying prayers and almost getting to the point of asking for forgiveness. But the more I learned in the prison mire about the human condition the harder it became to believe in God. The chaplain said that so long as I was contrite, so long as I was penitent, so long as I was remorseful, then God would forgive me. God would forgive me? What did He know of how I felt about my crimes? What could He know of what was in my head and in my heart? 'He knows everything,' the chaplain said. 'He knows everything and He will forgive you if you ask Him.' Much as I respected the chaplain for what he was achieving in that crazy prison, I could not accept his religious assurances. So I rejected his God talk and carried on the way I was, trying to do the best I could despite the tension, the pressure and the ever-present psychological weariness.

The time passed slowly in Long Lartin. Before my first year was out Eddie 'Teddy Bear' Watkins was dead. He took so many pills and smoked so much dope nobody knew whether he'd taken an overdose on purpose or not. I heard his door being opened over a teatime bang-up period. When I looked out through a crack in my cell-door observation flap I saw him being carried out in a black body bag. He was a big character in the prison. He'd shot and killed a customs officer while he was smuggling in a lorryload of cannabis. The officer was the first to be killed on duty in over a hundred and fifty years apparently. Watkins had only served ten years. I don't think he thought he had twenty-five in him.

On 1 April 1990 the Strangeways Riot exploded, raising the temperature in every prison in the country. Two days later a mass escape attempt from our jail was foiled by prison officers who apprehended almost a dozen men including a number of Cat As who had made it to the perimeter wall, but were thwarted when their makeshift ladder collapsed. As the officers and their dogs rounded up the would-be escapees somebody from my wing saw the action from the association room, smashed a window with a mop bucket and began shouting support for the runaways. Somebody heard the window smash and shouted, 'Fucking hell, it's a riot!' Riot fever quickly swept the wing and within minutes the prison officers had fled and the barricades were up.

Soon fires were burning and ripped-out water pipes were flooding the floors. On the opposite spur a number of sex offenders, including one known as the Vicarage Rapist, were cowering in fear. My neighbour in for killing five people went berserk. 'Let's burn the nonces!' He was raving and ranting. Men wearing home-made balaclavas which only had eye holes were running around brandishing lengths of pipe like spears. Another notorious sex offender known as the Barnsley Beast ran to his peers on his spur, corralled them into one cell and barricaded the door shut from the inside. There's no doubt he saved lives that night.

I bagged my books in a couple of pillowcases and guarded my cell door with a table leg. After some hours the IRA man Keenan and several of his comrades on our spur managed to calm the situation. Negotiations began with the riot squad in the early hours of the following day and after a fifteen-hour siege the wing was evacuated peacefully. Six months after that riot the man in for five killings hanged himself in high-security Full Sutton Prison near York.

Soon after the riot I received a letter from Nadine's solicitor. When I saw my daughter Nadia's name in bold on the reference line I thought she might have been asking for me and wanting to know me. She was eleven years old. What did she look like? How did she speak? I'd never tried to contact her, but rarely a day passed when I didn't think about her and her half-sister Louise and wonder how they were getting on. The rest of the letter brought me back to reality. Nadine was now in an established relationship with a successful businessman and he wanted to adopt Nadia. The letter contained a consent form.

I spent some days and nights thinking about how to respond. I didn't want to just sign her away to a stranger, but in my heart I knew I had to. I wrote a long letter to be given to her when she was older, telling her why I had signed. I loved her, he loved her. 'Because you are so loved', I explained.

That letter motivated me to make discreet enquiries about Louise. When I learned that she had been told I was dead I decided it would be better to leave her and her mother alone.

It wasn't all bad news at Long Lartin. The teachers in the education department were magnificent, even after some of the women who worked there had been sexually assaulted in the prison by prisoners. They still worked hard to bring some hope into the place. The chaplain brought staff and prisoners together to perform musicals in the chapel for elderly folk from the local community at Christmas. And in the gym young people with learning disabilities visited every Friday so a group of prisoners, including me, could work with them alongside the gym staff, giving them fun and exercise.

But life on the wings never stopped being challenging. Every other week somebody got stabbed or 'jugged' – scalded with a prison-issue jug of sugared boiling water, the sugar making the water stick so it would maximise the scarring. There were three prisoner-on-prisoner killings in two and a half years, half-a-dozen hostage-takings and numerous serious assaults on staff. I played for the prison rugby team and we often took on teams from the outside. Conflict on the field was a regular feature of the games, but mostly that meant games having to be stopped when players from the prison team attacked each other and had to be pulled apart, much to the visitors' bemusement.

All the time in my cell I focused on my studies and developed my interest in writing, and eventually I became known as 'the man who can write a good letter'. Writing for fellow prisoners letters home, parole representations or complaints to the Governor gave me a sense that I was doing something worthwhile amongst the chaos and the fear.

I was transferred to Cat B Nottingham Prison in January 1992. Another ageing Victorian jail, Nottingham had just one main wing, B Wing, which held two hundred prisoners, including around sixty lifers. It could be fierce living. Some called it the Wild West, others called it Beirut. Burn-outs, juggings and the occasional stabbing kept the tension high. But just like in the other prisons the teachers gave us hope. There were some great prison officers there too, old hands who knew the score and tried to make it safer whenever they could.

I worked as a cleaner in the prison hospital. Then I got a job in the yards, shovelling the shit parcels that were thrown from cell windows every night into a wheelbarrow. Shit parcels came in all shapes and sizes, mostly wrapped in newspaper, but there were jam jars, bean cans, even matchboxes, all filled with shit, and hurled out through the window bars. So much shit seemed to ooze out of that wing it was like a burst sewer. But it gave me a job which allowed me outside and gave me plenty of time to think.

I wrote letters to newspapers, challenging the idea that prisons in the UK were 'holiday camps' and correcting often misinformed and overly sensationalist reports about prisoners and prison life, several of which were published. In 1994 I graduated, majoring in history with the Open University, and the same year I had my first articles published in a national newspaper when Ruth Picardie and Genevieve Fox then at the *Independent* asked me to write something that would give a flavour of the reality of prison life. One article was about the man I knew in Wakefield who hanged himself. The other was about prisoner hierarchies entitled 'Rough Justice in the Jailbirds' Pecking Order'.

Nobody ever called me Erwin in prison. When asked I said I was Jim. I liked being a Jim. It was a name that seemed to describe somebody who was helpful, dependable – and dare I say it, trustworthy. Because I used the gym a lot I grew in physical stature. In Nottingham Prison they called me 'Big Jim'. Several reports written by staff described me as a 'gentle giant'. I liked that a lot. For my first articles in the *Independent* I used the pen name Jim Smith.

Seeing my words set free in print motivated me to pitch other articles and ideas to the press. Then I submitted an article to the annual Koestler Arts Awards, a competition founded by Arthur Koestler that attracted thousands of entries from penal institutions and special hospitals all over the country. There were hundreds of entries for the prose section and that year I won first prize. On the strength of that and my newspaper articles the Prison Service supported my application to the charity the Prisoners' Education Trust for a grant to undertake a distance-learning journalism course.

Writing made me feel I was really living. It also helped me to cope when the Governor called me to his office shortly after I'd finished my journalism course.

'Sit down,' he said. I could tell by his manner that it was bad news. I was determined to take any bad news standing. I braced myself to be told that my father had died. 'Please,' said the Governor, 'please, take a seat.'

The softening of his tone made me more determined not to sit. 'I'll take my bad news standing up, if you don't mind, Governor,' I said.

He moved round from behind his desk and passed me a letter. 'I'm sorry,' he said. His name was Graham Linney and he was one of the finest prison managers I had ever met.

I opened it and read the contents. It was from the Home Office. 'The Minister has decided you will serve a minimum of twenty-five years . . .' That was the gist of it.

Twenty-five years? At my trial the judge told me in open court that I would have to serve a minimum of fourteen years. Instantly I was transported back to the afternoon I first landed in Wandsworth Prison and the weight of my sentence crashed on my shoulders. This was the same sensation pressing down on me, buckling my knees and forcing me to sit. I read the letter again. I had been re-sentenced by a politician, a junior minister acting on behalf of the Home Secretary. The changes I'd made and the way I had lived over the previous ten years meant nothing. And why should they have? My crimes hadn't got any less serious. The pain and grief I had caused were surely still as agonising to the families and friends of my victims.

I'd started my prison journey with at least fourteen years to serve. I'd done ten and now I had at least another fifteen to go.

It takes a long time to change a whole life. I think it took me those ten years to make the changes necessary for me to become who I believed I should have been. By the time I received the re-sentencing letter from the Home Office I was already a long, long way away from who I had been when I stood trial at the Old Bailey.

I had never been a 'goody-goody' in jail but neither had I been a 'baddy-baddy'. I'd never made any plans for freedom. When I did think about it I naively considered that if any of the decision-makers in the Home Office were to take into account the changes I had made during my sentence they might think about releasing me around the fifteen- or sixteen-year mark. But it still wasn't a priority. Living well was what I was trying to do.

I became a Listener when I was at Nottingham, one of a group of prisoners trained by the Samaritans to be there to listen to and support fellow prisoners when they felt suicidal. I helped out in the education department and organised charity events, like sponsored runs around the exercise yard or sponsored training sessions in the gym. Helped by officers and teachers, we prisoners even put on Christmas 'porridge lunches' for local business people who were invited in to see how the prison operated and raise funds for a day centre for disabled children. In prison I had learned about the importance of helping others. Being helpful gave me a reason to justify my own life. Doing good was what I owed my victims. I never forgot what Joan Branton told me. Whenever there were big challenges in prison I remembered her words: 'You have a choice.' Back in my cell with the 'twenty-five-years' letter in my pocket I took out the card she gave me before she retired. 'Today is the First Day of the Rest of Your Life.'

Bless that good woman.

Twenty-five years was a big blow and maybe if I truly hadn't been thinking about the possibility of being released it would not have been such a shock. But in the end I had to be philosophical about it. We lived in a democracy and I had to accept that the people who had made this decision had the right to do so. I had to accept that this new term was what society wanted and I would just have to get on with it.

I never told my father that my minimum custodial term had been increased. I did try to tell him over the phone. A prison officer had allowed me to call him from the wing office. The officer was standing just a couple of feet away from me as I tapped in my father's number and waited. His phone rang out for ages.

I was about to give up when he answered. 'Aye . . . who is it?'

My heart sank. I could tell that he had been drinking. 'Dad,' I said, 'I need to tell you something.' I wished I hadn't called. His speech was low and slow and I could hear Hank Williams singing in the background.

'Erwin. . . whit is it, son?' I heard him take a drink.

'Dad, for fuck's sake,' I said. My head was spinning. I swore at him again.

He was quiet for a moment and then he shouted back at me, 'Who the fuck do you think you're talking to?'

My temper was rising. 'I'm talking to you. Just leave me alone,' I said. 'We're finished.'

From the beginning of my sentence my father had been loyal to me. He'd visited me and written to me over the years and never condemned me for what I had put him through. He must have loved me to have stood by me the way he did. But there was so much that was unsaid between us. There was so much I wanted to ask him, but I'd never had the courage. I wanted to know about my mother. I wanted him to explain his behaviour after she was killed. I wanted to know why he had treated me so badly when I was still a child, when I most needed to be loved. Why had he allowed me to be taken into care? Why had he given up my sister? I wanted to know why he hadn't kept us all together like he promised. Now I needed to tell him about this damned twenty-five years and he was sitting there drunk. All my frustrations with him came to a head. I slammed the phone down and walked out of the office back to my cell. It was the last time we ever spoke.

In doing my time I'd learned to walk the middle line and do what I needed to survive and achieve a way of living that I believed was authentic. But I didn't want to just survive. I searched out ways to do more than just time. I wanted to encourage and motivate those around me to achieve good things in prison in spite of our circumstances and despite the system's low expectations of us. I made some enemies. There were times when I had to stand my ground and act with some aggression to ensure I did not go under. But I never went out of my way to harm anyone. It would be no exaggeration to describe long-term prison life as animalising. But thankfully there is an army of good people who want prisoners to succeed in achieving the changes they need to make.

In 1998, four years after that phone call to my father, a prison officer called Dick Green came to my cell. It was over the teatime bang-up period. When I heard the key in the lock I thought at first it was a cell search, a 'spin'. I was sitting on my chair reading. As the door opened I looked up. Dick Green was one of the old-school officers. A real gentleman with decades of service under his belt who understood how to deal with prisoners in his charge and had more respect in the prison than he probably realised.

'Can I have a word?' he said. 'It's your dad. We've had a call. He passed away two days ago.'

Dick spent a little time with me. He told me about when his father died and the effect it had had on him. 'You'll dream about him,' he said. He told me that after his father's passing he had dreamed about him every night for weeks. 'It's quite comforting,' he said. He told me if I wanted he would see about the possibility of me attending my father's funeral, but there was no way I wanted to stand at my father's grave in chains and I declined the offer. I did so appreciate Dick's sympathetic consideration. It was a courtesy I never asked for or expected, but one I will never ever forget.

My father died alone in his little supported-housing apartment in Epsom, Surrey. I'd never seen his home. He had moved there from the bedsit in Reigate that I did know some years earlier. Dick said that one of my cousins had gone to visit him and found him dead on the living-room floor. He was only sixty-four. I hated the fact that he had died alone, but I think I always knew he would. Despite our fall-out I had hoped I would see him again and I had made up my mind that when I did we would clear the air and talk. His death meant we would never get the chance. There were only a few minutes before official evening unlock for association and Dick was kind enough not to bang me up when he left. But thinking about my father's lonely end intensified the loneliness of my cell. Now it was my turn to cry for us both. I sat on the end of my bed and quietly wept.

In the in-between years my writing activities had grown. I'd become involved in creative writing groups and helped to start prison magazines and organise debates. I still studied in my cell at night, embarking on a second degree with the Open University, this time focusing on sociology and psychology. My work as a cleaner in the prison hospital had made me aware of how big a problem self-harming was among prisoners – and by then I knew how prevalent suicide was in our prisons. In January 1998 I sent a chance piece to the *Guardian* about the record number of eighty-three self-inflicted deaths in prisons in England and Wales the preceding year out of a total prisoner population of just sixty-one thousand. I had been in prison twelve years and had known many fellow prisoners who had taken their own lives. But this was a shocking figure. My article was called 'Time of Grief'. It was my third to be published in a national paper and my first under the pen name Erwin James.

The modest writing success I'd had made me start to think that had things been different in my early life I might have ended up a journalist, a professional writer. I'd completed my journalism course and was awarded a fancy certificate. I often fantasised about what it would have been like to have been a real journalist. Nothing gave me more satisfaction than to sit and write something that might influence the thinking of other people, especially in relation to prison issues about which there was such a lack of trustworthy information in the media. The idea that thousands or even hundreds of thousands of people might be reading my words, sharing my thoughts while I lived in a concrete-and-steel box gave me a solid sense of achievement. But though I had found a way to live in prison, far better than the way I had lived outside, as I approached my fifteenth incarcerated year I felt I was flagging. Like everyone else in there I had to duck and dive and dodge and swerve, trying to keep the kernel of who I believed I was intact. Prison life confounds and perplexes even the most adept survivor.

Some years earlier the Prisoners' Advice Service, a charity that helps prisoners with matters relating to prison law, had made representations to the Home Office on my behalf about the change in the minimum term I had to serve. In 1999, just over a year after my father died, I had another letter from the Home Office informing me that following the PAS submissions the then Home Secretary, Jack Straw, had reduced my minimum term to twenty years. Suddenly I came back to life.

Then came a quirk of fate. A probation officer called Richard Spence paid me a visit. All lifers have outside probation officers whose job is to maintain contact and write the occasional report. A warm, good-natured chap, Richard expressed an interest in how I spent my time in prison.

'I like to write,' I said.

He seemed impressed. 'My next-door neighbour is a writer,' he said. 'His name is Ronan Bennett.'

I knew that Ronan Bennett was an Irish writer who had been convicted when he was eighteen years old for a murder he hadn't committed and had spent two years in Long Kesh Prison in Northern Ireland. Ten years later he was arrested for 'conspiracy with persons unknown' and spent some time on remand in Brixton Prison's A SEG unit, just like I had. On the conspiracy charges Bennett had defended himself and been acquitted. I'd read a book that Bennett had helped to write called *Stolen Years* by Paul Hill, one of the people convicted of the Guildford pub bombings of 1974 and sentenced to life imprisonment, later cleared of all charges and released after serving fifteen years. I had also read a novel by Bennett, *The Second Prison*. We talked about his writing. 'Why don't you drop him a line?' Richard Spence said. I did and to my delight Ronan and I struck up a regular correspondence.

I was downgraded to security Category C later that year and transferred to Littlehey Prison in Cambridgeshire. Shortly after I arrived I had a message from the landing officer to call Ronan. 'It's urgent,' said the officer.

Ronan told me that he had been talking to an editor at the *Guardian*. 'He's looking for a serving prisoner to write a regular column about prison life for the paper,' he said, 'and I've told him about you.' At that time Ian Katz was the editor of *G2*, the *Guardian*'s features section. I sent him some articles that I thought might work as columns. He wrote back and then came to see me.

'Well you can write,' he said, 'but I need to know more about you and why you are in here.'

It was a tense visit. I'd never met a newspaper editor before. He was a family man, a professional and a man of integrity. Instinctively I respected him. I hated having to discuss the worst aspects of myself with him – but I wanted him to know me and to trust me and so I opened up. I wondered after the visit whether he'd still want me to write for him. It was a big responsibility he was taking on, a big risk, to his reputation and to that of the *Guardian.*

Each day following Ian Katz's visit I waited anxiously for the post. A week passed before my name appeared on the letter board outside the wing office. I stuck my head in the door and saw an envelope on the desk bearing the *Guardian* logo. 'Cheers, guv,' I said as the landing officer passed it to me.

I raced back to my cell and tore it open. Katz was polite but brief. 'It was nice to meet you,' he wrote. 'We'd like you to write three columns of eight hundred words to start. We'll call it "A Life Inside".'

The Governor responsible for lifers at Littlehey was unimpressed when I asked for his approval. 'No prisoners allowed to contact the media,' he said. 'I'll give you fifty small nos or one big no but the answer will be the same.'

I felt my heartbeat rise. 'But,' I began, the words I wanted to say stuck in my throat. It took a massive effort to spit them out.

'I'm a writer!' I said finally, immediately feeling stupid and embarrassed. I was a convict, a lifer, a convicted murderer – who was I trying to kid.

I'd never said out loud to anyone before that I was a writer. The idea of being a writer, a real, professional writer, had been an off and on fantasy of mine for years, but I never dared hope for a chance like this.

I took a deep breath and repeated in a whisper, 'I'm a writer.'

The Governor looked at me as if I'd just told him I wanted to marry his daughter. 'I suggest you get another hobby,' he said.

His words hung in the air between us for a minute or so and then I picked up the evidence of my modest writing achievements to date that I had spread on his desk and began slipping them back into my folder. I felt rejected and hurt and I was about to slope out of his office when I remembered the journalism course I had done with the support of the Prison Service.

'Hang on a minute,' I said. I pulled out the course diploma and showed it to him. 'You supported me doing this.'

He looked a little shamefaced, lowered his eyes and said, 'We didn't expect you to do any real journalism.'

Persistent and determined I wrote to the Home Office, supported by Ian Katz, and eventually the then Prisons Minister, Paul Boateng, agreed I should be allowed to write the column. 'I'm content for this to go ahead,' were his precise words in an email to an aide. The inaugural column appeared in February 2000, entitled 'How Beggsy fell out with Bob' – a vignette about a fall-out over a newspaper between two prisoners in neighbouring cells. An editor's tag on the end of the column read: 'Erwin James is serving life imprisonment for two murders. He does not receive a fee for this column.'

I didn't realise it then but it turned out to be the first column of its kind in the history of British journalism. I received £20 a month from the *Guardian* for phone cards so I could telephone in my copy from the wing phone booth. There was a fee paid by the paper, but all of that went to charity. I'd never had anything, let alone the inclination, to give to charity before. Being able to do that was almost as satisfying as seeing my words printed regularly in a respected national newspaper. Overnight I went from being a prisoner who wrote to being a writer in prison.

The Governor was evidently impressed. One day some months after that first column he came to my cell accompanied by the Deputy Mayor of the local town who he had been showing around the jail. He opened my cell door and announced to his visitor, 'This is Erwin James. He writes for the *Guardian* newspaper!' He seemed proud of his prisoner writer. The hypocrite, I thought.

Like most of the people who work in our prisons the Governor was a decent man doing a difficult job. I spoke to him a couple of weeks later and asked him what he was up to. 'That was a bit hypocritical, wasn't it? After all you did to make sure I didn't get to write for the *Guardian*. "Fifty small nos", remember?'

He shook his head. 'I have to be honest,' he said, 'I'm amazed you're getting away with it. I keep expecting a headline in the *Mail* saying "Has the world gone mad?"' I think I half expected that too. 'Listen,' he said. 'As a society we believe in rehabilitation for prisoners – but the truth is, we're not sure how rehabilitated we want them to be! Do you see? My job is to keep you in here – to "protect the public" from you and all the others in here. We're expected to give you some *rehabilitation*, but anything that looks like you're getting a treat or a benefit from being in prison gets people's backs up. You writing for the national press? That's probably a little too much rehabilitation for some people to stomach.'

I understood his explanation. I'd seen press reaction to positive and innovative prison initiatives over the years. It was one of the reasons I wanted to write the column, so I could tell readers the truth. But the idea of limiting prisoner rehabilitation to some vague level that would stop the public being outraged seemed absurd to me. The outrage should have been directed at the waste of life in prison, the waste of time and money – the unnecessary misery inflicted on the vulnerable and the mentally ill and the lack of direction and purpose which led to so many released prisoners creating new victims, ending back up in front of the courts and back inside, costing society a fortune in the process. I so wished I'd had more help and support when I was a teenager in the detention centre, or later in the borstal system. I'd needed help so badly.

'Rehabilitation is the best way to protect the public, Governor,' I said. 'The more prisoners who achieve it, the fewer victims there will be when they are released. Surely people outside would understand that.'

*   *   *

After nearly eighteen years in closed prisons I was de-categorised again and made a Cat D. I'd run the whole gamut. All my reports had been favourable and the Home Office had decided that I was ready for 'open conditions'. Years previously I'd read about a prison in Kent called Blantyre House. It was a place where long-term prisoners convicted of serious offences were supported and given all the help they needed to get out and function well. One of only three resettlement prisons in the country, it sounded like the Shangri-La of the prison system. From my experience so far it seemed to me that most of the prison system was geared to dehumanise. Blantyre House from what I had read was designed to rehumanise. The fact I had been made a Cat D with nearly three years to the end of my twenty-year tariff meant the Home Office was minded to consider favourably the possibility of my release when my tariff was up. I decided to ask if I could be sent to Blantyre House.

I knew there had been problems there. Its good work had almost come to an end in May 2000 when it was raided by nearly a hundred prison officers wielding heavy tools who smashed the place up on the strength of false intelligence that the prison was 'awash with drugs' and the prisoners were 'running the place'. The Governor at the time was a good man called Eoin McLennan-Murray who went through hell after he was summarily removed from his post just hours before the raid took place. He was cleared of any wrongdoing in the running of Blantyre House by a Home Affairs Select Committee investigation five months later.

I got my move to Blantyre House and that was when I started to think about living my new life outside. The raid happened eighteen months before I arrived, but it was still fresh in the minds of many of the staff who had felt badly let down by what had happened. I could sense they were wounded by it. But the majority still championed the idea of resettlement and rehabilitation for long-term prisoners. They knew from their experience that what they were doing was making their prison work, and making society safer. They were still prepared to trust and to show some human decency to people like I had been.

The prison was set in the heart of the Weald, just a few miles from the village of Goudhurst. It was a big rambling mansion, formerly a Fegan's Home for orphans who were trained in agriculture and then shipped overseas to Australia, New Zealand or Canada. There were gardens and greenhouses, a football field and a lower grassy compound from which behind the high fence you could see right across a wooded valley. The views were spectacular. I hadn't looked at distances for so long: being in the lower compound was incredibly emotional. I'd forgotten how beautiful the world was. When I first went to prison the outside world held no attraction for me. Now I looked out with desire. I wanted to take part. I wanted to live out there, like a regular, decent, law-abiding citizen.

There was a high fence around the grounds, but there were no bars on the windows and instead of cells we lived in rooms that were never locked, unless we locked them ourselves with our own keys. Once I had been 'risk assessed' a number of times I was allowed to go out, escorted by a prison officer, on a work party to surrounding villages, undertaking supervised maintenance work on community buildings, the properties of elderly folk and even schools and medical centres. The first time I went out without handcuffs I couldn't stop swinging my arms. Being so close to freedom was intoxicating. Every day fifty or sixty men at a time were queuing at the gate to be let out to go to work. Some went on voluntary work placements, but most went to paid jobs. Minibuses took them to the station at Staplehurst where they got their train and some had their own cars in the prison car park.

I did my voluntary labouring in the village a couple of days a week and cleaned the corridors and shower block when I was in the rest of the time. I continued writing my column for the *Guardian* and had lots of positive feedback from readers. Even the Director General of the Prison Service at the time, Martin Narey, was supportive. When the column had been running fortnightly for a couple of years Narey wrote to me, 'Like many readers of the *Guardian* I have been fascinated by your diary . . . you do a remarkable job of capturing the immense difficulties of long-term imprisonment and the terrible uncertainty facing lifers.'

After a year and a half I wrote to the Prisoners' Advice Service and asked if there was any work I could do for them as a volunteer. I knew there were men in the prison who caught the train to London to work. The PAS office was in Holborn so I asked the Governor at Blantyre if he would let me go if PAS wanted me. 'Sure,' he said, 'I think that would be a great thing.' In my letter to PAS I wrote that I could touch type and, 'I can lift heavy things . . .' To my delight they wrote back and said yes, they would be happy to give me a voluntary work placement.

My first time on the train from Staplehurst to Cannon Street Station was so stressful, I was sure everyone could see I was a convict. My self-consciousness was overwhelming. But I settled into the routine, travelling to London twice a week and sitting at a desk in the PAS office, helping to file files and tidy boxes. When the time came for me to find paid work I applied for a part-time job at PAS as an assistant caseworker and got it. The final year I was at Blantyre House I was allowed to keep the money I earned from my *Guardian* column, coupled with my wages from a promoted job at PAS. I started to save, something I had never done before in my life. I was forty-six years old. Beckoning on the horizon I could see a brand-new beginning.

Ian Katz came to visit me at Blantyre House and asked me if I would like to go to the *Guardian* offices to write and file my column. I asked the Governor and again he agreed. The first day I went I got off the train at Cannon Street and walked up past St Paul's Cathedral, my usual route to the PAS office. But then I had to turn up Farringdon Road. As I drew closer to the *Guardian* building at 119 recognition of the area dawned on me. I nipped up a side street and emerged on to Leather Lane. Twenty-two years earlier this was a place I slept rough. There was a regular market here and it was on today. I remembered rummaging in the rubbish when the traders had left looking for food and good thick cardboard to keep me warm at night. If anyone had asked me then what a *Guardian* newspaper looked like they would have drawn a blank. I looked about and could see myself huddling in corners, shuffling in alcoves, trying not to be noticed and just wanting to get my head down and out of the way. A tramp. A drunken tramp with no hope and no life. A dangerous drunken tramp. I continued up to the *Guardian* building and as I walked through the doors and into the reception I could barely take in the journey I had made to get there.

Finally my parole answer came through in August 2004. The Parole Board had recommended my release and the Home Office had accepted the recommendation. Twenty years to the day since I was taken into custody by the gendarmes in Sainte-Maxime I walked out of the prison gate for the last time. I was still healthy, I had new skills and abilities, I had a means of earning a living and I had hope. I'd been going outside the gate regularly on voluntary work and paid work for over a year and I thought the moment of my release proper would not feel particularly special. But as I emerged into the light on that blazing summer's day it felt like I was climbing out of a hole as deep as a mountain. I'd survived the prison journey and with the help of some of the amazing people who worked in those places I'd managed to grab some opportunities along the way. The realisation that my life inside was over was overwhelming and humbling. But I didn't feel joyful. For I knew I would never be free of my crimes and those twenty years did not even make a dent in the debt I owed to my victims.

But at least I was free at last to be who I should have been.

It was the best I could do.

AFTERWORD

I'm grateful to live in a society that is still prepared to give people like I was a second chance. But I know in my heart that without the help of prison psychologist Joan Branton and a number of other significant people I met during my prison journey I would never have been able to make the changes I needed to so that I could function well in civilised society.

As soon as my release from prison started to look like a real possibility I vowed that once I was free I would try to find Joan. When my book, *A Life Inside*, was published in April 2003, Joan was the first person I thanked in the acknowledgements. I had no way of knowing if she would ever see it. But in any case I was desperate to thank her in person. I needed her to know how important the time I had spent with her during the call-ups in Wakefield Prison all those years earlier had been.

Joan retired before my transfer in 1989 from Wakefield to Long Lartin. I remembered she lived in Wakefield at the time but I hadn't a clue if she stayed on in the town after her retirement. It had been sixteen years since I saw her last. I didn't even know if she was still alive.

The people who work in our prisons do so for many reasons. Some just need a job to pay the bills, others see what they do as a vocation, a means of helping to change lives and make a difference. The transient nature of the prison population means that so often those who work hard in those places to try and make a positive impact on troublesome lives rarely get to see the end result. They can never be sure that the work they do has made any difference at all. Systematically prison is a cynical environment where on the whole expectation of failure prevails. But the staff who do their job well and exude an enabling, encouraging, supportive attitude towards prisoners – whether they are teachers, prison officers, counsellors or governors – they shine on wings and landings like beacons.

My impression over those twenty years was that, just like me, the majority of my fellow prisoners had the desire to change for the better. Despite the debilitating and corrosive effect of prison life most people I came across appreciated any kindness or help that was offered. But showing gratitude in those circumstances is often difficult. Familiarity between prisoners and staff is dangerous. A note, a handshake or a hug would be misconstrued in an instant. There was no way I could thank Joan properly when I was in Wakefield Prison. I was a Category A convict and she was just doing her job. Looking back I don't think I was even sure at the time just how much of a catalyst she had been. Now I knew and I needed her to know that the scale of the change I had managed in my life was primarily because of her.

In the late summer of 2004 I began my search. The internet brought up a blank. I tried the electoral register for Wakefield, but still could find no sign. I didn't know any of her friends or family. But then I vaguely remembered her telling me that she often attended services at Wakefield Cathedral. I found a number for the cathedral admin and called it. The woman who answered was polite, but when I said who I was trying to locate she became reticent about giving me any information. 'I can't just give out personal details over the phone,' she said. 'You could be anybody.'

I took a deep breath and explained exactly how I knew Joan and why I was searching for her. 'I really need to find her,' I said. 'She as good as saved my life.'

The woman went quiet. When she spoke again I immediately noticed a change of tone. 'I'm really sorry,' she said. 'Joan is in a nursing home. She's very poorly.'

She gave me the name of the nursing home and I called it straight away. The manager was sympathetic when I explained who I was. 'I'd like to visit Joan, if I may,' I said. He said he would pass on my message and that I could call again in a few days.

When I did I was devastated by what the manager told me.

'Joan cannot speak,' he said. 'She is very fragile. She communicates with a pencil and paper and has asked me to tell you that she is pleased you are free, but she would rather you did not see her in her present condition.'

I thanked him and put down the phone, squeezing my eyes tight in an effort not to cry. I berated myself for not trying to contact Joan sooner. Why did I think I had to wait until I was out of prison? If I could write a column for a national newspaper surely

I could have written letters, made enquiries, contacted agencies from my prison cell. She had been retired for years. Who could possibly have minded me being in touch with her? I was so angry with myself for having left it so late.

By then I was working full-time in London as a fundraiser and manager for the Prisoners' Advice Service and writing a weekly column for the *Guardian* called 'A Life Outside'. The weeks and months passed and I thought of Joan often. I sent her a copy of *A Life Inside* with her name in the acknowledgements underlined. I wrote to her and sent the occasional email to the manager of the home, asking for my warm thoughts and good wishes to be passed on. She had been a brilliant communicator, of ideas, solutions, hope. It was largely down to her that I had ended up being a professional communicator. Now she couldn't even speak. I wondered if the people who looked after her had any idea of what she had achieved in her professional life. Did they know that she used to work in a high-security prison and stroll without fear or judgement amongst some of the most dangerous men in the country? I hoped they did. I hoped they treated her with all the respect and veneration she deserved.

Christmas 2004, my first Christmas in the outside world for twenty-one years, I decided I was going to visit Joan. She didn't want me to see her the way she was, she'd said, but I was sure that once we met again she would know that how she looked was unimportant. Once I was holding her hand, she might even let me hug her gently. That was my plan, until I received the email from her solicitor informing me that Joan had passed away in the first week of January.

We all need champions, people who believe in us and who want us to succeed, whatever life path we find ourselves on. I found a champion in Joan Branton.

She made me believe I was redeemable.

Little Erwin '. . . a good wee boy . . .'

ACKNOWLEDGEMENTS

Alexandra Pringle, for your magnificent patience, your trust in me and your commitment to this book – thank you. And for their endeavours on my behalf, huge thanks to your brilliant Bloomsbury team. David Godwin, for your loyalty, patience and friendship – thank you. Ronan Bennett, you sent me a book once when I was in prison and in it you wrote that I was, 'a fine writer'. Back in my cell I had a little cry. You never knew how precious and timely, coming from you, those words were – thank you. Ian Katz – you took a hell of a chance when you took me on as a *Guardian* columnist, and stood by me when first as a writer in 2009 I almost went under, and then as a troubled paroled prisoner when I sank. You helped to bring me back to the surface – thank you. Emily Wilson – the time you were in my corner meant a lot – thank you. Bev Thatcher – when I was in prison you sent me John Healy's masterpiece, *The Grass Arena* – thank you. Richard Spence, among other books you also sent me *Soledad Brother: The Prison Letters of George Jackson* – thank you. Kathy Baker – you introduced the Listener Scheme into UK prisons and became a wonderful friend – thank you. My young comrade in arms, Robert 'Red Chief' Lewis – you never forgot me and your friendship brought much needed light during my first dark year – thank you. Long before I went to prison for life I thought I had nobody – but I had my Aunt Jean and Uncle Alex. I took you for granted but still you stood by me with visits and letters when I needed you most. You never closed a door on me – thank you. Aunty Jeanty, your big heart has always been open for me – for your twelve-hour-round bus trips to visit me, for new socks every prison Christmas and for your unconditional love – thank you. But most of all Margaret, you know the worst of me and brought out the best, for your steadfast nature and for all you have given me, especially your heart – well I could never thank you enough.

EJM

A NOTE ON THE AUTHOR

Erwin James is a *Guardian* columnist and author.
He has published two collections of essays: *A Life Inside:
A Prisoner's Notebook* and *The Home Stretch: From Prison to
Parole*. A trustee of the Prison Reform Trust and patron of a
number of offender rehabilitation charities, he has given keynote
adressess to the Royal Society in Edinburgh, the Probation
Union at the Danish parliament and the Festival of Dangerous
Ideas at the Sydney Opera House. He is a Fellow of the Royal
Society for the Encouragement of the Arts and an Honorary
Master of the Open University.

erwinjames.co.uk
@TheErwinJames